College Student Development

Theory and Practice for the 1990s

Don G. Creamer and Associates

American College Personnel Association
Media Publication No. 49

Distributed by University Press of America,® Inc.
4720 Boston Way, Lanham, Maryland 20706

Cover Design by Rebecca Crocker

Library of Congress Cataloging-in-Publication Data

Creamer, Don G.
College student development.
(American College Personnel Association media publication:
no. 49)
Includes bibliographical references.
1. College student development programs—United States.
I. Title. II. Series: ACPA media publication: 49.
LB2343.4.C74   1990   378.1'98

ISBN 1-55620-070-6 (pbk. : alk. paper)

 The paper used in this publication meets the minimum requirements of
American National Standard for Information Sciences—Permanence
of Paper for Printed Library Materials, ANSI Z39.48–1984.

Contents

About the Authors v

Part I   Introduction

Chapter 1   Progress Toward Intentional Student Development   3
             Don G. Creamer

Chapter 2   The Professional Practice of Student Development   9
             C. Carney Strange and Patricia M. King

Part II   Theoretical Foundations of Practice

Chapter 3   Recent Theories and Research Underlying Student
             Development   27
             Robert F. (Bob) Rodgers

Chapter 4   Assessing Development From a Cognitive-Developmental
             Perspective   81
             Patricia M. King

Chapter 5   Assessing Development From a Psychosocial Perspective ...   99
             Theodore K. (Ted) Miller and Roger B. Winston, Jr.

Chapter 6   Understanding and Assessing College Environments 127
             Lois A. Huebner and Jane M. Lawson

Part III   Applications of Developmental Theory

Chapter 7   An Integration of Campus Ecology and Student
             Development: The Olentangy Project 155
             Robert F. (Bob) Rodgers

Chapter 8   Use of a Planned Change Model to Modify Student
             Affairs Programs 181
             Don G. Creamer and Elizabeth G. Creamer

Part IV   Major Issues in Practice

Chapter 9   Ethical Practice in College Student Affairs 195
             Elizabeth Reynolds Welfel

Chapter 10   Student Outcome Assessment: An Institutional
             Perspective 217
             T. Dary Erwin

About the Authors

Don G. Creamer is professor in Graduate Studies in College Student Affairs and special advisor to the vice president for student affairs at Virginia Polytechnic Institute and State University. He earned his doctorate from Indiana University and his bachelor's and master's degrees from East Texas State University. Dr. Creamer's active involvement in the profession includes service as the first president of the Junior College Student Personnel Association of Texas and president (1978–1979), chair of the Commission on Two-Year College Student Development, member of the Executive Council, member of the Commission on Professional Preparation, and member of the editorial board of the *Journal of College Student Development* of the American College Personnel Association. He served on the board of directors of the National Association of Student Personnel Administrators and was awarded the senior professional Annuit Coeptis Award of the American College Personnel Association in 1989.

Elizabeth G. Creamer is co-director of the Liberal Arts and Sciences Advising Center, College of Arts and Sciences, and adjunct professor in Graduate Studies in College Student Affairs, College of Education, Virginia Polytechnic Institute and State University. She received a doctorate from Virginia Polytechnic Institute and State University, a master's degree from Colorado State University, and a bachelor's degree from Northwestern University. Her research interests include planned change in higher education, academic advising, and the effects of financial aid on college choice and access to higher education.

T. Dary Erwin is director of the Office of Student Assessment and associate professor of psychology at James Madison University. He was previously affiliated with Texas A & M University and the University of Tennessee. He received his bachelor's and master's degrees from the University of Tennessee and his doctorate from the University of Iowa. Dr. Erwin is past recipient of the Annuit Coeptis Award of the American College Personnel Association and of the Ralph F. Berdie Memorial Research Award of the American Association for Counseling and Development. He also served as chairperson of the Measurement Services Association.

Lois A. Huebner is director of the Counseling and Consultation Center and adjunct associate professor of psychology at Saint Louis University. Previously she was assistant professor of psychology at Virginia Commonwealth University and held both faculty and counseling center appointments at the University of Missouri-Columbia and the University of Iowa.

Patricia M. King is associate professor in College Student Personnel at Bowling Green State University. Previously she served as assistant vice president for student services at the Ohio State University and as senior research psychologist at the University of Iowa. Dr. King earned her PhD from the University of Minnesota and her bachelor's degree from Macalester College. Her major professional interests include studies in intellectual and moral development, with an emphasis on college student development; critical thinking, especially in the context of the Reflective Judgment model and ways in which faculty and student affairs staff can help students to think and reason more carefully and comprehensively; and ethical issues in student affairs.

Jane M. Lawson is staff psychologist at the Saint Louis University Counseling and Consultation Center, where she specializes in consultation with faculty on issues of teaching and learning. As a graduate student at the University of Minnesota, where she received her doctorate, she participated in the development of a model of faculty consultation. She is a single parent with an adopted son from India.

Theodore K. (Ted) Miller is professor in Counseling and Human Development Services at the University of Georgia, where he has served since 1967. He is currently director of the University of Georgia SACS Accreditation Reaffirmation Self-Study and chair of the Self-Study Steering Committee. Dr. Miller earned his degrees from Ball State University, where he received his bachelor's and master's, and the University of Florida, where he received his doctorate. His previous professional experience includes service as counselor to men and counseling psychologist. Dr. Miller has been active in professional associations and served as the first president of the Georgia College Personnel Association and president of the American College Personnel Association in 1975–1976. He was president of the Council for the Advancement of Standards for Student Services/Development from its inception in 1980 until 1989.

Robert F. (Bob) Rodgers is associate professor of education and psychology and director of the Student Personnel Assistant Program at The Ohio State University. He earned his bachelor's degree from Texas Tech University and his master's and doctorate from The Ohio State University. Dr. Rodgers's service to the profession includes 10 years as the American College Personnel Association representative to the Council for the Advancement of Standards for Student Services/Development. He served as a member of the editorial board for the *Journal of College Student Development* and the *National Association of Student Personnel Administrators Journal*, associate chair and member of the directorate body of the Commission on Professional Preparation, member of the directorate body of the Commission on Assessment of Student Development, and first chair of the Student Development Research Grant Program of the American College Personnel Association. During the past 20 years he has studied the applications of developmental theory. His current interests focus on testing selected theoretical hypotheses of developmental theory through studies such as the interaction of cognitive-structural and psychosocial development within various Jungian personality types, the role of autonomy for women and intimacy for men, and the measurement of personality types for educational environments. He also delivers workshops for faculty on the use of developmental concepts in teaching.

C. Carney Strange is associate professor and chair of the Department of College Student Personnel at Bowling Green State University, where he has been employed as a faculty member since 1978. Recipient of the Ralph F. Berdie Memorial Research Award from the American Association for Counseling and Development, Dr. Strange completed his bachelor's degree at St. Meinrad College of Liberal Arts and his master's and doctoral degrees at the University of Iowa. His teaching and research have focused on student development, the impact of educational environments, the needs and characteristics of returning adult learners, and factors that encourage student involvement in quality out-of-class experiences. An active member of several professional organizations, he has served on the editorial boards of the *National Association of Student Personnel Administrators Journal* and the *Journal of College Student Development*. He now serves as a member of the directorate body of the Commission on Professional Preparation of the American College Personnel Association.

Elizabeth Reynolds Welfel is associate professor of counselor education and director of doctoral studies in the College of Education at Cleveland State University. She received her doctorate in counseling and student personnel psychology in 1979 from the University of Minnesota. Dr. Welfel's publications span two research areas. The first is the development of reflective judgment in late adolescence and adulthood, and the second is professional ethics for counseling practitioners and student personnel administrators. Her ethics research centers on the ethical decision-making process and on the factors that impede the implementation of ethical decision making. Articles have appeared in the *Journal of College Student Development*, the *Journal of Counseling and Development*, and *The Counseling Psychologist*.

Roger B. Winston, Jr., is professor in Student Personnel in Higher Education and interim chair of the Department of Counseling and Human Development Services at the University of Georgia. He received his doctorate and his master's degree from the University of Georgia and his bachelor's degree from Auburn University. Dr. Winston serves currently as associate editor of the *Journal of College Student Development* and on the editorial board of the *Georgia Journal of College Student Affairs*. He was named senior scholar by the American College Personnel Association in 1989 and was awarded the senior professional Annuit Coeptis Award in 1987. He was recognized as "outstanding researcher" by the National Academic Advising Association in 1984.

PART I

INTRODUCTION

CHAPTER 1

Progress Toward Intentional Student Development

Don G. Creamer

Arthur Chickering asserted in *The Modern American College* (1981) that the ". . . idea of human development can supply a unifying purpose for higher education" (p. xxx). He and his associates argued that student (human) development is the principal aim of higher education and that its accomplishment is the overarching obligation of all college educators. There is scant evidence that *all* educators accept this obligation as a definitive statement of their roles, but many, if not most, student affairs educators do.

It would be imperceptive to declare that classroom educators and academic administrators reject any obligation to promote student development in its broadest sense. All educational roles may be seen as developmental by definition. At least they share the responsibility to advance intellectual growth by disseminating information or knowledge. Some teachers and academic administrators even recognize the striking similarities of the goals of liberal arts and those of student affairs, and, in this sense, not only acknowledge their goal-oriented kinship with student affairs, but structure their teaching responsibilities to contribute directly to these goals. But one reality of higher education is that most educators do not conceptualize their work in terms that reflect student (human) development intent. Only student affairs educators readily and willingly adopt a specific resolve to promote student development through their behaviors and programs.

HISTORICAL PERSPECTIVE

It has not always been true, of course, that student affairs educators conceptualized their work as intentional student development. *The Student Personnel Point of View* (*SPPV*) (American Council on Education, 1937, 1949) reflected a service-oriented perspective that challenged student affairs educators to meet

3

the needs of students through functionally discrete and bureaucratically fashioned administrative units. The resulting patterns of service delivery were driven by an individualistic, holistic, and humanistic philosophy that invited educators to assist students through a variety of educational strategies to become well-rounded citizens. In retrospect, the philosophy articulated in the *SPPV* was developmental in the sense that it focused on outcomes of citizenship in students; however, the remainder of the document clearly exhibited images that spotlighted the means of delivering service to students.

One of the most persistent images of student affairs professionals has been that of the parent-like dean. These officials personified *in loco parentis* responsibilities of student affairs, at least until the late 1960s when the legal relationship between the institution and its students was replaced by contract-like alliances. These officials also personified benevolent autocrats. They were autocrats who cared for students and who spent almost all of their time helping students solve problems and make the most of their educational opportunities. Simultaneously, they ruled single-handedly, and often sternly, on infractions of the institution's rules. There is some debate within the profession about whether these officials were most aptly described as "wardens" or "educators." (See "A Corrective Look Back" in *Pieces of Eight* [Appleton, Briggs, Rhatigan, & Associates, 1978] for a thorough discussion of these different points of view.) The burden of evidence suggests that these officials were honest, hardworking, and caring and taught students by example, but few would label their approach developmental.

It was during the decade of the 1960s that student affairs professionals turned their attention more specifically to the developmental focus of their educational activities. Selected actions of professional associations and groups centered on the question, "Can we promote development intentionally in higher education and specifically through student affairs activities?" One group, the Council of Student Personnel Associations (COSPA, 1983) published a paper in the early 1970s titled "Student Development Services in Post-Secondary Education" that contributed to widespread discussion within the profession about key concepts of the viewpoint. The American College Personnel Association (ACPA) sponsored a large-scale project called Tomorrow's Higher Education (T.H.E.) that was designed in phases to deal with central questions about the philosophy of student development. Brown (1972) responded affirmatively to the most basic question underlying the T.H.E. project about whether the accomplishment of student development can be demonstrated in higher education in a monograph entitled *Student Development in Tomorrow's Higher Education: A Return to the Academy*. A model for practice that focused on change in students was generated in 1975 and called the T.H.E. Model (Tomorrow's Higher Education Model, cited in Saddlemire & Rentz, 1983, pp. 410–422). It, too, resulted in widespread discussion in the profession. (A later model for practice that focused on change in the organization was formulated in draft form, but never received widespread distribution and discussion.) Miller and Prince (1976) prepared their book, *The Future of Student Affairs*, to reflect the essential components of the T.H.E. Model, and it was in this publication that the idea of intentionality was introduced into the professional language of student affairs.

Miller and Prince argued that ". . . the intentional student development approach seeks to meet the needs of all students, to plan change rather than react to it, and to engage the full academic community in this collaborative effort" (p. 21).

THEORIES AND RESEARCH

The decision to promote development in students intentionally calls into question some of the most vexing problems of the profession. Exactly what aspects of development do student affairs professionals intend to advance? To what extent do they agree on the targeted domains? How adequate are their theories of development in providing precise explanations of the targeted phenomena? How adequate are their assessment tools and methods in generating data about developmental status? What knowledge and skills are necessary to translate these developmental status data into programmatic interventions that meet the standard of intentionality? How strong is student affairs professionals' will to evaluate program success against developmental criteria?

The quest for answers to questions such as these formed a strong motive for publishing the forerunner to this volume—*Student Development in Higher Education: Theories, Practices, and Future Directions* (Creamer, 1980). That book presented a contemporary summary of theories relevant to promoting student development and a review of issues pertinent to translating these theories into practice. Rodgers's (1980) review of student development theories was definitive a decade ago and included some discussion of assessment procedures and instruments. The decade of the 1980s, however, witnessed further advances in theories of development, rapid accumulation of significant research findings about the theories, accelerating concerns about the profession's ability to assess developmental status, and progress in assessment instrumentation and methods. The current volume is fashioned from the knowledge of these developments and is intended to familiarize readers with the most recent thinking about developmental programming in student affairs. This book, then, represents a status report on the implementation of the principle of intentionality in developmental programming in student affairs. Readers should be cautioned that basic familiarity with developmental theory may be necessary to grasp the material covered in this book.

OVERVIEW OF TEXT

This volume is organized first to introduce an overarching conceptual orientation in developmental programming. In chapter 2, Carney Strange and Patricia King present a rationale for the professional practice of student development in student affairs and show how it is distinguished by the interlocking use of theory, research, practice, evaluation, and values. They demonstrate the application of these elements in student affairs and in other professions, provide general overviews of developmental theoretical models, discuss the nature of practice in applied fields like student affairs, and conclude with advice to professionals about how to prepare for the realities of practice. Chapter 2 also serves to orient the reader to basic concepts and ideas intrinsic to developmental programming in student affairs that are used throughout the book.

The second section of the book focuses on theoretical foundations of practice. Chapter 3, the lead chapter by Bob Rodgers on recent theories and research underlying student development, updates his earlier summary of the theories of student development. Rodgers argues in this review that intentional use of theory must be anchored in person-environment interaction to ensure its most professional application. He shows how the assessment of both person and environment is essential to adequate developmental programming. Rodgers's review of developments in theory incorporates the latest research findings about gender-related issues in both the cognitive-developmental and the psychosocial families of theory. In addition, he introduces theories not covered in the 1980 book, including the Kegan personality theory and the typological theories of Keirsey and Jung/Myers.

Chapters 4 through 6 were prepared by scholars who contribute to the review of the theoretical foundations of practice by clarifying the state of the art of assessing development from cognitive-developmental, psychosocial, and environmental perspectives. In chapter 4, Patricia King describes selected cognitive-developmental phenomena, and then demonstrates the benefits, disadvantages, and risks to student development practice associated with both formal and informal assessment approaches. She provides a list of available instruments to assess development from a cognitive-developmental perspective and discusses the characteristics of the instruments.

Ted Miller and Roger Winston, in chapter 5, describe the higher education context in which the assessment of psychosocial development must occur and offer a summary of germane findings about assessing ethnic minority students, nontraditional students, and international students. They also discuss gender-related issues of assessing psychosocial development. The complexity of psychosocial developmental processes is recognized in the review of significant issues associated with assessment. The authors conclude by reviewing work from the two major university centers—the University of Georgia and the University of Iowa—where scholars are concerned especially with the construction of instruments to assess psychosocial development.

Chapter 6 on assessing educational environments, prepared by Lois Huebner and Jane Lawson, concludes the section devoted to updating theory and assessing student development. Huebner and Lawson show that "there is nothing so complex as a simple idea." The simple idea is Lewin's notion that behavior is a function of the interaction of the person and the environment. In fact, not one of the definitions of person, environment, or interaction is simple. Thus, Huebner and Lawson explore the assessment of educational environments by reviewing literature from several strands of research associated with the idea of person-environment interaction and synthesizing this knowledge into useful terms. Chapter 6 is especially relevant as an extension of Rodgers's update on student development theory.

The third section of this book is devoted to two topics that deal with the application of developmental theory in practice. Chapter 7 features the Olentangy Project, in which Bob Rodgers illustrates the integration of campus ecology and student development. The project represents an attempt to solve significant problems arising from the poor architectural design of a large residence hall and the resulting undesirable consequences in student behavior and attitudes. Rodgers goes into great detail about the process of identifying the problem, assessing the students and the environments associated with the problem, designing interventions, executing the intervention plan, and evaluating the initiative. The complexity of person-environment interaction discussed by Huebner and Lawson is precisely demonstrated in this report of an actual student development practice.

Chapter 8, the second chapter of the applications section, is devoted to presenting and discussing the usefulness of a model of planned change in higher education. Resting on the assumption that the worth of a idea, such as replacing outdated and ineffective procedures with student development practices, is seldom sufficient to guarantee successful program innovation, Don Creamer and Elizabeth Creamer present a theoretical model to guide transitional procedures in practice. They present the theoretical underpinning of their model, called the Probability of the Adoption of Change (PAC), to describe the key variables that must be managed in intentional reform of student affairs practices. Several uses of the model are outlined, including its utility in strategic planning, in the assessment of environmental conditions that promote or inhibit change, in the selection of specific intervention strategies, in the assessment of external models that may be considered for importation, and in the design of case studies involving organizational development and change.

The concluding section includes two chapters that discuss some of the most pressing issues in the student affairs profession. The first is dedicated to ethics in college student affairs and the second is committed to student outcome assessment and the particular role of student affairs professionals.

In chapter 9, Elizabeth Welfel shows how ethics has emerged as a priority in the profession and how self-imposed standards can influence professional behavior. She reviews research literature related to ethical behavior and the emerging models of ethical decision making, noting especially some recent contributions by Kitchener (1985). Welfel concludes by delineating several persistent and emerging concerns, such as conflicts between responsibility to clients and to the institution, sexual harassment, dual relationships, confidentiality, and enforcement of published ethical guidelines.

Chapter 10 focuses on the issue of outcome assessment in college student affairs. Outcome assessment has received an enormous amount of attention on campuses in the last 5 years or so. It is a movement of sweeping proportions and seems to be an anchor for external constituents who are concerned with accountability in higher education. The issue is presented by Dary Erwin, who shows the widespread nature of the phenomenon in American higher education and the need of student affairs professionals to be involved in creating and managing outcome assessment systems. Erwin deals with how to get from where student affairs professionals are to where they want to be in the outcome assessment movement and offers some practical advice. Like other authors in this volume, Erwin also shows how complex the assessment issue can be and how much work may be necessary to accomplish the goal of direct involvement in campuswide systems to measure the effects of college on students.

CONCLUSION

Student affairs professionals are not yet able to promote predetermined forms of student development intentionally on a wide scale in higher education. It may never be possible to exercise all the necessary controls in very uncertain learning environments to achieve such a goal. As this volume shows, however, student affairs professionals have taken concrete steps during the past decade to expand their knowledge of theories of development; research on the effects of college on students; and practices that can, and do, result in developmental change in students. Even on a limited scale, promoting student development intentionally on American college campuses is a tall order. This book makes that point clearly and forcefully.

REFERENCES

American Council on Education. (1937). *The student personnel point of view.* Washington, DC: Author.

American Council on Education. (1949). *The student personnel point of view.* Washington, DC: Author.

Appleton, J.R., Briggs, C.M., Rhatigan, J.J., & Associates. (1978). *Pieces of eight.* Washington, DC: National Association of Student Personnel Administrators.

Brown, R.D. (1972). *Student development in tomorrow's higher education: A return to the academy.* Alexandria, VA: American College Personnel Association.

Chickering, A.W. (1981). *The modern American college.* San Francisco: Jossey-Bass.

Council of Student Personnel Associations. (1983). Student development services in postsecondary education. In G.R. Saddlemire & A.L. Rentz (Eds.), *Student affairs—A profession's heritage: Significant articles, authors, issues and documents* (pp. 384–395). Alexandria, VA: American College Personnel Association.

Creamer, D.G. (1980). *Student development in higher education: Theories, practices, and future directions.* Alexandria, VA: American College Personnel Association.

Kitchener, K.S. (1985). Ethical principles and ethical decisions in student affairs. In H.J. Canon & R.D. Brown, (Eds.), *Applied ethics in student services* (pp. 17–29). San Francisco: Jossey-Bass.

Miller, T.K., & Prince, J. (1976). *The future of student affairs.* San Francisco: Jossey-Bass.

Rodgers, R.F. (1980). Theories underlying student development. In D.G. Creamer (Ed.), *Student development in higher education: Theories, practices, and future directions* (pp. 10–95). Alexandria, VA: American College Personnel Association.

Tomorrow's Higher Education Model. (1983). In G.R. Saddlemire & A.L. Rentz (Eds.), *Student affairs—A profession's heritage: Significant articles, authors, issues and documents* (pp. 410–422). Alexandria, VA: American College Personnel Association.

CHAPTER 2

The Professional Practice of Student Development

C. Carney Strange and Patricia M. King

INTRODUCTION AND OVERVIEW

This chapter focuses on the purposes and functions of a theoretical knowledge base for the professional practice of student development in postsecondary education. It begins with a brief statement about the character of professional work and the role of theory and research in guiding it. This is followed by a summary of the status of the student development knowledge base and its implications for practice. Problems inherent to the nature of applied educational fields are then identified and issues related to the imperfect correspondence between theory and practice are discussed. Finally, several strategies are recommended to those involved in professional preparation and staff development for successfully connecting theory to practice in the course of graduate education and in-service programs.

Professionals at Work

"We make a difference or your money back!" the sign in bold letters says; "Call the professionals," another one reads; "Choose the experts," an advertisement suggests; "Skilled . . . certified . . . approved . . . accredited" banner lines in the yellow pages proclaim. All are claims of comfort we have come to rely upon in a consumer-oriented society. They are, in effect, promises of quality we expect from the person who changes the oil in our car to the individual who invests and manages our life savings. Attention to those assumed "to know" is more than good business or common sense, though. In a world where complexity exceeds the boundaries of any single individual's grasp, it is a matter of survival. Whatever the field or concern, it is characteristic of modern society to value and depend heavily on the input of those who are professionals at what they do.

What is the meaning of being a professional? By contrast, how does that differ from being a nonprofessional or amateur? The thesis proposed here is that professionals are clearly distinguished from nonprofessionals in reference to five criteria, and therefore, they have more to offer. Professionals can:

1. offer reasonable and believable explanations for the phenomena they purport to address (*theory*);
2. support the validity of their explanations with evidence (*research*);
3. respond to those phenomena on the basis of their explanations, and do so with methods, both unique or standard, that are generally endorsed by peers (*practice*);
4. demonstrate the success of their efforts with evidence (*evaluation*); and
5. articulate a clear sense of what is important and valuable in relation to the phenomena they address (*values*).

Each of these five criteria addresses an important component or tool of the professional at work. Explanations derive from *theory*; the validity of these explanations is supported through *research*; action flows directly from these explanations and is governed by standards of *practice*; and consequences are monitored and documented through *evaluation*. Above all, the *value* of the phenomena addressed is expressed through personal commitment.

The cyclical relationship between these elements is illustrated in Figure 1. For example, consider the familiar archetype of the professional at work—the family physician. Most of us have had the experience of limping off to the family doctor with a host of unpleasant symptoms, looking for some relief or, at the very least, a reasonable explanation for our private misery. Our choice of a doctor (rather than, say, a legal consultant) is obvious. First, we assume that, by virtue of the physician's professional preparation and training, she or he will see the connections between our symptoms and, in this case, drawing upon a knowledge of virology and bacteriology (*theories*), will be able to identify the probable cause of our illness. Second, we may further assume that the doctor has kept up with the latest issues of the *New England Journal of Medicine* and is abreast of the recent developments in this area, particulary concerning the current endemic strains of virus (*research*). Third, we expect the doctor to treat our illness based on an appropriate diagnosis and consistent with the accepted standards of practice. For example, the doctor may prescribe an antibiotic for bacterial infections, but may offer only symptomatic relief for viral infections (*practice*). Finally, we do expect to feel better, and if not, we are likely to go back for another explanation or perhaps even seek the advice of a different physician (*evaluation*). At the core of this whole process is our assumption that this physician clearly values good health and holds it as a goal of professional efforts (*values*).

STUDENT DEVELOPMENT EDUCATORS AS
PROFESSIONALS AT WORK

Student development, the power and promise of formal education to enhance the growth and development of individuals encountering life transitions, constitutes a

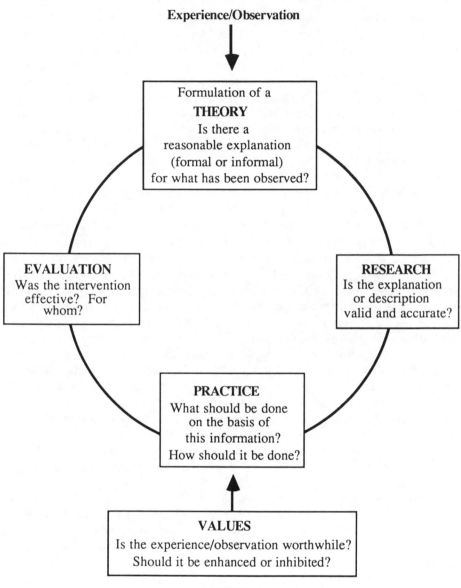

FIGURE 1
Relating Theory and Research to Practice

core *value* of the student affairs profession. Within the past two decades, the profession has articulated a knowledge base that more clearly enlightens the goal of student development. Student development *theories* help explain the complexities of students' behavior, change, and growth; these explanations, and the cumulative *research* that sharpens and validates them, constitute the "science of student development." Theory and research help us recognize that student behavior is not just a matter of chance and random effect; rather, many aspects of student behavior are observable, measurable, explainable, generalizable, and therefore, to some extent, predictable. The student development knowledge base has also yielded new ways of reaching the goal of intentional student development through the use of more effective strategies. The process of translating these explanations into professional *practice* by using various models, techniques, and methods constitutes the "art of student development." The notion of transforming ideas into practice is not new: Aristotle contrasted "artisans," those who did things well and knew why, from those who were "just lucky." The professional practice of student development, therefore, is an art informed by science, as is the profession of medicine.

Consider the case of a dean of students who is faced with a student considering leaving school during the first semester of her freshman year. In choosing how to respond, the dean may draw from a reservoir of knowledge about the developmental status of freshman students and the differential impact of various educational environments. The student's comments of "being confused about what to do with my life and what to major in" and about "not feeling that I belong" might quickly invoke the conceptions of Chickering's (1969) Developing Purpose and Identity vectors and Astin's (1984) involvement model that underscore the importance of a student's connection to the activities and structures of the institution. Perhaps the student's overly acquiescent manner and deference to the dean as an "authority who knows the answer" may also lead to hypotheses about developmental level, in this case, perhaps Dualistic (Perry, 1970) or Dependent/Conforming (Harvey, Hunt, & Schroder, 1961). All of these possible explanations, or *theories*, are useful for understanding this student's behavior and for anticipating her potential reaction, such as how she might respond to the dean's advice and whether or not she will stay in college. There is ample evidence in the attrition/retention *research* to suggest that, given her present characteristics and status, she is indeed a high-risk candidate for leaving school. Here, the dean is drawing from his knowledge of the science of his profession.

With the goal of student development in mind, and based upon the above explanations, several options for *practice* might be warranted. Three options the dean might consider are offered below. First, the dean could advise the student to enroll in a career decision-making class offered on campus. This recommendation might be based on two major theoretical assumptions: (a) that addressing resolution of questions of vocational purpose and direction often benefits other aspects of development, such as identity, sense of competence and self-esteem, and relationships with others (Chickering, 1969); and (b) that identification of the "ideal self," in this case one's occupational identity, provides a critical referent for evaluating the present environment (Pervin, 1968).

Second, the dean also may suggest that this student join an organization or group compatible with her interests. This second recommendation might be based on several theory-based assumptions: (a) that environmental attraction, personal satisfaction, and stability are enhanced in a congruent, differentiated environment (Holland, 1973); (b) that an individual increases his or her power to achieve a reinforcement by joining a group (Skinner, 1953); and (c) that student involvement on campus positively affects student persistence, self-esteem, and satisfaction with most aspects of college life (Astin, 1984).

A third option the dean may consider is to encourage more risk taking on the part of this student, supporting her attempts at self-reliance and judgment. The theoretical assumptions here are that tolerance of uncertainty and acknowledgment of self as a legitimate source of judgment are requisite changes in the achievement of more advanced levels of development (Harvey et al., 1961; Kitchener & King, 1981; Perry, 1970).

Each of these options incorporates elements common to the practice of intentional planned change. The student development goals to be reached are informed by theories of student development, an assessment of the current level or progress is made (formal or informal), and intervention strategies (instruction, consultation, environmental management) are planned to encourage growth (Miller & Prince, 1976; Morrill, Hurst, & Oetting, 1980). Which option or options the dean chooses and what methods of conveying and implementing the chosen option(s) will depend on his expertise in the art of student development.

Monitoring or *evaluating* the student's experience and progress with these recommendations may confirm the validity of the dean's response, or suggest alternative strategies. Evaluation also may suggest additional changes in policies and practices affecting other students that can be initiated in a more proactive, systematic manner, such as requiring students to complete an initial career planning assessment session as part of orientation to the freshman year, or establishing an institutional developmental transcript system to encourage and monitor student involvement on campus.

Another illustration of the student development educator as a "professional at work" might involve a program planning task such as orienting returning adult learners to a new Weekend College program on campus. Recent life-span literature (Levinson, 1978; Schlossberg, 1984) describes adult development in terms of a sequence of alternating periods of stability and transition (*theories*). The theoretical and research literature also has clarified the connection between the return to formal education and the experience of significant life transitions, most frequently those of a career or relationship nature (Aslanian & Brickell, 1980). In addition, adult learners also have been found to approach their return to school with memories of less-than-successful previous attempts, low self-esteem, and suspicion about the formal trappings of traditional classroom learning (Cross, 1981). The literature further shows that adults often expect a practical and concrete return for their efforts (*research*). These findings suggest that a successful orientation program for adults ought to acknowledge these concerns in some way. Opportunities for career interest assessment, exposure to various campus support services, and a chance to confront their reservations about returning to school in a nonthreatening, supportive atmosphere with other adults all are important components of interventions (*practice*) that are supported by theory and research. The successful matriculation, satisfaction, and retention of adult learners on campus will help determine the effectiveness of such interventions (*evaluation*).

The point of these illustrations is that theory, research, practice, and evaluation are integral components of a student development educator's professional repertoire in selecting a response that can be intentionally analyzed and implemented. Failure to effect a linkage between these components may yield a less than adequate explanation, unreasonable expectations, and, as a result, ineffective practice. Furthermore, the field itself cannot advance without the accumulated knowledge and experience of informed professional practitioners who understand these components and who communicate with each other about their successes and failures. The immediate risk is the failure of one program, but the long-term consequences are students' diminished developmental outcomes and the inability of educational institutions to fulfill their developmental mission and potential. The professional student development educator, as scientist and artisan, is an important link in addressing such questions on campus.

FORMAL THEORIES OF STUDENT DEVELOPMENT

Our collective knowledge about student development comes from a variety of sources, from individual informal hunches derived from personal experiences to formal theories with extensive research bases. We will focus on the formal theory base in this section. The role of informal theories will be examined later.

From the earlier writings of Erikson (1950) on identity development to current conceptions such as Kegan's (1982) charted path of the "Evolving Self," the student development literature has been enlightened by a host of theoretical models and schemes, each attempting to describe the course and processes of human development. Likewise, the pioneer works of Lewin (1936), Murray (1938), Stern (1970), and Holland (1973), as well as the more recent thinking of Moos (1979), have helped us understand more fully the power and dynamics of human environments. This accumulated body of knowledge from the behavioral and social sciences has collectively informed the student affairs field about changes in growth and development that are likely to occur across the life span, and how educational environments can either inhibit or enhance that process. Table 1 offers an overview of these theories for purposes of examining their implications for the practice of student development.

The central paradigm represented here is the differential interactionist perspective of Kurt Lewin (1936), who argued that scientific psychology must take into account the interaction of the person and the environment. Lewin's classic formula for examining and explaining human behavior is: "Behavior is a function of the interaction of person and environment," or $B = f(P \times E)$. This paradigm suggests that if we are to understand students' behavior and their progress toward the developmental goals we espouse, we must develop a language and a variety of concepts for describing both students' individual ("personological") differences and the important features of the various campus environments they experience ("environmental" characteristics). In the student development literature, various theoretical models have emerged that are helpful in understanding individual differences in

TABLE 1
A Theoretical Framework for the Professional Practice of Student Development

$$B = f(P \times E)$$
Behavior results from an interaction between persons and environments.

Personological Models identify differences in persons.
- *Life Structures and Psychosocial Tasks* describe specific age-related developmental tasks.
- *Cognitive and Interpersonal Styles* describe differences in the way individuals approach and resolve psychosocial tasks.
- *Cognitive-Developmental Structures* describe ways individuals explain their experiences and observations.

Environmental Models identify differences in environments.
- *Human Aggregates* describe differences according to the collective characteristics of individuals who inhabit environments.
- *Physical Features* describe influences of specified natural and synthetic characteristics of environments on human behavior.
- *Organizational Structures* describe effects of organized features related to goals and purposes of given environments.
- *Perceptual Interpretations* describe how individuals' evaluations of their environments affect their response and behavior.

Person-Environment Interaction Models identify predictions about behavior that results when certain types of individuals interact with certain types of environments.
- *Challenge:* environmental characteristics individuals find differentially stimulating, invigorating, or demanding.
- *Support:* environmental characteristics individuals find differentially comforting, familiar, or stabilizing.
- *Developmental Dissonance:* the degree of balance between environmental challenges and supports.

people, differences in human environments, and the consequences of specific person-environment interactions (Table 1). (See chapter 3 by Rodgers in this volume for a slightly different classification of theories.)

Personological Theories

With respect to personological differences, concepts from the *life structure and psychosocial models* (e.g., Chickering, 1969; Erikson, 1950; Gould, 1978; Havighurst, 1972; Levinson, 1978) underscore the importance of the ascendancy and resolution of specific developmental tasks in individuals' lives. Cyclical periods of transition and stability, generally a function of chronological maturation, offer opportunities for teachable moments when the learning tasks are personally relevant. The *cognitive and interpersonal style models* (e.g., Heath, 1964; Holland, 1973; Kolb, 1984; Myers, 1980; Witkin, 1976) suggest that individuals approach these tasks in characteristically different ways; they tend to exhibit different styles and patterns that must be taken into account when designing and presenting learning tasks. And finally, the *structural developmental models* (e.g., Harvey et al. 1961; Kohlberg, 1969; Kitchener & King, 1981; Perry, 1970) give us a view of how individuals differ in the way they organize and assign meaning to the events around them. These qualitative, hierarchical patterns are important for understanding the goals of development (i.e., independence/self-reliance, principled reasoning, reflective judgment, commitment) as well as the stepwise paths leading to those goals. Collectively, these personological models provide a means for understanding and assessing "where students are, where they are going, and how they get there" in terms of their own growth and development.

Environmental Theories

With respect to environmental differences, the *human aggregate models* (e.g., Astin, 1968; Holland, 1973; Myers, 1980) suggest that environments are transmitted through people and reflect the collective characteristics of the individuals who inhabit them. Environments also select and shape the behavior of individuals over time in a coercive manner, depending on the degree of differentiation and consistency of both the person and the environment. Concepts from the *physical models* (e.g., Heilweil, 1973; Michelson, 1970) note that the natural and synthetic features of environments set limits on the behavior that can occur within them. The *structural organizational models* (e.g., Blau & Scott, 1962; Etzioni, 1964; Hage & Aiken, 1970; Price, 1968) underscore the importance of the goals and purposes of environments that give rise to various organizational structures which, in turn, encourage or discourage certain behaviors (e.g., innovation, effectiveness). Finally, the *perceptual models* (e.g., Moos, 1979; Murray, 1938; Pace & Stern, 1958; Pervin, 1968; Stern, 1970) acknowledge that a critical element in understanding how individuals experience an environment is their subjective interpretation of that environment. Collectively, these environmental models help us understand how various aspects of educational environments attract, sustain, and satisfy students (Strange, in press).

Person-Environment Interaction

A final set of theories emerging in the student development literature describes the dynamics of person-environment interaction. Sanford's (1966) principle that development occurs when challenges in the environment are balanced by environmental supports is paramount. This concept is also referred to as "developmental dissonance" (Festinger, 1957). Here, too little challenge under highly supportive conditions is assumed to result in no developmental change, as there is little or no stimulus to alter present behavior. The opposite condition, that is, too much challenge accompanied by too little support, also may result in no developmental change because of overstimulation. Each of these conditions is a function of the interaction between personological characteristics and environmental conditions which, in combination, influence how the individual evaluates and responds to the environment, and, in short, whether development occurs as a result of the interaction. In other words, as Chickering (1969) noted, the impact or effectiveness of a given learning experience depends on the characteristics of the person who encounters it. Such differences may include, for example, learning style, assumptions about knowledge and learning, self-confidence, and willingness to take personal and intellectual risks.

These dynamics hold several implications. First, there is no single best method for promoting student development: What is effective will depend on the characteristics of the individual student and the specific features of the educational environment. Second, because students differ, a single experience can have different developmental outcomes. By the same token, different experiences can have similar outcomes. Third, the impact of a given experience depends on the *time* at which it is introduced because time is related to development (e.g., readiness to learn, willingness to be challenged, being in a period of stability or transition).

In summary, according to the interactionist paradigm, the greatest opportunities for growth and development occur when students are "matched" with appropriate environmental conditions. Designing such conditions (the art of student development) requires using the knowledge of concepts about the person and about the environment and how such elements interact to influence behavior (the science of student development).

THEORY AND PRACTICE IN APPLIED FIELDS

Lewin (1936) asserted that there is nothing so practical as a good theory, and Cross (1981) contended that, although theory without practice is empty, practice without theory is blind. Both claims affirm the importance of a theory and research base and its linkage to practice as essential for professional effectiveness. Yet, linking theory and practice, and incorporating a theory and research base in the professional preparation of student affairs practitioners, is problematic for several reasons. The problems with the linkages are hypothesized to be: (a) the inherently imperfect correspondence between theory and reality; (b) the difficulties of translating theory to practice; (c) the nature of applied fields; and (d) the nature of individuals attracted to people-oriented, applied fields.

Theory and Reality

As stated above, theory is a believable explanation for reality; it serves to organize and delineate the relationships between observed facts. A theoretical concept or model is derived from an abstraction of a potentially infinite number of specific and concrete variations of a phenomenon. For example, Kolb (1984) described the complex variations in the way students learn in terms of four patterns: (a) divergence, with its emphasis on concrete experience and reflective observation; (b) assimilation, emphasizing reflective observation and abstract conceptualization; (c) convergence, with a preference for abstract conceptualization and active experimentation; and

(d) accommodation, with an emphasis on active experimentation and concrete experience. No single individual's learning style can be completely captured by any one of these patterns, yet the presence of each of these is clearly evident in given populations. In this sense, theory cannot be an accurate description of any specific reality, but only an approximate representation of many.

Theory and Practice: The Role of Informal Theories

Parker (1977) addressed succinctly the difficulty of translating theory into practice in student affairs. He stated that such a task presents a dilemma to theorists and practitioners alike, that it is, in fact, paradoxical, and that it is therefore problematic. The dilemma, according to Parker, is that:

> In order for us to create a researchable model of the person [i.e., a theory] we must abstract from a very complex wholeness those parts which we wish to study. When we do so we ignore the rest of the person, which is interrelated in a complex and systemic way. . . . Workable models are too complex to research and researchable models are too simplified to be useful in practice. (p. 420)

The paradox Parker identified is that although "the nature of theory is such that it does not lead directly to practice, . . . the nature of practice is such that it does not proceed without theory" (p. 420) or ". . . some fairly set ideas about what is important, how those elements are related to each other, and what should happen" (p. 420). To understand the paradox, he drew the distinction between formal theory and informal "theories in use" (Argyris, 1976). Formal theories comprise:

> . . . explicit conceptualization[s] of the essential elements of a particular phenomenon, the hypothesized relationships among those elements, and the procedures by which those relations may be validated. Such theories are shared in the scientific community and tested in the laboratory or in natural settings. (Parker, 1977, p. 420)

Informal theory refers to the "body of common knowledge that allows us to make implicit connections among the events and persons in our environment and upon which we act in everyday life" (Parker, 1977, p. 420). Parker suggested that:

> . . . it is precisely because of our tendency to not self-correct that we cannot rely solely on our informal theories. Formal theories and their validation are crucial as counterforces to our highly personal world. It is the process of formal theory building and testing that corrects and adds to the body of knowledge common to a group or a culture, in our particular case, the group of professionals who work in student affairs. (p. 420)

Parker's solution is to recognize the problem of learning how to translate formal theories into informal theories-in-action, in effect, using formal theories to "tune our ears" and to adapt "to the needs of individual students (reading and flexing) through understanding the ways they personally construe their life and environs" (1977, p. 424).

The Nature of Applied Fields

The problem of linking theory to practice, it is hypothesized, is also a function of the nature of applied fields and the types of individuals attracted to them. Success in an applied field tends to be gauged in terms of what an individual has done. Accomplishments accumulated over time lead to a successful "track record" which, in turn, becomes the mark of an experienced and "seasoned practitioner." Individuals must "pay their dues" as an apprentice, learning from those who have "been there." Advancement is contingent upon a succession of responsibilities and assignments. Basic knowledge, such as theory, that is acquired through traditional schooling is both a source of mistrust and perhaps even a threat to those already practicing in the field. It may be a source of mistrust for several reasons. Claims of expertise, grounded in "what you know" rather than "what you have done," will predictably be met with suspicion in an applied field. This is especially true of a field like student affairs where interaction with people is paramount. Nothing substitutes for experience and maturity in terms of learning about and responding to the complexities of human behavior. Consequently, a status claim based on "what you know" (e.g., knowledge of current theory) rather than "what you have done" is understandably threatening because it tends to undercut the experiential foundation of the field.

This phenomenon is exacerbated by the already imperfect relationship between theory, reality, and practice. Moreover, the debate sharpens particularly at a time when the theory and research base of the field is expanding rapidly, such as is presently the case in student affairs. It is difficult to find time to stay current with all the new developments in the literature, and, unfortunately, support for continuing education and professional development is too often seen as a luxury item and therefore is the first to go when budgets tighten. Theory and practice are continually juxtaposed in an applied field, and the tension created by this dynamic is inevitable.

Practitioners Attracted to Applied Fields

Assumptions about the nature of applied fields are also important in understanding the type of individuals who are attracted to them. The notion that different occupational settings create characteristic environments that, in turn, differentially attract individuals to them is not a new idea. Holland (1973) has written extensively on this topic and claims that environments select and shape the behavior of people within them. Those who more closely resemble the dominant type within an environment are most likely to be attracted to it, and once within it, to be more satisfied and stable. A host of other studies examining differences in psychological type (Provost & Anchors, 1987), cognitive style (Messick & Associates, 1976), and learning style (Kolb, 1984) lend additional support to the validity of the notion of person-environment congruence.

An implication of this dynamic for the present discussion is that the dominant group of individuals attracted to a people-oriented applied field like student affairs may simply not value a theory and research base because they are essentially "doers." In the parlance of the Myers-Briggs model (Myers, 1980), they may be "extroverts," "sensors," "feelers," and "judgers," each characteristic representing an aversion to abstract, logical analysis and prescription. From Witkin's (1976) vantage point, the dominant group may tend toward "field dependence," seeing the whole rather than the parts. Alternatively, according to Kolb (1984), many student affairs professionals may be "accommodators," with a preference for active experimentation and concrete experience as principal modes of learning. Furthermore, using Holland's (1973) model, the individuals in the dominant group are often characterized as "Social," "Enterprising," and "Artistic" and derive occupational satisfaction from people rather than data, ideas, or things. The point of this analysis is that student affairs may attract a dominant group of individuals who are not particularly interested in manipulating concepts and ideas, and who are skeptical about the value of theory and research components in professional preparation criteria or staff development programs.

THEORY AND PRACTICE IN THE EDUCATION OF STUDENT DEVELOPMENT PROFESSIONALS

The following recommendations are offered for addressing the treatment of theory in staff development opportunities and in graduate preparation of professional student development practitioners. The suggestions are derived both from formal theory and 10 years of our own accumulated informal "theories in use" as graduate faculty members. The recommendations are offered to increase students' and practitioners' awareness of the role of theory in their actual situations, not as final solutions to the four hypothesized problems just discussed. The importance of a theory and research base for professional practice is not compromised, but the inherent difficulty of transmitting such a value is acknowledged. The three basic proposed recommendations follow.

1. *Encourage the role of "personal theorist."* This strategy recognizes that theory building is a very natural activity for practitioners. To wonder how something functions, or why something worked well or did not work, is a normal step in the day-to-day decisions a practitioner must make. Encourage the role of "personal theorist" by having students or staff members first focus on identifying their informal "theories in use." Within the context of a formal course or staff development workshop, for example, appropriate activities might include addressing basic questions like: "Do college students change over the course of their undergraduate years?" "In what ways?" "To what can you attribute such changes?" "What is the connection between those changes and the programs and activities we sponsor in our office?" There is an inevitable period of struggle in addressing such questions because informal theories are never completely clear and are invariably difficult to articulate. Group discussions that focus on synthesizing disparate "hunches" and developing a consensual framework (e.g., a descriptive model of the changes that take place among students during the college years) seem to work well. It is important to do this before any formal theories are introduced. Articulating and owning a personally generated explanation is critical to successfully initiate the "personal theorist" role. This is also an important step in recognizing the need for a more adequately articulated and supported perspective, namely, formal theory. Our own experience over the years with this exercise suggests that, collectively, a

group of students or staff members will generate an informal theory model in response to the above task that is very close to what they will later come to know as a formal theory. This compatibility is an affirming process and helps them gain confidence in recognizing and using their own informal theories.

2. *Move from the concrete to the abstract, from practice to theory.* This second recommendation recognizes that formal theory rarely introduces a completely new idea, but rather, it more often helps to organize and articulate better what we intuitively know or already have observed. For example, interacting with an individual who approaches issues from an absolute, authoritarian, simplistic, and black-and-white perspective is not an uncommon experience for most of us. The concept of Dualism, as described by Perry (1970), is immediately recognizable and helps us identify more clearly the nature of that pattern of thinking, as well as its sequence in an overall scheme of development (in this case, a requisite step to Multiplicity and Relativism). Good theories allow us to incorporate extant knowledge. The best theories seem to be almost self-evident, as if anyone could have developed and written them.

The best place to start, then, in presenting theory is with the concrete experience of students and staff members. Inductive methods, where the task is to move from particulars to general principles, are most effective at this point. For example, guiding students or staff members through an actual moral dilemma and having them synthesize and organize the various choices and responses builds an important informal theory base that will leave them much more receptive to the formal stages of moral reasoning identified by Kohlberg (1969). The use of case studies, focusing on the development of an explanation for individual differences (e.g., how two students responded differently to the same class or editorial), is another effective technique.

3. *Move from the abstract to the concrete, from theory to practice.* At first glance, this seems to contradict the recommendation above. However, it is offered as a suggestion for completing the learning cycle. Going from the particular to the general, from the concrete to the abstract, from practice to theory, is important for the initial acquisition of concepts. To fully understand the concepts, though, the process must come full circle, moving from the general to the particular, from the abstract to the concrete, and from theory back to practice. Kolb (1984) addressed in greater detail the sequence and effectiveness of this cycle of learning. Kolb described a learning model in terms of four sequential points on a cycle, beginning with *concrete experience*, leading to *reflective observation*, followed by *abstract conceptualization*, and then by *active experimentation*.

A quick reference to the children's television show "Mr. Wizard" makes the model easy to remember. The classic scene begins with a curious member of the neighborhood in Mr. Wizard's kitchen-laboratory being asked to "try something out" (concrete experience). A flash of excitement occurs (many times literally!) and Mr. Wizard challenges the naive participant to think about what happened (reflective observation). Following a brief moment of puzzlement, Mr. Wizard comes to the rescue with a succinct description and explanation of the basic principles involved and proceeds to unravel the mysterious underlying elements of cause and effect (abstract conceptualization). Now having understood what is likely to happen in this situation, or even a variation thereof, the participant is challenged to "try it again" (active experimentation), and the learning cycle is complete. Strategies that capitalize on the last two steps of this cycle (i.e., moving from abstract conceptualization to active experimentation) might include using a particular theoretical model to critique current campus policies or practices, or generating a program intervention designed to stimulate developmental growth. The focus of such a task should be on examining the implications inherent in the way a particular theory explains the phenomenon it purports to address. For example, developmental differences identified by the Conceptual Systems theory (Harvey et al., 1961) imply that a "Dependent-Conforming" individual requires more environmental structure for growth than one who is "Independent Self-Reliant." How can those structural differences be reflected in the way a class is taught? In a counseling/advising approach? In variations of a program design? In terms of critiquing policies or practices, for example, the method used to assign roommates or to deliver career counseling services might be examined in reference to a typology model like the Myers-Briggs model (Myers, 1980). Too often theory is presented as a revealed, abstract conceptualization, with little reference to the reality that initially generated it. Starting from the concrete, moving to the abstract, and then going back to the concrete can bridge the critical gap between theory and practice. These strategies are applicable to any phase of professional preparation, from an entry-level degree program to opportunities for continuing education and staff development.

In summary, the relationship between theory and practice in an applied field is not a problem to be solved; it is a concern that can be managed. Enabling practitioners to go beyond the present generation's experience and respond in more creative and informed ways in the future, and making the relationship between theory and practice more explicit, are signs of a mature profession.

REFERENCES

Argyris, C. (1976). Theories of action that inhibit individual learning. *American Psychologist, 31*, 638–654.

Aslanian, C., & Brickell, H. (1980). *Americans in transition: Life changes as reasons for adult learning.* New York: College Entrance Examination Board.

Astin, A.W. (1968). *The college environment.* Washington, DC: American Council on Education.

Astin, A.W. (1984). Student involvement: A developmental theory for higher education. *Journal of College Student Personnel, 25*, 297–308.

Blau, P.M., & Scott, W.R. (1962). *Formal organizations: A comparative approach.* San Francisco: Chandler.

Chickering, A.W. (1969). *Education and identity.* San Francisco: Jossey-Bass.

Cross, K.P. (1981). *Adults as learners.* San Francisco: Jossey-Bass.

Erikson, E. (1950). *Childhood and society.* New York: Norton.

Etzioni, A. (1964). *Modern organizations.* Englewood Cliffs, NJ: Prentice-Hall.

Festinger, L. (1957). *A theory of cognitive dissonance.* New York: Row, Peterson.

Gould, R.L. (1978). *Transformations: Growth and change in adult life.* New York: Simon & Schuster.

Hage, J., & Aiken, M. (1970). *Social change in complex organizations.* New York: Random House.

Harvey, O.J., Hunt, D.E., & Schroder, H.M. (1961). *Conceptual systems and personality organization.* New York: Wiley.

Havighurst, R.J. (1972). *Developmental tasks and education.* New York: McKay.

Heath, R. (1964). *The reasonable adventurer.* Pittsburgh: University of Pittsburgh Press.

Heilweil, M. (1973). The influence of dormitory architecture on residence behavior. *Environment and Behavior, 5,* 377–412.

Holland, J.L. (1973). *Making vocational choices: A theory of careers.* Englewood Cliffs, NJ: Prentice-Hall.

Kegan, R. (1982). *The evolving self: Problem and process in human development.* Cambridge, MA: Harvard University Press.

Kitchener, K.S., & King, P.M. (1981). Reflective judgment: Concepts of justification and their relationship to age and education. *Journal of Applied Developmental Psychology, 2,* 89–116.

Kohlberg, L. (1969). Stage and sequence: The cognitive developmental approach to socialization. In D. Goslin (Ed.), *Handbook of socialization theory and research* (pp. 347–480). Chicago: Rand McNally.

Kolb, D.A. (1984). *Experiential learning: Experience as the source of learning and development.* Englewood Cliffs, NJ: Prentice-Hall.

Levinson, D.J. (1978). *The seasons of a man's life.* New York: Ballantine.

Lewin, K. (1936). *Principles of topological psychology.* New York: McGraw-Hill.

Messick, S., & Associates (Eds.) (1976). *Individuality in learning.* San Francisco: Jossey-Bass.

Michelson, W. (1970). *Man and his urban environment: A sociological approach.* Reading, MA: Addison-Wesley.

Miller, T., & Prince, J. (1976). *The future of student affairs.* San Francisco: Jossey-Bass.

Moos, R. (1979). *Evaluating educational environments.* San Francisco: Jossey-Bass.

Morrill, W., Hurst, J., & Oetting, E. (1980). *Dimensions of intervention for student development.* New York: Wiley.

Murray, H. (1938). *Exploration in personality.* New York: Oxford University Press.

Myers, I.B. (1980). *Gifts differing.* Palo Alto, CA: Consulting Psychologists Press.

Pace, C.R., & Stern, G.G. (1958). An approach to the measurement of psychological characteristics of college environments. *Journal of Educational Psychology, 49,* 269–277.

Parker, C.A. (1977). On modeling reality. *Journal of College Student Personnel, 18*(5), 419–425.

Perry, W.G. (1970). *Forms of intellectual and ethical development in the college years: A scheme.* New York: Holt, Rinehart & Winston.

Pervin, L. (1968). Performance and satisfaction as a function of individual-environment fit. *Psychological Bulletin, 69,* 56–68.

Price, J.L. (1968). *Organizational effectiveness: An inventory of propositions.* Homewood, IL: Irwin.

Provost, J.A., & Anchors, S. (1987). *Applications of the Myers-Briggs type indicator in higher education.* Palo Alto, CA: Consulting Psychologists Press.

Sanford, N. (1966). *Self and society: Social change and individual development.* New York: Atherton.

Schlossberg, N. (1984). *Counseling adults in transition.* New York: Springer.

Skinner, B.F. (1953). *Science and human behavior.* New York: Macmillan.

Stern, G. (1970). *People in context: Measuring person-environment congruence in education and industry.* New York: Wiley.

Strange, C. (in press). Managing college environments: Theory and practice. In T.K. Miller, R.B. Winston, and W. Mendenhall (Eds.), *Administration and leadership in student affairs.* Muncie, IN: Accelerated Development.

Witkin, H.A. (1976). Cognitive style in academic performance and in teacher-student relations. In S. Messick and Associates (Eds.), *Individuality in learning* (pp. 38–89). San Francisco: Jossey-Bass.

PART II

THEORETICAL FOUNDATIONS OF PRACTICE

CHAPTER 3

Recent Theories and Research Underlying Student Development

Robert F. (Bob) Rodgers

Treated simplistically, the concept of "student development" entails characterizing a *student* and characterizing *development* and then applying the concept of development to a student. Student development comprises, in this context, the ways that a student grows, progresses, or increases his or her developmental capacities as a result of enrollment in an institution of higher education. The concept of student development has come to represent more, however, than this descriptive meaning suggests. The concept is used, for example, to represent the body of research and theories on late-adolescent and life-span adult development. In particular, works in the families of theory termed *person-environment interaction, psychosocial, cognitive-developmental,* and *typological* are called the theories of student development (Knefelkamp, Widick, & Parker, 1978; Rodgers, 1980).

The concept of student development can also be used as a philosophy. Student development can be considered as the ideological basis for actions or the rationale for programs. In the *Student Personnel Point of View* (American Council on Education, 1937, 1949) and the reports of the Council of Student Personnel Associations (Cooper, 1971, 1972), for example, this ideological use is plainly stated and openly advocated. The philosophical usage is prescriptive. It takes a value stand on the purpose of higher education and on the question of what higher education ought to seek as an outcome. In this usage, student development is synonymous with student affairs' central, historical educational value, *concern for the development of the whole student.*

A third usage of the concept of student development is programmatic. Student development is what student affairs staff and faculty members do to facilitate learning and development. It consists of the environments (i.e., services, workshops, classes, programs, policies) provided. This programmatic usage may or may not use the theories and research on student and adult development as the bases for

27

programmatic efforts. In this chapter, however, it will be assumed that programmatic efforts are based on these theories and research about them, and the chapter will concentrate on an update of the families of theory and research that can be used to plan those programmatic efforts. Because the major reviews of these theories and research occurred in the late 1970s (Drum, 1980; Knefelkamp et al., 1978; Rodgers, 1980), this update will emphasize theories and research published since 1980 and thus will supplement those major reviews.

PERSON-ENVIRONMENT INTERACTION THEORIES

In the 1980s, it became clear that in using developmental theories without the person-environment interaction perspective, student development efforts tacitly focused mostly on the person (P) and often neglected the environment (E) and the interaction $(\times)$. Similarly, in using the person-environment perspective without using developmental theories, campus ecology projects did not assess, redesign, or evaluate for development per se. The two approaches are compatible and integratable, that is, student development can be *integrated into* the person-environment way of thinking, with both approaches profiting as a result. Campus ecology $[B = f(P \times E)]$, therefore, has become the most basic way of thinking about the work of student affairs, and theories of adult development give the ecology model developmental substance. The following will elaborate on these points using recent research and evaluation studies.

Campus Ecology Without Student Development

William Perry (1970) opened his book *Forms of Intellectual and Ethical Development in the College Years* by describing and analyzing three students' reactions to a classroom lecture. Building upon Perry's hypothetical scene, let's imagine these three students are once again headed for class. Each student is thinking about an announced history lecture on the causes of the Civil War while walking toward the lecture hall. Student A is thinking, "Well, the professor is going to tell us why we had the Civil War. As he lectures, I'll write down the answers in my notes. Later I'll memorize my notes, and then on the test I'll prove to the professor that I've learned why we had the Civil War."

Student B thinks, "Well, I want to know why we had the Civil War so I can make a good grade in this class. I hope the professor gives us the answers. If he does, I'll take good notes and then give the answers back to the professor on the test. Professors, however, sometimes want you to learn to think critically rather than just learn the facts. So, instead of giving you the answers, which they could do, they give you a set of questions and criteria, lecture on various views of what happened, and then expect you to work out the correct answer. That is all right as long as the material is not too vague. I wonder what our professor is going to do today?"

Student C assumes, "I'm going to class to learn about the various points of view on the question of why we had the Civil War, the evidence that supports the various theories, and their limitations. After the lecture, I'll read the important sources, and then I'll try to work out a synthesis of why I think we had the Civil War.''

The professor has to lecture from some point of view. Let us assume he covers four theories on the causes of the Civil War, does a devastating critique of each one, and then says, "Class dismissed!" Let us assume all three of our students have the same academic advisor. After class, student A rushes to see the advisor. "I want out of my history class," he says. "I don't understand anything the professor is saying. You cannot learn anything in the class. I have no idea why we had the Civil War after listening to the professor's lectures. I know I can't pass a test in this class. Why did the university hire him anyway? He doesn't know very much about history. I am so confused. I want to drop this class."

The next day Student B arrives at the advisor's office. "I need to talk," he says. "I don't know about history. I think I understand the questions about the causes of the Civil War, but I'm really confused about which theory is correct. The professor is so difficult to understand. I don't know if I can handle this class or not!"

A week later Student C visits the advisor. "I can't tell you how much I'm enjoying history," Student C says. "The professor is so stimulating. You should have heard his wonderful lectures on the Civil War."

At this point the academic advisor is scratching his or her head and thinking, "Could this have been the same professor on the same day in the same set of lectures with the students reacting so differently?" Evaluation using the Perry scheme, of course, makes this range of reactions possible. Students A, B, and C are making meaning of their experience in the same history class in different ways; they are at different positions of intellectual development. Nevertheless, the advisor, who is not familiar with Perry's work but is familiar with the ecosystems model of examining person and environment interaction, decides to visit the history professor, and they discuss Students A, B, and C, the class, and the possibility of studying the situation. The professor agrees to join the advisor in studying the environment of the history class using an ecosystems methodology. A working group of students, the professor, and the advisor design a tailor-made instrument to assess the syllabus, reading list, each major assignment, the tests, the professor's lectures, and the recitation discussion groups. Students are asked to evaluate their degree of satisfaction with each of these elements in the class environment. For items with a high degree of dissatisfaction, students are asked through an Environmental Referent (ER) form for suggestions to correct the situation. Data are collected and analyzed, with the following results:

1. On the ER, a majority of the 150 students in the class report that the professor's lectures are confusing. They have difficulty understanding him and judging which point of view is the right one. They recommend simpler lectures. "Tell us clearly," says one student, "which theory is the right view on the topic." "Be more straightforward," says another.

2. A majority of the students also say that the discussions in the recitation sections are a waste of time. "We don't learn anything in these so-called discussions," says a representative student. "It would be better, especially for passing tests, if the teaching assistant lectured and made sure we've learned the material for the tests."

3. The students report having difficulty with the professor's tests. Each test is half essay and half objective questions. The students do not like the essays and recommend that they be dropped and the entire test be clear-cut and objective.

Should the class be redesigned based on these recommendations? Should the professor simplify his lectures and present a single point of view clearly and carefully? Should he switch to objective tests and make the recitation sessions into lectures to prepare students for the tests? Upon *what grounds* should the planning group or the professor make decisions? Would the recommended changes be appropriate for the development of the students? For satisfaction with the class? For better grades?

This illustration is typical of most ecosystems studies that were completed and published in the 1970s and 1980s. These person-environment interaction studies were mostly atheoretical studies of students' perceived dissatisfactions with a given environment. They assumed that reducing the perceived dissatisfactions would result in improved satisfaction, performance, and development. These assumptions may or may not be valid. In terms of development, for example, reducing perceived dissatisfactions would facilitate development if the recommendations were congruent with the environmental conditions that seem to facilitate development. In the illustration, the recommendations are largely incongruent with the kind of classroom environment that seems to facilitate intellectual development for students making meaning in dualistic or relativistic ways, but may be congruent with improved satisfaction for dualists and perhaps improved performance in terms of making higher grades. Hence, if the recommendations for the history class were implemented, satisfaction might improve for many but not all students in the class. Performance in the class might improve provided the goals of the course were compatible with the changes, or the professor amended the goals to be compatible with the changes. It is doubtful, however, that the ability to think in more complex ways (i.e., intellectual development) would be enhanced.

Assessment of Ecosystems Studies

Although the intent of campus ecology studies has been to assess and then, if needed, redesign campus environments for increased satisfaction, better performance, and personal, intellectual, and social development (Banning & Kaiser, 1974; Blocker, 1974; Fawcett, Huebner, & Banning, 1978; Huebner, 1979; Huebner & Corazzini, 1978; Kaiser, 1978; Morrill, Hurst, & Oetting, 1980), most of the published works and dissertations on campus ecology have not mirrored these intents. In residence halls, for example, Schuh's (1979), Livingston's (1980), Fries's (1983), and Reynolds's (1984) studies are atheoretical assessments of students' perceived satisfaction with the environment, not studies of development or performance per se. Schroeder's (1976, 1980a, 1980b, 1981; Schroeder & Belmonte, 1979) works with residence halls are theoretically based. He used theories of territoriality, person-environment interaction, and Jungian personality type in his assessments and environmental redesigns. His pre- and posttest measures of the impact of redesigned environments, however, focus on perceived satisfaction, behaviors on administrative indices such as renewal and damage rates, or Moos's (1979) perceived social climate. None of these measures are developmental per se.

Dietrich's (1972) ecosystem study of campus ministries, Sabock's (1980) ecosystem assessment of intercollegiate athletic academic support services, Treadway's (1979) report on a campuswide assessment and redesign project, and Mintz's (1976) assessment of a national Greek pledge educational system similarly are atheoretical assessments of perceived environments without using any criteria derived from developmental theory. With the exception of Treadway's study, these studies also have not reported on satisfaction, group performance, or developmental outcomes that may have resulted from redesigned environments. Treadway reported on a follow-up atheoretical campuswide assessment after redesign. The redesigns did not use criteria derived from developmental perspectives, and the evaluation did not examine developmental changes that may have occurred.

Huebner, Royer, Moore, Cordes, and Paul (1979) and Hurst and Ragle (1979) advocated the use of developmental perspectives in assessments and evaluations of outcomes; however, the projects they described failed to implement these recommendations. Huebner's work on stress and medical school environments and Hurst and Ragle's brief descriptions of ombudsman and minority student assessments all used tailor-made local instruments, interviews, or institutional atheoretical data bases for assessments. No studies of redesigned environments were reported.

Hence, most campus ecology studies seem to have used tailor-made, local, atheoretical environmental assessments or, when theories have been used, they have not been developmental theories. Reports on evaluations of environmental redesigns are less numerous but also have not included developmental variables. At best, therefore, published studies have assumed that redesigned environments based upon recommendations from students' atheoretical perception of the environment would result in development. The studies have not dealt with the issue of development directly, and the assumption that development occurs may or may not be the case. Hence, in the 1980s the question became, *How might student development principles be integrated directly into campus ecology methodologies* (Rodgers, 1984a)?

Integrating Student Development and Campus Ecology Principles

The integration of student development and campus ecology theories and methodologies initially requires an analysis of the basic constructs of both. Campus ecology examines the interaction of students and their campus environments or subenvironments. Given the same environment, some students may succeed (Student C in the history class), whereas others may fail (Students A and B). Some may be satisfied (Student C), and others (Students A and B) may not be. Some may develop (Student C); others (Students A and B) may not.

The *student*, the *environment*, and their *interaction* are involved in these differential outcomes, not just the student or the environment. Students have different genetic heritages and histories of development. These students can experience the same environment differently. Similarly, when the environment is altered, development, performance, and satisfaction also may be altered for different students differentially. In short, the essence of the ecological perspective is a belief that human behavior results from the *interaction* of the *individual* and the *campus environment*.

In one of its three usages, student development is a name given to deliberate attempts to help students learn and develop by designing campus environments using adult developmental theories. The *deliberate* and *theory-in-practice* nature of these efforts often are put into operation through the use of process models (Rodgers, 1980). *Process models* are conceptualizations of the steps that help practitioners use theory in practice. They are not developmental theories per se. They cannot tell deans or counselors anything about the nature of development, how development is facilitated, or how it is measured. The theories themselves inform the practitioner of the types of development possible for college students, the criteria for deliberately designing environments that facilitate development, and the instruments or other means for measuring development. The means of measurement link the theories to developmental assessments of persons and evaluations of redesigns. The criteria for designing facilitative environments link theories to environmental assessments and redesign efforts. Process models tell the practitioner *when* and *how* to use the theories, their criteria for designing facilitative environments, and the means of measurement.

Campus ecology studies often have used ecosystems (Aulepp & Delworth, 1978) or related process models (Fawcett et al., 1978; Huebner & Corazzini, 1978) to implement their projects. Similar to all other process models, ecosystems models cannot define student development, specify criteria for facilitating developmental change, or specify means for measuring student development. Ecosystems models specify the nature and order the steps needed to assess an environment, redesign the environment, and evaluate the results of redesign. As indicated, when theories have been used in campus ecology, these theories have been person-environment interaction theories such as those of Moos (1979), Stern (1970), or Pervin (1967, 1968). These theories are not developmental per se (Rodgers, 1980). Hence, the campus ecology studies completed and published so far have not focused on student development per se and have not used developmental theories as criteria for designing facilitative environments or as means of measurement in the steps of their process models.

To correct the situation, Lewin's (1936) famous equation

$$B = f(P \times E) \tag{1}$$

can be restated in a more complex form as follows:

$$B_p = f(P_d \times E_s) \tag{2}$$

where, B_p is the probability of facilitating growth in a specific kind of development [e.g., intellectual development as defined by the Perry (1970) scheme] or two or more kinds of development [e.g., development on the Perry scheme and psychosocial development as defined by Chickering's (1969) vectors]; f represents the phrase "is a function of"; P_d is the developmental level of a person in a given developmental area(s) such as the Perry scheme or Chickering's vectors; E_s is the external stimuli of the environment as described by criteria for facilitating development derived from the developmental area(s) under consideration (e.g., the Perry scheme or Chickering's vectors); and $\times$ is the interaction defined by the degree of compatibility between a person and the environment as evaluated by the criteria for facilitating development derived from the theories under consideration. It is important to note that *both* the person and the environment are assessed, not just one or the other, and *both* are evaluated in terms of *interaction* as defined by the *same developmental theories*.

When student development and campus ecology are combined, both P_d and E_s can be defined by various kinds of developmental theories. For example,

$$P_d = f(P_{cd}, P_{ps}, P_{pei}, P_t, \text{ and/or } P_s) \tag{3}$$

where P_{cd} represents cognitive developmental theories of human development such as those of Perry (1970), Kohlberg (1984), and Kegan (1982); P_{ps} represents psychosocial theories of development such as those of Erikson (1968), Chickering (1969), Levinson (1978), Josselson (1987); P_{pei} represents person-environment interaction theories and models such as those of Moos (1979), Pervin (1967), Barker (1968), and Stern (1970); P_t represents typological models and theories of personality type such as those of Jung (1971), Kolb (1976), Keirsey and Bates (1978), and Heath (1964); and P_s represents academic and life coping skills and attitudes such as assertiveness, problem-solving, interpersonal care-giving, and reading or note-taking skills.

Similarly, for E_s

$$E_s = f(E_{cd}, E_{ps}, E_{pei}, E_t, \text{ and/or } E_s) \tag{4}$$

where the subscripts represent the same families of theory as P_d.

Figure 1 summarizes this integration of student development theories into the person-environment interaction perspective. The person, the environment, and their interaction can be conceptualized and assessed from behavioral, psychosocial, cognitive-structural, humanistic-existential, person-environment, or typological points of view. The *same theoretical perspective(s) need to be used for all three assessments* (P, E, and X) and not one or the other. Mutual assumptions, constructs, and research bases ailow for consistent interpretation of assessments, goal setting, environmental design criteria, and evaluation of outcomes.

If campus ecology is to focus on development in environmental redesign, then at least *one developmental theory* must be used in assessing the persons and the environment, in analyzing their interaction, in making decisions about redesigning the environment, and in evaluating the outcomes of the redesigned environment. It is important to note, however, that the use of *several theoretical perspectives* permits more sophisticated person-and-environment assessment and environmental design than the use of a single theory or no theory at all (Rodgers, 1983).

To sum up, in order to integrate student development within campus ecology and to focus on student development as an outcome, the following recommendations and observations are offered:

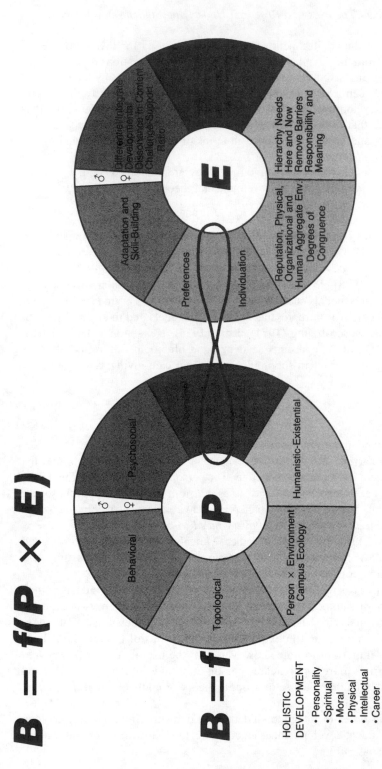

FIGURE 1

Integrating Student Development With Person-Environment Interaction

34

1. Use the person-environment interaction as the basic general paradigm for your work and then integrate developmental and other relevant theories into it;
2. Person-environment interaction models serve as reminders to assess three things, not just one or two of the following: (a) the *students*, (b) their *environment*, and (c) the degree of congruence or incongruence in their *interaction*;
3. Use theory, including at least one developmental theory, in making campus developmental and other theoretical ecological assessments; do not limit assessments to common-sense and atheoretical variables;
4. If *multiple types* of developmental and other theoretical frameworks are used, the degree of individuation in environmental designs can be increased;
5. To determine whether or not environmental redesign is needed, use criteria derived from theories and your educational values to analyze and make judgments on the interaction data;
6. If redesign is needed, the nature of the redesign also derives from the assessment data as evaluated by theoretical criteria; and finally,
7. Evaluate outcomes of redesigned environments using measures of the developmental and other theories and atheoretical variables selected for a given project.

COGNITIVE-DEVELOPMENTAL THEORIES

Cognitive-developmental theories attempt to describe the increasing degrees of complexity with which individuals make meaning of their experience with moral questions (Kohlberg, 1984), questions of knowing and valuing (Kitchener & King, 1981; Perry, 1970), questions of faith (Fowler, 1981), and questions of what is self and object (Kegan, 1982; Loevinger, 1976).

During the 1980s, with the exception of the theories of Carol Gilligan (1982, 1986a, 1986b) and Robert Kegan (1982), major new cognitive-developmental theories were not introduced as they were in the 1960s and especially in the 1970s. The past 10 years have been more of a period of testing the validity of these theories. More specifically, during the last 10 years some researchers have been examining questions of possible gender and cultural-ethnic differences in cognitive structural development. Other researchers have been conducting longitudinal studies in order to validate theoretical constructs or propositions.

Gender-Related Research

If you were planning a career development workshop, if you were counseling a married couple, if you were teaching a history course, if you were contemplating a set of policies and processes for student retention, or if you were mediating a residence hall roommate conflict, and if you were trying to use your students' cognitive-developmental levels as a guide to doing your work, would your work inherently be biased against women? Because many cognitive-developmental theories were developed using male subjects, the question has been raised whether cognitive-structural theories are gender-biased in favor of men. In other words, if you use cognitive-structural theories to plan your practice, are you inherently helping the development of men more than the development of women?

This issue of whether men and women make meaning in similar or different cognitive-structural ways has been the focus of research and speculation throughout the 1980s. The most famous theory in this regard is Gilligan's (1982) two voices of development, and the best known debate or discussion involves Kohlberg (1984) and Gilligan (1986a, 1986b). Kegan's (1982) theory and the Perry scheme (1970), however, also have been foci for research on gender issues.

Gilligan's Theory and the Kohlberg-Gilligan Debate/Discussion

While Gilligan was studying the relationships between moral reasoning and moral behavior using as subjects women who were considering whether or not to have abortions, she discovered a form of moral reasoning that she believed to be different from the reasoning described by Kohlberg (Gilligan, 1982). She called this different way of reasoning the *care and responsibility voice*, and, following Kohlberg's use of language, she called his descriptions of reasoning *the justice voice*.

The *care voice* may be characterized (Gilligan, 1982; Lyons, 1983) as emphasizing relationships between persons and seeing self and others as embedded in their specific situations. Within these situations care seeks to understand what the other needs and then to respond to these needs as defined by the other and not by the self. Moral dilemmas, therefore, are seen in terms of relationships, collaboration, maintaining and restoring relationships, and preventing psychological or physical harm, and are resolved through actions of support, healing, and care. On the night before he died, for example, Jesus of Nazareth is reported to have ministered to his disciples. He washed their feet, expressed love and care for them just as they were to love and serve others, and tried to prepare them to maintain their relationships with each other and with him through a new ritual of bread and wine. At the same time he claimed that one disciple would deny and another betray their relationship.

The *justice voice*, in contrast, is characterized as emphasizing the effects of moral choice on the self or on the other as the self would see it from the other's shoes. These effects are evaluated through rules and principles of fairness and relationships of reciprocity. Moral dilemmas are analyzed in terms of issues and conflicting claims among competing individuals or options. Duty and obligation are the result of impartial analysis using rules and principles of justice. For example, on the night before his death, in contrast to Jesus, Socrates and his friends engaged in a dispassionate analysis of the competing options open to him to escape or to stay in prison and face death. Using starting principles and logical analysis, Socrates concluded that he should not escape but stay in prison and die. His duty was clear.

Although the care voice was discovered using a female sample, Gilligan was careful to point out that subsequent research indicated that all men and women use both voices, but everyone prefers one voice over the other. The preferred voice is used most often and is probably better developed; the other voice is used sometimes even though it is not preferred. In the research reported by Gilligan and her colleagues (Gilligan, 1982, 1986a, 1986b; Lyons, 1983) most (about 80%) but not all women preferred the care voice, and most (about 70%) but not all men preferred the justice voice. Some women (about 20%) preferred the justice voice and some men (about 30%) preferred the care voice.

These associations of voice with majority and minority gender groups were not overridden even when care-voiced persons of both sexes were presented with a hypothetical dilemma that was formulated in terms of conflicting rights, and justice-voiced persons of both sexes were presented with a dilemma of conflicting responsibilities and relationships (Gilligan, 1986a; Johnston, 1985; Langdale, 1983). Both kinds of reasoning were used by both voices in response to both dilemmas. The care-voiced persons' use of justice reasoning increased on the justice dilemma and the justice-voiced persons' use of care reasoning increased on the relationships dilemma. Nevertheless, individuals' preferences were not overridden by the nature of the dilemma. Both groups still preferred and used most often the preferred voice. Hence, the situation (the nature of the dilemma) does affect reasoning, but does not seem to cancel voice preferences.

Kohlberg's scoring system uses justice-oriented dilemmas as the stimuli to which subjects respond, and his scoring manual is based on justice criteria for assigning stages to protocols. If such stimuli bring forth more justice responses, even from care-voiced persons, and if such rating criteria bring forth scores representing a care person as lower in developmental level than comparable justice persons, then there may be a systematic bias against the care voice in Kohlberg's theory and measure. Gilligan (1982, 1986a) believed that these biases do exist, and that care-voiced persons are handicapped within Kohlberg's theory and measurement system.

Kohlberg rejected Gilligan's proposition that his theory is biased and not universally applicable both to women and men. He argued (Kohlberg, 1984) that there is one justice structure of moral reasoning with two *styles* of expressing it. Gilligan's care voice is not a separate cognitive structure but a style that is similar to his substage A. Similarly, Gilligan's justice voice is his substage B, a second style for the *same* stage structures. Furthermore, if age, occupation, and educational level are held constant, then Kohlberg maintained that the research (Denny, 1988; Gibbs, Arnold, & Burkhart, 1984; Walker, 1984) does not support the conclusion that men score higher than women using his or Gibbs's (Gibbs & Widaman, 1982) scoring systems.

Countering, Gilligan (1986a, 1986b) claimed that in two recent studies (Baumrind, 1986; Haan, 1985) where educational levels were controlled, women scored lower than men. In addition, Langdale (1983) performed a third study controlled for age, occupational level, and educational level; she found that persons with care orientations (86% women, 14% men) had significantly lower Kohlberg stage scores than did individuals with predominantly justice orientations (69% men, 31% women). This suggests ". . . that gender differences reported in Kohlberg's measure derive not from the fact of gender per se but rather from the greater tendency of females (and some males) to frame and resolve moral problems in the care orientation. . . . This finding in turn reflects the fact that Kohlberg conceived moral judgment within the single perspective of the justice orientation'' (Gilligan, 1986a, p. 45).

So, the debate continues. The issues are not yet resolved. Is there one structure with two styles, or are there two structures? Is Kohlberg's measurement biased against the care orientation? Or, as he claims, do substages A and B correct for this criticism?

The debate is important because the differences in the two voices have practical implications for student affairs. Is it possible that *most* college teaching, student affairs programs, and even educational policies help one voice (justice) to be a detriment to the other (care)? For example, if classroom or workshop procedures focus only on the adequacy of a student's justice reasoning and perhaps use a debate as a forum for learning and as a stimulus for cognitive development, then that classroom or workshop is based on the assumption that care-voiced students learn best in the same environment as justice-voiced students. The development of care students has been equated with their ability to accept the questions, definitions, and teaching methods of the justice voice. Such processes may not be optimal for facilitating development of a care-oriented student.

Care-voiced persons seem to prefer *dialogue discussions*, where students rely on each other and their teacher or facilitator for understanding, comfort, and support (Gilligan, 1986a, p. 50). They prefer collaborative, supportive discussions instead of competitive debates. They prefer an interdependent atmosphere that empowers them to build and evolve relationships with each other and staff members and then to learn from one another by listening to each other. They do not prefer hierarchical classrooms or organizations that are structured around dominance and subordination or autonomous competition.

Gilligan (1986a; Lyons, 1983) also believed that the two voices have consequences beyond cognitive-structural development per se. There also may be two kinds of *identity formation*, two different processes for *resolving psychosocial issues* such as vocational choice, and two different ways of *constructing problems, making decisions*, and *resolving conflict*. Identity formation for a care-voiced person, for example, may best be facilitated within a framework of relationships and dialogue. Such a dialogue process places emphasis ". . . on speaking and listening, on being heard and making oneself understood, ties self-definition to an active engagement with others and turns attention to the process of communication'' (Gilligan, 1986a, p. 51). In short, counseling rather than objective critical self-analysis would be a more appropriate paradigm for facilitating identity formation for care-voiced persons.

Gilligan argued that the two voices cannot be integrated into a single, unified entity. They are always in tension with each other. They are complementary processes for development, ways to construct problems and find solutions, and forms of identity. Sometimes justice might benefit from the *inclusiveness* of care; sometimes care might benefit from the *rational analysis* of justice. Nevertheless, to educate both voices requires student affairs to use processes applicable to both

orientations and to give up what Perry (1970) might call the
road to development.

Finally, if many women and some men prefer the care
said about the origins of the voices? Gilligan (1986b) d
activities that might lead women behaviorally to a care perspective, w....
Rodgers (1988) conceptualized the problem in terms of Jung/Myers personality
types. Rodgers hypothesized that the underlying distinction between the two
voices may be the Thinking (T) and Feeling (F) judgment preference as defined
by Jung (1971) and Myers (1980). He studied the voice orientations of equal
numbers of dominant male and female Fs and dominant male and female Ts.
Without exceptions, so far, he has found all of the Fs (both male and female)
to be care-voiced and all of the Ts (both male and female) to be justice-voiced
using Lyons's (1983) interview to measure voice. It is important to note that
the T and F scales are the only dimension of the Myers-Briggs Type Indicator
that also has revealed a gender difference in the population. Similar to Gilligan's
findings, about 75% of the women have F preferences and 25% have T preferences, and about 75% of the men have T preferences and 25% have F preferences. These preliminary findings lend some support to an interpretation that
the two voices originate in personality type at birth rather than in social conditioning. Cultural expectations for the sexes may bring experiences that reinforce personality type preference voices (e.g., female Fs and male Ts) or make
some voices/types "swim upstream" (e.g., female Ts and male Fs). The voices
of college students, therefore, may be exemplifications both of personality type
preferences and social conditioning.

Robert Kegan's Theory

Robert Kegan's (1979, 1980a, 1980b, 1982) theory of ego development attempts
to describe how we make meaning of *what is self* and *what is other*. That is, his
theory describes the processes of differentiating *self* from *other* and then integrating
self with *other* as the ego evolves throughout the life course. In addition, his work
also helps clarify some of the issues that divide Gilligan and Kohlberg.

Kegan posited six cognitive structural stages similar to but broader than Kohlberg's
stages. Kegan called his stages *temporary truces*—an equilibrium people establish for
a time that provides the boundary between self/subject and other/object. Stages, therefore, are the ways a person settles the issue of what is *me* and what is *other*. It is the
psycho-logic of individuals' meaning making. It is their *truth*. It defines *who they are*.

Thus, for example, at the stage of interpersonalism (Stage 3, the stage of many
college students), people *are* their relationships. They are, in Kegan's terms, embedded in mutuality with their primary peer group. They cannot *be* without being in
relationship. Hence, for many college students, nothing is as influential as the peer
group, for "who they are" is defined by their relationships in these groups. Therefore, in a property damage situation in a residence hall, the self would rather help

.ne damages than risk disapproval of the group by reporting the person actually ₃ponsible.

When the Stage 3 self evolves or develops, people differentiate the self as interpersonalism and make the psycho-logic of interpersonalism into an object. As individuals move to Stage 4 (institutionalism), they *have* relationships with peer groups as opposed to *being* those relationships. However, at Stage 4, the self is embedded in ideology, autonomy, and competence. People are now autonomous, ideological selves and self-consistency with their ideology is more important than relationships. Hence, they may act in opposition to peer norms and report the person responsible for damages. However, the institutional way of defining the self cannot be differentiated; this self cannot yet examine itself as an object.

The stages of the evolving self are summarized in Table 1, which begins on page 42. The underlying tension in the evolution of the self outlined in Table 1 is the yearning toward *inclusion* and *connectedness* (Gilligan's care voice) and the yearning toward *autonomy* and *independence* (the justice voice). The nature of the self's boundaries emphasizes one and then the other yearning as individuals progress through life. Stages 1, 3, and 5 emphasize inclusion and connectedness. Stages 0, 2, and 4 emphasize separateness and autonomy.

Kegan argued that this alternating emphasis has significant implications for relationships, working with groups, and counseling. As indicated, at the interpersonal stage, college students are embedded in mutuality, in their relationships. They cannot separate who they are from their relationships. If their relationships with lovers or fraternal groups come to an end, they may have strong feelings of dependency and loss of self. They may leave school rather than face peers without their lover or without being pledged to the right fraternal group.

Students at Stage 3 cannot settle or resolve conflicts between different but important interpersonal relationships. For example, the peer group and parents may have different norms on the issue of drinking alcoholic beverages before being of legal age. The student may behave one way with peers and another way at home. In each case, the student behaves according to the norms of the group, even though they are inconsistent. If these two worlds come together, however, such students often report feeling sad, wounded, or incomplete, but not angry at their friends or parents. They may become *depressed* and express their depression as feeling lonely, deserted, betrayed, and strained. The tension behind the depression results from being both vulnerable to what peers and family think of them and yet feeling selfish and uncaring if they begin to put themselves and a new set of values first.

Similarly to this analysis of Stage 3 and parallel with transitions between different stages of ego development, Kegan postulated three kinds of depression, each corresponding to the failure or inadequacy of a previous stage of ego development (see Table 2, on page 44).

Sensitive staff and counselors can use both the stages and forms of depression in understanding and intervening with college students. The stages help them understand how students may be defining "self" and "other" as they attempt to resolve psychosocial developmental tasks. Emotional autonomy, for example, may require a student to move from seeing self as his or her relationships (Stage 3) to

having relationships and *being* his or her autonomous ideology (Stage 4).
resolving the emotional autonomy aspect of Chickering's "developing auton
may require a Stage 3 to Stage 4 cognitive-structural transition as a necessary
not sufficient condition for psychosocial developmental change.

The three forms of depressions may help student affairs professionals understand
the pain often associated with cognitive-structural change. Students resist growth-
because what must be given up is who they are, their being, their truth. Transition
from one stage to another is a slow, painful, and sometimes *depressing* process.
Kegan's theory (1982) helps student affairs professionals understand the differential
kinds of depression students often experience and how to support them differentially
through their process of change.

Gender Research on Intellectual or Epistemological Development

Just as Gilligan explored possible gender differences in moral development, similar
gender-based questions have been explored for the Perry scheme and to some degree
for Kitchener and King's (1981, 1985a, 1985b; King, 1982; King, Kitchener,
Davison, Parker, & Wood, 1983; Kitchener, 1986) Reflective Judgment model.
Do college women systematically score lower than college men on intellectual or
epistemological development? If you use Perry's or Kitchener and King's theories
to plan your practice, are you inherently helping men more than women? Do women
reason with different epistemological structures than men? Or, if they do not use
different structures, are there different styles of making meaning within the same
structures? If there are different structures or styles, what difference does it make
for professional practice?

Upon entry to college, generally women have scored slightly higher than men
on intellectual development in several studies at various institutions (Heidke, 1982;
Omahan, 1982; Rodgers, 1974–1988), or no differences have been found between
the genders (Baxter Magolda, 1987, 1988a, 1988b, 1989; Brabeck, 1984; Kitchener
& King, 1985a; Kitchener & King, 1985b; Moore, 1982). First-year students have
scored predominantly at Position 2, between 2 and 3, or at Position 3, using both
theories.

Seniors, on the other hand, generally have scored between Positions 3 and 4 or
at Position 4, also on both theories, with men usually scoring slightly higher than
women (Heidke, 1982; Kitchener & King, 1985a, 1985b; Omahan, 1982; Welfel
& Davison, 1986). Hence, it seems that women start college slightly ahead of or
equal to men; however, they finish college slightly behind. Institutions of higher
education, therefore, seem to have more effect on the intellectual or epistemological
development of men than the development of women. Why is that? What in the
environment of the college experience might account for this difference? Are there
two structures or styles of epistemological development, and is the college experience biased toward one more than the other? Belenky, Clinchy, Goldberger, and
Tarule (1986) and Baxter Magolda (1987, 1988a, 1988b, 1989) explored these
issues, and their works deserve careful consideration and analysis.

TABLE 1
The Evolving Self

Stage	What is Self? Subject? "I am this way of making meaning."	Become Object	What is Other? Object "I relate to these old s
0: Incorporate Self	I am my reflexes such as moving, sensing. → *new self*	↗	None.
1: Impulsive Self	I am my impulses and perceptions. → *new self*	↗	I can relate to and consciously manipulate my reflexes, moving, sensing. →
2: Imperial Self	I am my needs, interests, and wishes. → *new self*	↗	I now have and can consciously control my impulses and perceptions. →
3: Interpersonal Self	I am my interpersonal relationships, mutuality. → *new self*	↗	I now have needs, interests, and I can control them. →

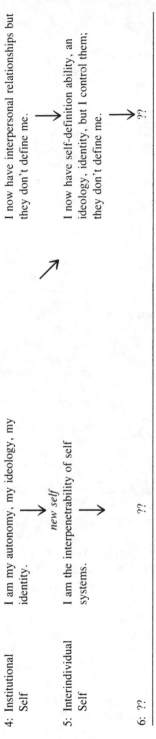

4: Institutional Self   I am my autonomy, my ideology, my identity. → *new self* → I now have interpersonal relationships but they don't define me.

5: Interindividual Self   I am the interpenetrability of self systems. → I now have self-definition ability, an ideology, identity, but I control them; they don't define me.

6: ??   ?? → ??

TABLE 2
Types of Depression

Type of Depression	Transition	Characteristics
Type A	Concerns transition from Stage 2 to 3	Concern over loss of needs; unhappiness at cost of meeting needs; feels constrained, controlled, yet feels compromised.
Type B	Concerns transition from Stage 3 to 4	Concern with loss and damage to interpersonal relationships; feels lonely, deserted, betrayed, abandoned; feels tension between being vulnerable to fusion with others and feeling selfish, heartless, and cold if puts self first. "If I lose my relationships, I will cease to be."
Type C	Concerns transition from Stage 4 to 5	Concern with failure to meet own standards, to control oneself or perform as one should or is expected to perform. Feels humiliated, out of control; life is unfair and meaningless. Feels tension between self-criticism and isolation and feeling out of control, ineffective, and evil.

*Adapted from Kegan (1982). Adapted with permission of the publisher. From *The Evolving Self: Problem and Process in Human Development* by Robert Kegan, Cambridge, MA: Harvard University Press. Copyright © 1982 by the President and Fellows of Harvard College.

In *Women's Ways of Knowing*, Belenky et al. (1986) described five ways of knowing derived from their study of women. Their five positions seem to share epistemological structures with Perry's scheme; however, there are significant differences in how Perry's men and Belenky's women come to change their ways of knowing and how the positions are expressed once known. Table 3, which begins on page 46, summarizes *both* schemes and contrasts their similarities and differences.

An analysis of this table indicates that the differences in men and women occur in the categories of View of Self and View of Authority. They do not occur in the View of Knowledge. The structural category is View of Knowledge, whereas View of Self and View of Authority are behavioral correlates with the structures. Hence, the differences found by Belenky et al. (1986) seem to be *stylistic* rather than *structural*. Baxter Magolda (1987, 1988a, 1988b, 1989) independently reached similar conclusions.

Baxter Magolda (1988a, 1988b) is studying possible gender differences longitudinally with a male and female sample using her measure of the Perry scheme, the Measure of Epistemological Reflection (MER), and a semi-structured interview. The MER (Baxter Magolda & Porterfield, 1985) was developed and normed using both men and women; therefore it should be sensitive to stylistic differences between the sexes. The interviews were designed to examine possible structural differences. After 2 years in college, her sample has revealed stylistic but not structural differences during both years. Specifically, Position 2 women wanted authorities to provide them with answers while they listened, wanted a relaxed and nonconfrontive atmosphere, wanted others to ask the questions, and advocated studying together in groups. They saw areas of uncertainty as places where authorities had different opinions about the facts. Men, on the other hand, felt authorities expected them to look up answers and not just listen, expected learning to be interesting, and saw evaluation as a time to be corrected. Uncertainty was seen as caused by different degrees of detail among authorities.

At Position 3, women gained a new perspective through discussions, sought the support of teachers, preferred experiential learning and organized classes, and believed they would find answers to uncertainties sometime in the future or by adding up positive factors associated with options. Men emphasized being forced to think, identified with their teachers, sought fairness in evaluation, and evaluated using logic. Hence, Baxter Magolda's findings are similar to the results of Belenky et al. and Gilligan.

To sum up, Belenky et al. and Perry seem to describe two different styles of knowing within one epistemological structure. Baxter Magolda's MER seems to be sensitive to both styles, and she also finds similar stylistic differences between her male and female students, but not structural differences. Stylistic differences are important because of their implications for differential ways of teaching and offering student affairs programs. Given that men seem to enter college behind or equal to women in intellectual development and leave college ahead, there is some support to conclude that the environments of colleges cater more to the male, Separate, or T style than to the female, Connected, or F style. As Gilligan emphasized, if one voice, style, or type goes untutored due to biased learning environments, then everything we do in student affairs and college teaching may need to be systematically redesigned to accommodate two voices, styles, or types.

Recently Astin (1987) and Palmer (1987) seemed to agree. They characterized the environment of higher education as competitive rather than collaborative, individualistic rather than communal, objective rather than related, and exclusive rather than inclusive. They called for radical reform, not just of structures but also of higher education's inherent *ways of knowing*. If the way of knowing stays in the *separate* style, they believed reform efforts would fail. Reform efforts should, from their viewpoint, accommodate the care voice, the connected and communal way of knowing, and the F form of judgment. Furthermore, the reform efforts must manifest themselves in the reward structures, desired outcomes, how programs are taught and what programs and services are offered, and who is hired as faculty and staff.

PSYCHOSOCIAL THEORIES

Psychosocial development refers to the issues, tasks, and events that occur throughout the life span, and to a given person's pattern of resolution of the issues and

TABLE 3
Perry Scheme Compared to *Women's Ways of Knowing*

Position	Perry	Belenky et al.	Similarities	Differences
	Name	Name		
1	Basic quality	Silence	*View of Knowledge* • Single absolute right and wrong answers. Cannot perceive authority as making errors • Knowing is observing, hearing without evaluation, and then obeying *View of Authority* • Tell you what to do, not why *View of Self as Learner* • Concrete and not conceptual • Silent, passive, obedient • Dependent on authorities and obey blindly • Authorities are right and overpowering	
2	Multiplicity Prelegitimate	Received Knowledge	*View of Knowledge* • What is known is true, absolutely • Good authorities have truth; bad ones do not • Learners receive truth from authorities • Questions are right or wrong, true or false	

	Perry only			
3	Multiplicity Subordinate	• You collect right answers; you do not construct them • Facts are true; opinion does not count • Diversity is due to poor authorities who are wrong; therefore, diversity is an illusion *View of Authority* • Have right answers and give them to you • Bad authorities are mistaken or wrong *View of Self as Learner* • Listening is the way to learn • Receive knowledge, not source of it • Intolerant of ambiguity; literalist in interpretation • Prefer clarity, predictability, structure, precise and detailed expectations • Perceive diversity of opinion exists	Comparable position not described *View of Authority* • (W) are awed by authorities; do not identify with authorities; authorities are they, not we • (M) do identify with authorities; authorities are we *View of Self as Learner* • (W) not confident of ability to contribute • (M) speak up to let authorities know that they've learned • (W) listen to authorities or to discussions of peers who know; listen actively; dislike debate • (M) listen and argue or debate; discussion is waste of time because only authorities have truth; peers do not	None because no equivalent position is described *Male View of Knowledge* • Some knowledge is known absolutely; all is knowable in principle

(continued)

47

- We may not know yet; someday we will
- When we know, it must be right. If we don't know yet, then how do we search? Absolutize the method of search
- Diversity of opinion is legitimate in areas where don't know yet

View of Authority
- Authorities tell us what is right when we know, and teach us how to search when we don't know

View of Self as Learner
- Receive by listening, observing when we know; helping search when we don't know
- Learn methods of searching and use them because they are the right processes

3
Belenky
et al.

No such
position

4 Perry	Multiplicity	Subjective knowledge	*View of Knowledge* • No longer absolute right or wrong • Is subjective, right only for me and nobody else • All opinions are of equal value because there are no absolute criteria for deciding • Each person has own truth *View of Authority* • Not absolute authorities • Redefine authority as just another outside opinion no better than mine • Do not have to accept what they say • Their opinions can be bad for you *View of Self as Learner* • Active explorer for own opinions and beliefs • Liberated from tyranny of absoluteness • New sense of autonomy and self-directedness • Can hold contradictory beliefs	*View of Self as Learner* • (W) Self's truth is personally intuited and perhaps uncommunicable • (M) Self is defender of everyone's *right* to have own opinion; resist authorities who pretend to have answers; publicly give their opinion • (W) Style is less public; opinion held inside and often not expressed; fear open expression of opinions and desires • (W) Less confident about their opinions and beliefs and want others to affirm their views *(continued)*

- (W) Subjective truth is felt and is not thought about logically; tolerate differences rather than being an advocate for rights. Advocation can lead to unpleasant conflicts
- (W) Distrust logic and analysis
- (M) Opinions tend to be expressed and thought out logically

4
Belenky
et al.

Relativism

Procedural
knowledge

View of Knowledge
- Results from use of nonabsolute criteria such as reasoned reflection
- Subjective truth can be wrong or hurtful
- Move from subjective to rational criteria for making judgments on what is known

View of Self as Learner
- Try new way of thinking that authority recommends

5
Perry

View of Self as Learner
- (W) *Procedural preoccupation* with obtaining and passing on knowledge; especially prefer a sensitive counselor/teacher

- (M) New way to think is a logical argument to meet standards of an impersonal authority in the field; need to master a field objectively
- (W) New way is an inner need to understand and to have a personal connection with knowledge, to develop a commitment to it
- (M) *Separate knowing style*

  Be doubting: doubt and apply logical criticism, especially to ideas based on feelings

  Use reason: learn to analyze and evaluate arguments. Use critical discourse with others, whether know them or not

  Debate: paradigm of desired adversarial process of learning and growth is a debate

  Be adversarial and competitive: learning procedures are adversarial, but with fair rules. Competitive comparisons are emphasized

  Public: public presentation of views for criticisms by others is emphasized

  Separate self from ideas (objective): impersonal analysis is valued; must learn to divorce self

(continued)

from your ideas; personal beliefs or commitments are excluded and not trusted

- (W) *Connected* learning style

  Experiential base: The most trusted knowledge comes from personal experience. How does one gain access to the experiential and personal bases of others' views of a theory?

  Empathetic: Empathetic listening, drawing out, and clarifying are preferred means of knowing and developing. Establish connected knowing groups before sharing and learning together

  Conversation, not debate: Clinical-like interview is paradigm of the valued procedure. Tell one's story without interruption, then clarify. Question only when relationship is established and listening and clarification has occurred

			Clarify, don't judge: Listen, draw out, understand but don't judge others' views. Must build trust to have a relationship. Must have relationship to get at understanding. Judgment destroys trust. That is, judgment is a threat to connectedness
			Collaborative and personal: Bring tentative ideas to a connected group and collaboratively work on them. Nurture ideas given and help clarify them. Person and ideas stay connected in a personal journey for knowledge
5	Relativity	Constructed knowledge	*View of Knowledge* • Constructed: Knowledge is constructed and knower is part of known • Contextual: Knowledge is contextual and answers of better or worse vary due to context in which question is asked and personality and experience of person asking • Never-ending: Search for truth is a never-ending construction
Both Belenky et al. & Perry			

(continued)

View of Self as Learner and View of Authority

- Self and authorities are on a joint journey to construct truth
- Competence, not role, defines authority

View of Self as Learner

- (W) *Passion and commitment:* Passionate pursuit and commitment of self to understand and connect with others' constructions. Attend to others, feel related to them, and seek to understand their assumptions and experience. Encounter them only after hearing their story and clarifying it.
- (W) Self is related to what it is trying to understand and know
- (W) *Connected learning style*
- (M) *Separate knowing style*

tasks, and adaptation to the events (Rodgers, 1984b). Some of the issues, tasks, and events are *age-graded*, that is, their timing, duration, and nature are similar for many individuals of the same chronological age. For example, most 18- to 23-year-olds in our culture struggle to determine who they are (identity), who they will love (sexuality and intimacy), and what they will believe (values and lifestyle). Some of the issues, tasks, and events are *history-graded*, that is, they are normative for a given age group due to the group's unique historical experience. The civil rights era or Great Depression, for example, are unique historical events that have influenced the development of a given cohort of college students but not others. Finally, some are *unanticipated life events*. For example, an unexpected illness or death of a parent can influence the development of a college student in negative ways.

College environments (e.g., programs, relationships, policies) appropriately challenge and facilitate the resolution of tasks and adaptations to events or get in the way and hinder development. The *content* of the tasks and events, the *skills* needed to cope with them, and the dynamics or *processes* involved in resolution and adaptation all provide the criteria for evaluating or designing college environments. A review follows of selective research on psychosocial age-graded tasks of college students in terms of content, skills, and processes.

Similar to the cognitive developmental family of theory, research on psychosocial development during the 1980s concentrated more on testing and validating theories than on introducing new theories. Gender, socioeconomic, and cultural-ethnic differences once again were the foci of research. Studies examined the degree to which the psychosocial development of men and women, Blacks and Whites, rural and urban populations, or individuals in various socioeconomic classes is the same or different. Each of these issues is important and will be viewed selectively.

GENDER RESEARCH

In research on women, Baruch, Barnett, and Rivers (1983) studied the sources of feelings of mastery and pleasure in women's lives, Straub and Rodgers (1986) and Straub (1987) the development of autonomy, and Josselson (1987) the development of identity. In research on men, Farrell and Rosenberg (1981) studied development in the 20s and 40s age ranges for various socioeconomic classes in both urban and rural environments. Finally, for both sexes, Branch-Simpson (1984) studied the developmental tasks of traditionally aged Black college students and compared the results with Chickering's vectors.

Baruch and Barnett (1980) and Baruch et al. (1983) studied how the number and types of roles in a woman's life may act as moderating variables in how women adapt to life events and resolve adult developmental tasks. The patterns of life roles under study were: (a) never married, (b) married with children, (c) married without children, and (d) divorced with children. The sample was randomly selected from a single town in Massachusetts. All the never-married and divorced women in the sample were employed, as were half of the married women selected. Random selection led to approximately equal numbers of high-, medium-, and low-prestige jobs.

Generally, Baruch and Barnett sought to describe the sources of pleasure and mastery in the lives of women in the different role patterns. They found that 88% of all these women had a strong sense of pleasure and mastery. The main source of mastery was competent skill in a job that had high prestige. The main sources of pleasure were relationships with spouse, children, family of origin, friends, or work colleagues. Many women in all of the life patterns reported satisfying lives; however, the right combination of roles seemed to be the key to well-being.

Divorce as a life event forced the divorced women in this study to grow. It forced them to provide both materially and psychologically for themselves. These women became more instrumentally and emotionally self-sufficient rather than dependent.

Marriage and children generally were sources of pleasure; however, if a woman overidentified with her spouse or her children, she was vulnerable. The loss of spouse or children would leave such a woman without an identity because she defined the self almost exclusively in terms of others. Married women at home with children were satisfied but also felt that current society viewed their traditional combination of roles negatively.

Never-married women scored lower than married women; however, single women with high-prestige jobs scored high enough to have very satisfying lives. The problem for single women, therefore, was not being single per se but the combination of being single combined with a low-prestige job. This combination of roles yielded the lowest sense of pleasure and mastery.

The best combination of roles was wife, mother, and high-prestige job holder. These women reported the highest levels of pleasure and mastery, and they did not report the high levels of stress predicted for this combination of roles.

It seems, therefore, that counselors and student affairs staff should note that both single women with careers and women with husbands, children, and jobs can have satisfying lives. There was not a single psychosocial pattern of well-being for women in this study. In addition, the work implies that the development of instrumental and emotional autonomy (Chickering, 1969) during the college years may be especially important for the well-being of women in later adulthood.

Straub and Rodgers (1986) and Straub (1987) studied the achievement of autonomy in women, and their work can help illuminate the types of experiences that have helped women internalize the capacity for instrumental and emotional self-sufficiency. Using the Bem Sex Role Inventory, Straub and Rodgers (1986) found that college women with androgynous and masculine orientations tended to resolve the tasks of instrumental and emotional autonomy during college. Feminine and Undifferentiated women, on the other hand, not only did not become autonomous individuals during college, but they tended to remain dependent well into their late 30s. Is it the case that Feminine and Undifferentiated college women become the mothers Baruch and Barnett (1980) described who overidentify with their spouses and children and are dependently vulnerable at mid-life? Additional research is needed to answer questions such as this.

Straub (1987) followed up with the women who scored high in autonomy. She conducted critical incident interviews with these women to discover the types of events that contributed to their development of autonomy and the aspects of those events that were significant or meaningful. Briefly, the categories of events associated with achieving autonomy included: (a) significant relationships with men or parents (38.5%), (b) educational experiences (37%) both in the classroom (15.5%) and student affairs areas such as residence halls or student organizations (21%), (c) work experiences (4%), (d) uprooting family experiences (10%), and (e) personal experiences with counseling or personal growth workshops (8%). The significant aspects of these experiences were: (a) having to be "on their own" in a residence hall and then in an apartment (33%), (b) "taking risks" that lead to insights about oneself and about sources of personal stress (24%), (c) "overcoming obstacles" in academic or job achievement (7%), and (d) learning that dependence on men or parents results in enormous personal losses in areas such as career, educational pursuits, and personal identity (17%). Seventy three percent of the events related directly to instrumental or emotional autonomy as conceptualized by Chickering (1969), and 27% related to developing autonomy through freeing interpersonal relationships with significant others or parents.

In terms of the college environment, 22% of the experiences related to classroom or academic obstacles and 29% related to experiences with student affairs programs and services outside the classroom. Combining classroom and student affairs experiences, 51% of the events occurred in the college environment and 49% occurred in other environments.

Finally, Josselson's (1987) longitudinal study of identity development in women from their first year in college through age 34 seems especially significant. Josselson's research is based on Marcia's (1966, 1976, 1980; Marcia & Friedman, 1970) model and research on identity statuses. Guided by Erikson, Marcia described two dimensions in identity formation: (a) conscious experience of an identity crisis to be resolved and (b) commitment to a sense of self or identity after deliberate exploration of options. The combination of the two dimensions yields four paths as summarized in Table 4.

Each of these paths has important characteristics and dynamics that student affairs professionals could profit from knowing.

Foreclosed

At the end of college, 24% of Josselson's women were "foreclosed." (The percentages are based upon 34 of the original 60 subjects in the study.) They had made commitments to an identity without experiencing a crisis or deliberately exploring options. These women needed *to feel loved and cared for.* They saw only one course for their lives—getting married, having children, and having close family relationships. Security and harmony were prominent needs. A close-knit family, turned in on itself, was their source of security. Childhood identifications with family of origin seemed to be the source of their foreclosed identity. They held

TABLE 4
Marcia's Identity Model

| | | Conscious of an identity crisis and its issues | |
		NO	YES
Commitment to identity after exploring options	NO	Diffuse	Moratorium
	YES	Foreclosed	Achieved

Notes.

Foreclosed: Women who have never felt an identity crisis or explored options but who are rigidly committed to a childhood vision of their identity.

Diffuse: Women who never experienced an identity crisis in college, never explored options, and have not committed to an identity at the end of college.

Moratorium: Women who felt an identity crisis during college, explored identity issues, but left college still exploring and unresolved.

Achieved: Women who felt an identity crisis during college, explored options, achieved an individualized sense of self, and have committed to an identity.

their goals rigidly and without doubt. These women were going to continue the beliefs, sex-role orientations, and values on sexual behavior of their parents without rethinking or testing them in any way. They resisted the influences of the classroom, extracurricular college experiences, and peer influences during college. They did not change.

These foreclosed women had histories of difficult peer relationships and never identified with a primary peer group during college. They had possessive and fearful mothers and warm fathers. They passed through college remaining close to their mothers, did not experiment, and graduated seeing things as their mothers did. They were judgmental rather than empathic, and their judgments were absolutely right or wrong.

At age 34 these foreclosed women had high self-esteem and low anxiety. They seemed to be functioning well and still held rigidly to their college views of an ideal life. They had not changed at all. They had resisted today's pluralistic culture just as they had resisted college's potential influences for change. Many had full-time jobs but cared only about their private family lives. Career success was not a goal in their lives. They had a strong sense of duty to family and conservative moral values. Their identities continued to be assigned from the outside and held rigidly. They had not resolved issues of autonomy or interdependence. The only hint of Baruch and Barnett's vulnerability for overidentified women was found in those who experienced divorce. Divorce precipitated an identity crisis on foreclosed women, forcing them to change to deal with issues of self-sufficiency.

Hence, from the freshman year in college until age 34, foreclosed women apparently derive both a sense of mastery and pleasure from relationships in their families. They make meaning in Perry's dualism during college and adulthood.

They are not autonomous or interdependent. They identify totally with their families and rigidly hold conservative values. Most were functioning well and satisfied with their lives at age 34, but the clouds of mid-life were on the horizon.

Diffuse

At the end of college, 23% of Josselson's women were identity diffuse. They had not experienced a crisis, explored options, nor committed to an identity. Josselson differentiated this group into four (4) subgroups (see Table 5).

The subgroup labeled *severe psychopathology* and *previously unresolved tasks* had histories of traumatic abuse or neglect by unhealthy parents. By their freshman year, nothing was working in their lives. They had undifferentiated sex-role orientations. They were impulsive (similar to Kegan's Stage 2 of ego development), tried to avoid feeling guilty, and were unstable and unreliable. They failed to develop the inner capacities for intimacy, autonomy, or interdependence. The self fluctuated widely and there was no inner sense of self. They were at the mercy of today's experiences and impulses without the capacity to learn from their experiences.

The *moratorium diffuse* subgroup (19%), in contrast, had experienced an identity crisis; however, their crises were deeper than those of most of the other women in the study. They struggled with deep philosophical questions about the meaning of life and explored radical options involving drugs, sex, and religious sects. Their college years were characterized by movements in and out of moratorium and diffusion.

The *foreclosed diffuse* subgroup (31%) were characterized as acting on the demands of their immediate situation without a consistent sense of direction. This group's parents were also diffuse and left all decision making in the hands of their daughters. The parents could offer neither guidance nor role models. The women seemed to cling to what little security their families could provide and then waited to see what fate would bring. They adopted, in turn, whatever came. They graduated with nowhere to go and had no idea how to proceed with their lives.

By age 34, the moratorium and foreclosure subgroups had been in and out of counseling on several occasions. Their solution to the identity issue was to not solve it. They moved in and out of jobs and accepted whatever the environment seemed to be saying that they should be. Various authority figures organized a

TABLE 5
Four Patterns of Diffusion

Subgroup name	(Percentage)		Percentage
Severe psychopathology	(Not reported)		
Many unresolved previous developmental tasks	(Not reported)	[Combined]	50%
Moratorium diffuse	(19%)		
Foreclosure diffuse	(31%)	[Combined]	50%

temporary self for them. From the four combined subgroups, 33% briefly tried to create identities and then fell back into diffusion; 33% established some kind of identity through the help of authorities who structured their lives; 22% died in their 20s, and 11% were still trying to establish identity.

Moratorium

At the end of college, 29% of the longitudinal sample were classified as being in *moratorium*. As college students, these women were aware that they had to make choices to define themselves but they were not yet able to do so. They seemed to be paralyzed in their crisis and awareness.

   These women were concerned about social problems, had a capacity for empathy, and were concerned about philosophical questions. They had dreams of careers in helping others and solving social problems but did not know how to make their idealistic dreams become reality. They tested and searched. They had lower self-esteem and greater levels of anxiety than achieved or foreclosed women. By age 34, three had achieved identity, one was still struggling in moratorium, and six had retreated into more-or-less foreclosed identities similar to those of their childhood families.

   The dynamics of the college years for moratorium women are especially important for student affairs professionals because they may provide cues for developmental interventions. Women classified in moratorium did loosen family ties, unlike foreclosed and diffuse women. They tended to find boyfriends who were different from their families. The boyfriends they chose, however, often became substitute parents. That is, the women remained dependent or even more dependent on their controlling boyfriends than they had been on their parents.

   Like the foreclosed women, the moratorium women had overprotective mothers who indulged them, and they felt guilty over betraying the norms of their mothers, especially in sexual behavior. Those who were able to tolerate their guilt went on to achieve identity; those who could not, retreated toward foreclosure.

   These women would daydream rather than really exploring careers. They needed relationships to bolster their self-esteem and to show them how to be different or uniquely themselves. They needed healthy models, but more often chose and obeyed controlling boyfriends with different sexual values. They were not yet autonomous or interdependent at graduation and usually chose the wrong resources to help them achieve these inner capacities. They needed supportive rather than controlling relationships during college.

Achieved

Twenty four percent of Josselson's longitudinal sample were identity achieved. These women had felt an identity crisis, separated from their families, explored options, and chosen their own identities and life-styles. Although the content of their identities differed, they used a common process.

   All of the achieved women were able to separate themselves from needing parental or peer group sanctions. They became individualized persons, capable of inner self-reliance. This internal liberation involved several common ingredients: These women did not retreat from rejections, even though they were painful; they developed an internalized sense of competence in and out of the classroom; and they had the capacity to tolerate their sense of guilt as they explored options.

The common process also involved a common pattern; that is, all of these women defined the self as a *self in relationships*. They emphasized interdependence rather than autonomy. Their identity was a related identity, usually with a boyfriend with whom they had a mutually supportive, interdependent relationship. Their boyfriends were not controlling but supportive.

As adults, the achieved women had consciously examined and reworked their identities by age 34. They had the highest self-esteem and low levels of anxiety. They were flexible, open to new experiences, self-confident, and not dependent on external sources for meaning. Work was a source of mastery and pleasure but was not the key ingredient in their identity as it was for men of this age (Levinson, 1978; Vaillant, 1977). The adult self was a *balance* of work, relationships, and other interests, with *relationships* being the key ingredient in the balance.

Summary and Comparison

Each of Baruch and Barnett's role combinations (married with no children, married with children but no job, married with children and job, single) are found in each of the four different identity statuses of Josselson's women. One could infer from Josselson's data that the pattern of roles may not be as important in the well-being of women as the identity status of the individual. For example, a woman in her mid-30s could be married with children and be foreclosed, diffuse, achieved, or in moratorium. Only foreclosed and achieved women seemed to have a sense of well-being, and a high-status job did not seem to be a central issue for either.

Of Kegan's two basic issues in life, *separateness* and *togetherness*, togetherness, or connectedness, was central to the identity development of most of Josselson's women. Those who achieved identity opted to stay attached as they became self-confident, assertive, and masters of their own lives. Their problem was how to separate, how to be different, and yet how to stay connected as they went through this process.

The process and nature of identity formation for Josselson's women were different, therefore, from those of men. Whereas men often separate from their families as they form and live their identities, these women tended to stay connected. The issues that concern men and women as they separate also tended to differ. Whereas Josselson reported that men focus on politics, religion, and careers in separating themselves from their families, her women were concerned with religious traditions, whom to choose as friends, sexual behavior, and whom and when to marry. Most of Josselson's women used relationships with men, staff, or friends to help them separate from their mothers' priorities.

Work was important but secondary in the lives of Josselson's women, and even avocational interests could be more important than careers in defining the self. When career was the most important thing in a woman's life, the woman had a mentor with whom she had a supportive, facilitative relationship. The absence of a mentor had significant consequences for using career as an anchor for identity. In order to be an anchor for identity, ". . . work has to matter to someone who matters to her" (Josselson, 1987, p. 177).

Many identity achieved women became disillusioned with work. Most of these women's career goals included "helping others," and this goal often was not a top priority of the bureaucracies and businesses in which they worked. As a consequence, for these women, avocations rather than their jobs often became the outlet for this goal.

Finally, friendships were the anchor relationships for identity achieved women only if other relationships were tried and rejected. Friends came to play some of the same roles as husbands and mentors, that is, they were people with whom the women could discuss a problem, find support, and obtain logistical help.

Farrell and Rosenberg's (1981) study of men offers the closest comparative study to Josselson's women. Farrell and Rosenberg studied 500 men, 200 between 25 and 30 years old and 300 between 38 and 48. They identified urban, suburban, and rural districts in the northeast zone of the United States, and then classified each area by socioeconomic class (SEC). Districts, neighborhoods, blocks, and houses were then selected randomly by SEC, and the authors studied the men who lived in the houses selected. The resulting sample was statistically representative of the general population of men in this country.

Generally, regardless of SEC or rural-urban background, Farrell and Rosenberg found that a common set of issues tended to confront each of their subjects at mid-life. Some of these issues seemed to be biologically determined, but the majority seemed to be derived from psychological or societal motivations.

Mid-life was a time of fundamental reassessment but not necessarily a crisis for the men in this study. They reexamined their careers, their marital relationships, and relationships with their children, parents, and friends. Approximately 33% of the sample confronted and resolved these issues. Most (approximately 67%) denied or avoided the issues. The common set of issues and differential outcomes are especially instructive.

In their 20s, regardless of SEC or urban or rural background, the men in this study were absorbed in their world of work. Whether their careers were foreclosed, unstable and drifting, purposefully in exploration, or mature commitments, identity and relationships were *organized around work*. For many men, however, work was a source of defeat rather than success. Socioeconomic class and past developmental history correlated with differential career outcomes.

At mid-life, most of these men felt committed *both* to work and family relationships; however, internal self-experience became more focused on the family for the first time. That is, many of these men began to view wife, children, and material characteristics of the home as expressions of and support for the self, a self often frustrated at work. At mid-life, however, children were beginning their separation or individuation from the family, and spouses often were becoming more autonomous and achievement-oriented. Many wives in this study wanted to move away from being expressions of and support for their husbands, just as the husbands wanted "nothing to change." Thus, for many men in this study, the development of family members disrupted their use of family to make up for career frustrations. They were being asked to facilitate and support the others rather than use the others as their refuge. They, in effect, were being asked to switch to a more connected identity from a separate identity, to support more rather than be supported. The problem was to establish intimate, care-oriented relationships with spouse, children, and parents; for these men, this was a more complex and difficult task than their career problems. Work, however, also was a mid-life issue.

Career possibilities were shrinking at mid-life for these men. There were fewer illusions about advancement, fewer openings, and stiffer competition. Dreams were measured against realities, whether the men were foreclosed, searching, diffuse, or achieved. The expansive future of youth gave way to particular options in the present, or lack thereof.

At mid-life, biological or physical body decline was clearly present. This decline also affected these men's images of themselves and how they related to the world.

Finally, just as men were expected to be at their height of social and family responsibility and to be pillars of emotional strength for others, they needed a moratorium in order to explore the changes that were going on within themselves. They needed to negotiate a new or revised identity.

A factor analysis of data received from these men yielded four styles of coping with the demands of mid-life and four outcomes. The two dimensions that define the four styles are as follows: (a) alienation—integration, and (b) denial—openness. The four developmental pathways are summarized in Table 6.

TABLE 6
Four Developmental Pathways for Men

	Denial	Openness
	Punitive-Disenchanted	**Crisis Type**
Alienation	Deny issues and stresses Alienated Unstable and bigoted	Openly confront stress and issues Alienated, with a developmental history of unresolved issues
	Pseudodeveloped	**Generative**
Integration	Deny issues and stresses Satisfied and trying to prevent changes	Openly confront stress and issues Have a positive developmental history Have resolved issues and integrated a revised identity

*Adapted from Farrell & Rosenberg (1981). Used with permission. From *Men at Midlife* (pp. 32, 75) by Michael P. Farrell and Stanley Rosenberg, Dover, MA: Auburn House, an imprint of Greenwood Publishing Group, Inc. Copyright © 1980 by Auburn House Publishing Company.

Generative

Professional, middle-class men who lived in urban areas had the best internal and external resources to resolve the issues of mid-life, and this group made up most but not all of the 33% who successfully negotiated mid-life. Careers and autonomy became less important for these men, whereas intimacy and interdependence with spouse, children, and parents became more important. They reformed their identities, adjusted their life structures (Levinson, 1978), became or stayed open to feelings and new experiences, and facilitated the individuation of their young adult children. They paralleled Josselson's identity achieved group, although the nature of their issues differed.

Punitive-Disenchanted

Unskilled laborers in rural and urban locations had the least internal and external resources to deal with mid-life. These men had the same personal disorientations and psychopathology as Josselson's diffuse women. They began the college years developmentally behind and they never recovered. In their 20s these men were alienated, unstable, and prejudiced. By mid-life they denied that they had faults and projected the negative happenings in their lives onto minority groups and their own children. They were authoritarian, reported high degrees of anxiety and depression, and had many physical illnesses. They roamed from job to job and did not have stable relationships. They were in serious physical and mental decline.

Pseudodeveloped

The majority of the sample were lower- and middle-class skilled workers, clerical personnel, and owners of small businesses. These men divided into two groups, one called "pseudodeveloped" and the other "crisis type." The "pseudo-developed" group resembled Josselson's foreclosed group in their psychological makeup. They *denied* that they were experiencing the stress and issues of mid-life and *tried to avoid* dealing with them. They claimed to be satisfied with their lives, yet their attitudes were rigid and prejudiced. They denied feelings. They exhibited a great deal of authoritarianism and covert depression and anxiety. They avoided new situations, people, or ideas, and rigidly tried to hang onto their highly structured and self-centered lives.

Crisis Type

The crisis type resembled Josselson's moratorium group. These men were very well aware that they were in a total identity crisis, but their poor developmental histories left them highly handicapped. They cast themselves as anti-heroes trying to find a sense of wholeness and ability to cope, but they were failing. Being highly dependent but self-aware, they lamented their lack of ability to deal with the growing demands of their wives, children, and parents. They had, in essence, given up on themselves. They had a vivid sense of futility and were in depressive decline.

Summary and Implications

As with Josselson's women, the casualty rate for men at mid-life is high. Only one fourth to one third of the group remain developmentally healthy at mid-life. The distinguishing variables seem to be societal expectations, internal psychological resources, and life circumstances.

Our society's norms for men seem to be externally and materially defined. Most young men strive for identity through external achievement in school, work, athletics, and marriage. These norms may neglect or even punish a care orientation and the inner capacity for intimacy. At mid-life, however, the capacity for care and intimacy must be developed if the issues are to be resolved.

Past developmental history also seems to affect mid-life outcomes. Previous developmental success affects men's openness to the experiences, stresses, and needed psychological capacities of mid-life. If the tasks of previous stages have been more rather than less resolved, then men have a better chance of resolving the issues of mid-life.

Socioeconomic class and educational level, in turn, also seem to affect the experiences that influence resolution of tasks. Urban, educated, middle- and upper-class men have better chances of dealing with adult developmental tasks than rural, less educated, and lower socioeconomic class men.

In higher education, it may be important to reflect on these findings. For example, it may be important to support alternatives to the dominant social expectations for men and women during adulthood. Identity through autonomous achievement may leave care, support, and intimacy retarded in adolescence. The college years are critical for developing capacities for free and intimate interpersonal relationships as well as autonomy (Chickering, 1969). For men, freeing interpersonal relationships is swimming upstream to dominant societal norms, and apparently many men leave college without resolving these issues. Nevertheless, for men at mid-life, a capacity for care and intimacy is critically important. Must many men wait until mid-life to develop these capacities? Could more men develop them during the college years as many women apparently do?

RESEARCH WITH BLACK STUDENTS

Branch-Simpson (1984) studied the degree to which Black students' psychosocial developmental tasks were similar to those reported by Chickering (1969) as well as other theories based on White subjects. Instead of using Chickering's vectors as a basis for studying Black students, the author conducted psychosocial biographical interviews with Black male and female college students and used content analysis to identify developmental tasks descriptive of their experience. She found many areas of overlap with Chickering's vectors; however, there were some differences, which are highlighted in Table 7.

Although Branch-Simpson's (1984) work is very preliminary, it is interesting to speculate on the implications of this work for student affairs. For example,

TABLE 7
Black Student Development Compared to Chickering's
Vectors and Ways of Knowing

Issue	Chickering	Branch-Simpson
Competence	Sense of competence is resolved during first 2 years if student stays in college.	Sense of competence is an issue throughout undergraduate years. Continued stress and hard work.
Autonomy	Separation from family is part of process of developing emotional and instrumental autonomy. Women develop these capacities well ahead of men. Women stay related to parents as they separate.	Both sexes tend to stay connected to family and supports development of autonomy, women more so than men. Women develop these capacities well ahead of men.
Intimacy	Women develop these capacities well ahead of men.	Women develop these capacities well ahead of men. Many men graduate without developing these capacities.
Values	Religion is seldom mentioned in humanizing or personalizing issues.	Religion or spiritual dimension is part of both sexes' lives and is used to resolve values questions.
Identity formation	Separate and achievement-oriented for men; relationship-oriented in a balanced pattern of relationships for women.	Identity is achieved in relationships with extended family, including deity, for both sexes. Men more instrumental and career achievement oriented than women. Role models are Black humanitarian figures or family members.
Ways of knowing	Separate knowing for most men and connected knowing for most women.	Connected learning for men and women. Knowing must be personal. Students want relationships with their teachers, men less so than women, however.
*Weltanschauung*** (Worldview)	Value acquisition of objects. Knowing is cognitive. Justice logic dominates. Trust in technology and science.	Value interpersonal relationships. Knowing is symbolic imagery. Logic is a union of opposites. Trust networks of human and spiritual interrelationships.

*Worldview is not a part of Chickering's theory (see Nichols, 1988).

the religious and spiritual dimension was prominent in the developmental processes these Black students described. Spiritual or faith development has not been a major focus of Euro-American psychology or student affairs programs. Amendments may be needed. Also, Branch-Simpson found the theme of interpersonal relationships in several psychosocial domains and in ways of knowing. Although there were differences between the Black men and women in the degree of this emphasis, clearly this theme was more pervasive than it is in descriptions of the development of White men, if not White women. Or, considering the pervasive influence of the family and extended family on Black students, student development educators may need to study the family's influence and family development much more seriously if they are going to use theory to design programs and services for Black students.

TYPOLOGICAL THEORIES

Typological theories describe permanent or semipermanent stylistic, temperament, or personality type preferences. There is not a single unifying theoretical perspective for these theories, and, with the exception of the theories of Jung (1971) and Myers (1980), they are not developmental per se. They relate to college student development, however, because psychosocial and cognitive-structural development takes place within a type or style, and type or style affects preferred ways of learning, being motivated, relating with others, and being satisfied. If student development programs are to be appropriately challenging and supportive, then how students learn, are motivated, relate with others, and are satisfied should be taken into account.

Because Claxton and Murrell (1987) published a recent major review of typological theories and because one of the typological models is used more than the others in student affairs, this section will focus on recent theoretical debates related to the most used and general of the typological instruments, the Myers-Briggs Type Indicator (MBTI) (Myers & McCaulley, 1985). The debate centers on whether theories of *type* or theories of *temperament* are more valid for interpreting and predicting behavior. For example, MBTI preferences can be interpreted in terms of Jung/Myers (Jung, 1971; Myers, 1980) personality *types* or Keirsey (Keirsey & Bates, 1978; Keirsey, 1988) or other (Osmond, Siegler, & Smoke, 1983) personality *temperaments*. Type and temperament not only offer differing interpretations of MBTI preferences, but also sometimes offer different prescriptions for practitioners. Hence, the assumptions and major propositions of each need to be examined.

Keirsey's Temperaments

Temperament theory (Keirsey, 1988; Keirsey & Bates, 1978; Keirsey & Brownsword, 1983) asserts that persons are *systemic, self-regulating wholes*. Personality has an inborn pattern of or propensity toward certain behavior, and it is the total pattern that is called *temperament*. The focus is on the governing whole, not the parts.

These patterns are socially imprinted or conditioned, however (Keirsey & Brownsword, 1983). That is, the patterns emerge, survive, and flourish if the social environment facilitates their emergence and growth. If not, various pathologies emerge (Keirsey, 1988). The environment does not create the pattern, however. "The pattern is there from the start" (Keirsey & Brownsword, p. 6). Temperament, therefore, is an inborn propensity for constancy of behavior.

Keirsey (1988) divided temperaments into MBTI Sensors (concrete and component perceivers) or Intuitives (abstract and wholistic perceivers) and subdivided these two subgroups each. The letters in the Keirsey Temperaments' box correspond to Jungian/Myers names for mental functions and attitudes to be covered later in this chapter; however, Keirsey believes that persons function as patterned wholes and he does not accept the concepts of mental functions and attitudes per se. Nevertheless, the letters in the box are used symbolically as follows: S stands for Sensors, N for Intuitives, E for Extroverts, I for Introverts, T for Thinkers, F for Feelers, P for Perceptive type, and J for Judgment type.

KEIRSEY TEMPERAMENTS			
S	SJ	Epimethian or Guardian Temperament	
		ISTJ	ISFJ
		ESTJ	ESFJ
	SP	Dionysian or Artisan Temperament	
		ISTP	ISFP
		ESTP	ESFP
N	NT	Promethian or Rational Temperament	
		INTJ	INTP
		ENTJ	ENTP
	NF	Apollonian or Idealistic Temperament	
		INFP	ENFP
		INFJ	ENFJ

The four Jungian types listed under each temperament subgroup are believed to share common behavior patterns, and the common pattern guides behavior more than do differences among patterns. The SJ temperament, for example, has a strong sense of duty. SJ type individuals establish and maintain social institutions such as family, church, or corporations. Belonging to such organizations must be earned. Structure, order, and planning are valued and reflected in their behavior. These individuals relate to others in terms of their status and roles in structured hierarchies. They are not risk takers; they are conservers. They desire stability and predictability. They are stable, responsible, dependable, and practical in their behavior. Hence, they learn and develop best in environments that are preplanned, concrete, experiential, routine, sequential, structured, and inductive—that is, proceeding from a particular instance to the generalization.

The SP temperament, on the other hand, wants to be free and spontaneous. SP type individuals do not want to be preplanned, restricted, or obligated. They are action-oriented. Spontaneous action based on here-and-now impulses is characteristic of their behavior. Hence, they enjoy life and its sensual pleasures. They are fun-loving, exciting, generous, and congenial. They are competitive and take risks. If they have goals and plans, these would be highly pragmatic, formulated at the last moment, and changeable. They learn best, therefore, through sensual involvement with spontaneous action in competitive contexts that also provide enjoyment, some risk taking, and excitement.

Among the two Intuitive temperaments, NT type individuals are centered on competence. They search for intellectual understanding, explanation, prediction, and control. They enjoy abstract reasoning and intellectual achievement. They read and build abstract theories or systems, and are interested in the principles that underlie their theories and not the facts or specifics of particular instances. Generally, they are competent with language and complex problem solving. Hence, they learn and develop best in environments that involve impersonal analysis, exploration of ideas, critique, debate, classification, and exploration of the possibilities of underlying principles.

Finally, NF temperaments characterize people in the process of becoming. Their goals are self-development and self-actualization. They are emotive, sensitive, and skilled in interpersonal relationships. They search for meaning in their experiences and value authenticity rather than role behavior or facades. They are abstract reasoners and have a personal flair for influencing others with their speech or writing. They learn and develop best in environments that involve the exploration of possibilities with people, understanding of self and others, empathic discussions, development of personal relationships, creativity and imagination, and personalization of knowledge.

Given these four basic patterns of behavior, Keirsey (Keirsey & Brownsword, 1983) believed that the parts of the whole that Jung called mental *functions* and *attitudes* have meaning mostly in relationship to the total pattern, not by themselves. In other words, temperament precedes type. A particular function in one temperament may mean a different behavior in another temperament. For example, Jung/Myers described ISTPs and INTPs as similar "introverted thinking" types. They share the same dominant function, T, and it is expressed in an introverted manner for both types. Hence, both share a propensity, according to Jung/Myers, for introverted logical analysis (one of concepts and the other of sensual facts). Keirsey (Keirsey & Bates, 1978) claimed that "even a cursory observation of a few clear-cut ISTPs will show how striking the contrast, and how trivial the resemblance" (p. 203). ISTPs are interested in doing, not thinking, in spontaneous real-world action, and do not reflect even on their sensations. The primary differences between ISTPs and INTPs are their symbolic-abstract *intuition* and real-concrete *sensations*, not the sharing of the Jungian dominant function of Thinking and attitude of Introversion. Temperament precedes type.

Jung/Myers Types

In contrast to Keirsey's *holistic* emphasis on static patterns of behavior, Jung/Myers (Jung, 1971; Myers, 1980; Myers & McCaulley, 1985) emphasized a *dynamic parts* theory whose constructs *develop* over the life span. Their theory, therefore, is a dynamic model of ego development involving four functions (Sensing, Intuition, Thinking, Feeling), two attitudes (Extroversion and Introversion), and two lifestyles (Judgment and Perception).

The four functions attempt to describe the functioning and development of the ego. Sensing (S) and Intuition (N) are polar processes for taking in information, for perceiving. Everyone has both processes within themselves but everyone prefers to use one more often than the other. Sensing is the taking in and coordinating of concrete, here-and-now experiences through the five external senses and through the internal body senses. Sense perceiving is believed to be spontaneous, concrete, linear, accurate, and concerned with components of the whole. In contrast, Intuition (N) is the spontaneous perception of the significance of experience, that is, the insights generated by experience. It is the perception of symbols, images, ideas, and abstractions rather than the concrete components of experience. Intuition is an ideational process concerned with abstract, symbolic, nonpractical, holistic comprehension. That is, it allows individuals to grasp the symbolic and abstract whole, and it probably exceeds their capacity to express it with language (Newman, 1986).

Thinking (T) and Feeling (F) are polar rational processes of judgments that everyone is capable of using. One process is preferred, however, and it is used most often and is better differentiated than the nonpreferred alternative. Thinking is judgment based on an objective, impersonal, and logical sorting and analysis. Thinking relates perceptions to existing knowledge and allows them to be expressed in a logical manner. Behaviorally, thinkers are critical and believe personal considerations should be left out of decisions. Feeling, on the other hand, is an experiential process of judgment based on a complex coordination of a variety of emotional reactions to perception and value-oriented criteria. It is sensitive to and coordinates the feelings of self and others and regulates individuals' emotional life. It is associated with cognitive capacities to image and visualize, control body states, and think with metaphors (Newman, 1987). Behaviorally, Fs use personal consideration in making decisions, and are good at projecting the impact of decisions on people.

The two attitudes, Extroversion and Introversion, are basic and fundamentally different ways of relating the self to the world. One is preferred and more differentiated, although everyone experiences both. Extroversion focuses on the external world of people, places, and things, whereas Introversion relates to the internal world of thought, awareness, and reflection. Behaviorally, Extroverts need more outside involvements, seek affirmation and confirmation of themselves from others, are comparatively good at meeting people and at interpersonal interaction, speak often at meetings, and in fact speak in order to sort out judgments. Introverts need more time alone, seek inner understanding, and must internally sort and analyze before they speak. They often have better writing than verbal skills, and are more difficult to get to know than Extroverts.

Finally the two life-styles are polar opposite preferences for Judgment (T or F) or Perception (S or N) in individuals' extroverted environment. Judgment (J) prefers an organized, planned life-style. Js like to get things settled, dislike interruptions or changes in the schedule, and get things done on time. Perceivers (P) prefer flexibility and therefore adapt better to changing circumstances. Ps are open to new perceptions, make decisions more slowly, start more often than finish, and are often late in finishing if they finish at all.

Unlike Keirsey in the use of Sensing and Intuition, Jung first divided types on Extroversion and Introversion, and then added the functions, and Myers added the life-styles. In addition, Jung believed that one of the four functions is the *dominant* function in ego development and expression. This is the most important function in personality and its development. The *auxiliary* function also is preferred but is not dominant. Rather than being in opposition to the dominant function, however, Jung believed the auxiliary serves the dominant function but is less differentiated.

Jung's constructs yield 16 personality types. They represent 16 different tracks of development toward wholeness or individuation. During the first half of life (until age 40), development ought to focus on the dominant function and a fairly well-differentiated auxiliary. In the college years, the opposite of the auxiliary (called the third function) can become the object of development, while the inferior function, the opposite of the dominant, is more consciously felt and is differentiated only after mid-life. Hence, for Jung/Myers, an ISTP type has T as a dominant function and S as the auxiliary. For good type development, Thinking is expressed introvertedly, whereas Sensing is expressed extrovertedly. During college, therefore, development would be facilitated by a major calling for introverted, logical reflection on concrete external data from Sensing. The third function is Intuition, the opposite of Sensing, and some experiences differentiating this function also would be prescribed. Feeling processes probably should be minimized during college for this type.

Summary and Comparison of Temperament and Type

To sum up, Keirsey would interpret MBTI preferences in terms of four temperaments, SJ, SP, NF, and NT. These, he believes, are systemic, holistic patterns of behavior, not particular mental functions. The patterns of behavior are static and not developmental per se. The patterns are more important and override the influence of any particular mental function, if such exists. Temperament precedes and overrides type.

In contrast, Jung/Myers would interpret MBTI preferences in terms of particular psychological cognitive processes or functions, attitudes, and life-style patterns. The 16 types have different dynamic paths for development. Type development includes having a clearly preferred and differentiated perceiving and judging function, attitudes, and life-style. The dominant function operates mainly in the preferred attitude, whereas the auxiliary provides attitude and functional balance and operates mainly in the nonpreferred attitude. Early in life, development should concentrate on the dominant function, along with the supporting auxiliary. Later the third and inferior functions should receive attention. Behavior is influenced by all four preferences, not just the pairs Keirsey highlighted. Keirsey's temperaments in fact are only four of several preference combinations that could be used to describe patterns of behavior. Osmond et al. (1983), Arthur (1985), and Brownsword (1988), for example, described the behavior of functional pairs (NT, NF, ST, SF), whereas Brownsword (1988) also described the behavior of attitude pairs (EJ, EP, IJ, and IP) and extroverted pairs (SP, NP, TJ, and FJ). All combinations of preferences could be considered as temperaments; they do not precede or override type, however. They simply highlight selected behavioral aspects of type.

What seems to be needed in order to clarify some of the differences between Keirsey and Jung/Myers is research on the actual behavioral characteristics of types and temperaments. Berens (1985) cautioned that valid interpretation of such research on Ss, Ns, Ts, Fs, Es, Is, Ps, Js, or any combination of letters cannot be made unless samples include balanced representation from all of the other preferences. The study of the behavior of SPs for example must include balanced representation of ESFPs, ISFPs, ISTPs, and ESTPs, and not be biased by the absence or overrepresentation of any one of the SP types. Given the above, McCarley and Carskadon (1986) and Ruhl and Rodgers (in press) asked college students of all 16 types to rate the accuracy of each individual element in Keirsey and Bates's (1978) and Myers's (1980) type descriptions. Both studies found the ratings of Myers's and Keirsey's descriptions virtually identical in accuracy; hence, on the preliminary data available, neither theory seems to be more accurate than the other in describing behavior. Both interpretations of MBTI preferences, therefore, seem to be acceptable as a basis for planning student affairs programs.

Keirsey and Brownsword (1983) agreed that both are useful and that a practitioner's choice is not "either-or" but "both." This can be illustrated by analyzing the behavior of an ESTJ and ESFJ student leader. These two leaders would have similar SJ temperaments, but would be very different functional types.

The ESTJ leader has a "no-nonsense, impersonal, sometimes hot tempered style" (Keirsey & Brownsword, 1983, p. 8.). This leader is socially active but also decisive, dependable, and demanding. She believes she is right on most issues and she does not easily compromise her rightness for harmony among members of her group. She gives orders, makes assignments, and gets things done.

On the other hand, the ESFJ leader could take over a student government that is full of conflict and within a few weeks everyone would be working harmoniously together (Keirsey & Brownsword, 1983). Before meetings, this leader spends much time figuring out how to minimize conflict and maximize harmony and commitment. The ESFJ leader rarely gives orders, rarely speaks in a commanding way, and is likely to ask for information when the intent is to ask the other to do something. Type, therefore, would predict these T versus F differences in leadership emphasis and style. Temperament would not. Both of these leaders, however, also share the SJ traditionalist or guardian temperament. Both respect the university governance system and keep their organizations within policy guidelines. They follow rules, get things done on time, and accomplish the details of organizational life. Temperament works, also.

Using MBTI, Type, and Temperament

To use the MBTI, type theory, and temperament theory, practitioners must know the theories and instrument well and use them (Rodgers, 1983). Self-analysis is a good way to start. Look at your own behavior through the perspectives of type and temperament. Similarly, look at the behavior of the students with whom you work. This usually leads to greater understanding of self and other, acceptance of what cannot be changed, and awareness of what can be changed. It also can lead to designing programs that facilitate psychosocial and cognitive-structural development through the use of type characteristics. This student development use of type has been aptly demonstrated in teaching (Golay, 1982; Lawrence, 1982), counseling (Provost, 1984), retention (Kalsbeek, 1987), residential programs (Schroeder & Jackson, 1987), student activities (Provost & Anchors, 1987), academic advising (Anchors, 1987), career development (Golden & Provost, 1987; Myers & Mc-Caulley, 1985), and student development as defined by Chickering's vectors (Lynch, 1987).

USE AND ABUSE OF THEORY

As this review of recent theory and research underlying student development concludes, a few remarks about the abuse of theory may be in order. Brownsword (1987) provided a brief synopsis of this important topic. He reminded student affairs professionals that thorough knowledge of theory is both professionally powerful and subject to abuse. If professionals use knowledge to stereotype or limit themselves or others, then they are abusing their knowledge of theory.

"Oh, he's only a Kohlberg Stage 3, we can't pick him."

"She's an ISTJ, she'd never make a career in student affairs."

Similarly, when a professional uses knowledge of theory as an excuse for behavior, he or she is abusing theory.

Other: "You missed our appointment again."

Self: "What can you expect, I'm a P!"

"He's a Kegan 3 and that's why he let his friends into the back gate of the concert. What else can you expect?"

Awareness, understanding, appreciation, and facilitation of the growth of developmental and typological differences are not the same as excuses, stereotypes, and preemptive limitations. Seek the former; avoid the latter.

REFERENCES

American Council on Education. (1937). *The student personnel point of view.* American Council on Education Studies, Series 1. Washington, DC: Author.

American Council on Education. (1949). *The student personnel point of view* (rev. ed.). American Council on Education Studies, Series 6. Washington, DC: Author.

Anchors, S. (1987). Academic advising. In J. Provost & S. Anchors (Eds.), *Applications of the Myers-Briggs Type Indicator in higher education* (pp. 109–123). Palo Alto, CA: Consulting Psychologists Press.

Arthur, S. (1985). The most closely related types. *Bulletin of Psychological Type, 8*(1), 24–25.

Astin, A.W. (1987, Sept./Oct.). Competition or cooperation. *Change, 19*(2), 12–19.

Aulepp, L., & Delworth, U. (1978). A team approach to environmental assessment. In J.H. Banning (Ed.), *Campus ecology: A perspective for student affairs* (pp. 51–71). Washington, DC: National Association of Student Personnel Administrators.

Banning, J., & Kaiser, L. (1974). An ecological perspective and model for campus design. *Personnel and Guidance Journal, 52*, 370–375.

Barker, R.G. (1968). *Ecological psychology: Concepts and methods for studying the environment of human behavior.* Stanford, CA: Stanford University.

Baruch, G., & Barnett, R. (1980, December 7). A new start for women at midlife. *New York Times Magazine*, pp. 196–201.

Baruch, G., Barnett, R., & Rivers, C. (1983). *Lifeprints.* New York: Signet.

Baumrind, D. (1986). Sex differences in moral reasoning: Response to Walker's (1984) conclusion that there are none. *Child Development, 5*(2), 511–521.

Baxter Magolda, M.B. (1987). A comparison of open-ended interview and standardized instrument measures of intellectual development on the Perry scheme. *Journal of College Student Personnel, 28*, 443–448.

Baxter Magolda, M.B. (1988a). Measuring gender differences in intellectual development: A comparison of assessment methods. *Journal of College Student Development, 29*, 528–537.

Baxter Magolda, M.B. (1988b, March). *Validity of the measure of epistemological reflection for assessing gender differences.* A paper presented at the annual conference, American College Personnel Association, Miami, FL.

Baxter Magolda, M.B. (1989). Gender differences in cognitive development: An analysis of cognitive complexity and learning styles. *Journal of College Student Development, 30*, 213–220.

Baxter Magolda, M.B., & Porterfield, W.D. (1985). A new approach to assess intellectual development on the Perry scheme. *Journal of College Student Personnel, 26*, 343–351.

Belenky, M.F., Clinchy, B.M., Goldberger, N.R., & Tarule, J.M. (1986). *Women's ways of knowing: The development of self, voice and mind.* New York: Basic Books.

Berens, L. (1985). Differences that make a difference: Theory and research. *MBTI News, 7*, 8–10.

Blocker, D.H. (1974). Toward an ecology of student development. *Personnel and Guidance Journal, 52*(6), 360–365.

Brabeck, M. (1984). Longitudinal studies of intellectual development during adulthood: Theoretical and research models. *Journal of Research and Development in Education, 17*, 12–27.

Branch-Simpson, G. (1984). *A study of the patterns in the development of black students at The Ohio State University.* Unpublished doctoral dissertation, The Ohio State University, Columbus.

Brownsword, A.W. (1987). *It takes all types!* Washington, DC: Baytree.

Brownsword, A.W. (1988). *Psychological type: An introduction.* Washington, DC: Baytree.

Chickering, A.W. (1969). *Education and identity.* San Francisco: Jossey-Bass.

Claxton, C.S., & Murrell, P.H. (1987). *Learning styles: Implications for improving educational practices,* Report 4, ASHE-ERIC Higher Education Reports. Washington, DC: ERIC Clearinghouse on Higher Education.

Cooper, A.C. (1971). *A proposal for professional preparation of the college student development educators.* Report from Commission on Professional Development, Council of Student Personnel Associations. Washington, DC: Council of Student Personnel Associations.

Cooper, A.C. (1972). *Student development services in higher education.* Report from Commission on Professional Development, Council of Student Personnel Associations. Washington, DC: Council of Student Personnel Associations.

Denny, N. (1988). *Socio-moral development variability: Comparisons of Kohlberg's moral reasoning stages for Jung's Thinking-Feeling student process, educational level, and gender.* Unpublished doctoral dissertation, The Ohio State University, Columbus.

Dietrich, M.K. (1972). *Goal setting for The Ohio State University Campus Ministry Association using The Delphi Technique as a data-based intervention strategy.* Unpublished master's thesis, The Ohio State University, Columbus.

Drum, D. (1980). Understanding student development. In W.H. Morrill, J.C. Hurst, & E.R. Oetting (Eds.), *Dimensions of intervention for student development* (pp. 14–38). New York: Wiley.

Erikson, E.H. (1968). *Identity, youth, and crisis.* New York: Norton.

Farrell, M.P., & Rosenberg, S.D. (1981). *Men at midlife.* Dover, MA: Auburn House.

Fawcett, G., Huebner, L.A., & Banning, J.H. (1978). Campus ecology: Implementing the design process. In J.H. Banning, (Ed.), *Campus ecology: A perspective for student affairs* (pp. 32–50). Washington, DC: National Association of Student Personnel Administrators.

Fowler, J. (1981). *Stages of faith.* New York: Harper & Row.

Fries, S. (1983). *Black and white students' perceptions of the Olentangy Residence Halls: An ecosystems approach.* Unpublished master's thesis, The Ohio State University, Columbus.

Gibbs, J.C., Arnold, K.D., & Burkhart, J.E. (1984). Sex differences in the expression of moral judgment. *Child Development, 55,* 1040–1043.

Gibbs, J.C., & Widaman, K.F., with A. Colby. (1982). *Social intelligence: Measuring the development of sociomoral reflection.* Englewood Cliffs, NJ: Prentice-Hall.

Gilligan, C. (1982). *In a different voice: Psychological theory and women's development.* Cambridge, MA: Harvard University Press.

Gilligan, C. (1986a). Remapping development: The power of divergent data. In L. Cirillo & S. Wapner (Eds.), *Value presuppositions in theories of human development* (pp. 37–61). Hillsdale, NJ: Lawrence Erlbaum Associates.

Gilligan, C. (1986b). Reply by Carol Gilligan. *Signs: Journal of Women in Culture and Society, II,* 304–333.

Golay, K. (1982). *Learning patterns and temperament styles.* Fullerton, CA: Manis Systems.

Golden, V. & Provost, J. (1987). The MBTI and career development. In J. Provost & S. Anchors, (Eds.), *Applications of the Myers-Briggs Type Indicator in higher education* (pp. 151–179). Palo Alto, CA: Consulting Psychologists Press.

Haan, N. (1985). With regard to Walker (1984) on sex "differences" in moral reasoning. Mimeographed paper. Berkeley, CA: University of California, Berkeley, Institute of Human Development.

Heath, R. (1964). *The reasonable adventurer.* Pittsburgh, PA: University of Pittsburgh Press.

Heidke, J. (1982). *A study of cognitive-intellectual and psychosocial development of women at Kenyon College and The Ohio State University*. Unpublished doctoral dissertation, The Ohio State University, Columbus.

Huebner, L.A. (1979). Emergent issues of theory and practice. In L.A. Huebner (Ed.), *Redesigning campus environments* (pp. 1–21). New Directions for Student Services Series, No. 8. San Francisco: Jossey-Bass.

Huebner, L.A., & Corazzini, J.G. (1978). Eco-mapping: A dynamic model for intentional campus design. *Journal Supplement Abstract Service, Catalogue of Selected Documents on Psychology, 8*(9), 9.

Huebner, L.A., Royer, J.A., Moore, J., Cordes, D.L., & Paul, S.C. (1979). Stress management through an ecosystem model in a school of medicine. In L.A. Huebner (Ed.), *Redesigning campus environments* (pp. 51–67). New Directions for Student Services Series, No. 8. San Francisco: Jossey-Bass.

Hurst, J.C., & Ragle, J.D. (1979). Application of the ecosystem perspective to a Dean of Students office. In L.A. Huebner (Ed.), *Redesigning campus environments* (pp. 69–84). New Directions for Student Services Series, No. 8. San Francisco: Jossey-Bass.

Johnston, D.K. (1985). *Two moral orientations—two problem-solving strategies: Adolescents' solutions to dilemmas in fables*. Unpublished doctoral dissertation, Harvard University, School of Education, Cambridge, MA.

Josselson, R. (1987). *Finding herself: Pathways to identity development in women*. San Francisco: Jossey-Bass.

Jung, C.G. (1971). *Psychological types*. In H. Read, M. Fordham, G. Adler, & W. McGuire (Eds.), R.F.C. Hull (Trans.), *Vol. 6 of Collected works*. Bollingen Series, *XX*. Princeton, NJ: Princeton University Press.

Kaiser, L. (1978). Campus ecology and campus design. In J.H. Banning (Ed.), *Campus ecology: A perspective for student affairs* (pp. 24–31). Washington, DC: National Association of Student Personnel Administrators.

Kalsbeek, D. (1987). Campus retention: The MBTI and institutional self-studies. In J. Provost & S. Anchors, (Eds.), *Applications of the Myers-Briggs Type Indicator in higher education* (pp. 31–63). Palo Alto, CA: Consulting Psychologists Press.

Kegan, R. (1979). The evolving self: A process conception for ego psychology. *The Counseling Psychologist, 8*, 5–34.

Kegan, R. (1980a). Making meaning: The constructive-developmental approach to persons and practice. *The Personnel and Guidance Journal, 58*, 373–380.

Kegan, R. (1980b). *There the dance is: Religious dimensions of a developmental framework. Toward moral and religious maturity*. Morristown, NJ: Silver-Burdett.

Kegan, R. (1982). *The evolving self: Problems and process in human development*. Cambridge, MA: Harvard University Press.

Keirsey, D. (1988). *Portraits of temperaments*. Del Mar, CA: Prometheus Nemesis.

Keirsey, D., & Bates, M. (1978). *Please understand me: Character and temperament types* (3rd ed.). Del Mar, CA: Prometheus Nemesis.

Keirsey, D., & Brownsword, A. (1983). Temperament theory and the theory of functions. *MBTI News, 6*(1), 5–10.

King, P.M. (1982, November). *Perry's Scheme and the Reflective Judgment model: First cousins once removed*. Paper presented at the Annual Conference of the Association for Moral Education, Minneapolis, MN.

King, P.M., Kitchener, K.S., Davison, M.L., Parker, C.A., & Wood, P.L. (1983). The justification of beliefs in young adults: A longitudinal study. *Human Development, 26,* 106–116.

Kitchener, K.S. (1986). The reflective judgment model: Characteristics, evidence, and measurement. In R.A. Mines & K.S. Kitchener (Eds.), *Adult cognitive development: Methods and models* (pp. 76–91). New York: Praeger.

Kitchener, K.S., & King, P.M. (1981). Reflective judgment: Concepts of justification and their relationship to age and education. *Journal of Applied Developmental Psychology, 2,* 89–116.

Kitchener, K.S., & King, P.M. (1985a). *Reflective judgment theory and research: Insights into the process of knowing in adulthood.* (ERIC Document Reproduction Service No. ED 263 821.) Denver: University of Denver.

Kitchener, K.S., & King, P.M. (1985b, June). *The reflective judgement model: Ten years of research.* Paper presented at the Beyond Formal Operations Symposium, Boston, MA.

Knefelkamp, L., Widick, C., & Parker, C.A. (1978). *Applying new developmental findings.* San Francisco: Jossey-Bass.

Kohlberg, L. (1984). *Essays on moral development: Volume II—The psychology of moral development: The nature and validity of moral stages.* San Francisco: Harper & Row.

Kolb, D.A. (1976). *Learning Style Inventory technical manual.* Boston: McBer.

Langdale, S. (1983). *Moral orientations and moral development: The analysis of care and justice reasoning across different dilemmas in females and males from childhood to adulthood.* Unpublished doctoral dissertation, Harvard University, School of Education, Cambridge, MA.

Lawrence, G. (1982). *People types and tiger stripes* (2nd ed.). Gainesville, FL: Center for Applications of Psychological Type.

Levinson, D.J. (1978). *The seasons of a man's life.* New York: Knopf.

Lewin, K. (1936). *Principles of topological psychology.* New York: McGraw-Hill.

Livingston, M.D. (1980). *An ecological assessment of the residence halls' environment at the University of Iowa.* Unpublished doctoral dissertation, Michigan State University, East Lansing.

Loevinger, J. (1976). *Ego development: Conceptions and theories.* San Francisco: Jossey-Bass.

Lynch, A. (1987). Type development and student development. In J. Provost & S. Anchors (Eds.), *Applications of the Myers-Briggs Type Indicator in higher education* (pp. 5–29). Palo Alto, CA: Consulting Psychologists Press.

Lyons, N.P. (1983). Two perspectives: On self, relationships, and morality. *Harvard Educational Review, 53,* 125–145.

Marcia, J.E. (1966). Development and validation of ego identity status. *Journal of Personality and Social Psychology, 3,* 551–558.

Marcia, J.E. (1976). Identity six years after: A follow-up study. *Journal of Youth and Adolescence, 5,* 145–160.

Marcia, J.E. (1980). Identity in adolescence. In J. Adelson (Ed.), *Handbook of adolescent psychology* (pp. 159–187). New York: Wiley.

Marcia, J.E., & Friedman, M. (1970). Ego identity status in college women. *Journal of Personality, 38,* 249–263.

McCarley, N., & Carskadon, T.G. (1986). The perceived accuracy of elements of the 16 type descriptions of Myers and Keirsey among men and women: Which elements are most accurate, should the type descriptions be different for men and women, and do the type descriptions stereotype sensing types? *Journal of Psychological Type, 11,* 2–29.

Mintz, R.B. (1976). *Goal setting for the future: An application of context evaluation to fraternity life*. Unpublished master's thesis, The Ohio State University, Columbus.

Moore, W. (1982). *The measure of intellectual development: A brief review*. Baltimore, MD: University of Maryland, Center for Application of Developmental Instruction.

Moos, R.H. (1979). *Evaluating educational environments*. San Francisco: Jossey-Bass.

Morrill, W.H., Hurst, J.C., & Oetting, E.R. (1980). *Dimensions of intervention for student development*. New York: Wiley.

Myers, I.B. (1980). *Gifts differing*. Palo Alto, CA: Consulting Psychologists Press.

Myers, I.B., & McCaulley, M.H. (1985). *Manual: A guide to the development and use of the Myers-Briggs Type Indicator*. Palo Alto, CA: Consulting Psychologists Press.

Newman, J. (1986). Intuition as a cognitive process. *Bulletin of Psychological Type, 9*(1), 4–6.

Newman, J. (1987). Thinking as a cognitive process. *Bulletin of Psychological Type, 10*(2), 13, 25–27.

Nichols, E.J. (1988, July). *Managing in a multicultural community*. Paper presented at the 14th annual Richard F. Stevens NASPA/ACE Institute on Leadership and Administration of Student Affairs in Higher Education, Annapolis, MD.

Omahan, D. (1982). *Cognitive-intellectual and psychosocial development of male students at a small private college and a large public university*. Unpublished doctoral dissertation, The Ohio State University, Columbus.

Osmond, H., Siegler, M., & Smoke, R. (1983). Typology revisited: A new perspective. *MBTI News, 5*(2), 1, 10–13.

Palmer, P.J. (1987, September/October). Community, conflict, and ways of knowing. *Change, 19*(2), 20–25.

Perry, W., Jr. (1970). *Forms of intellectual and ethical development in the college years: A scheme*. New York: Holt, Rinehart & Winston.

Pervin, L.A. (1967). A twenty-college study of student x college interaction using TAPE: Rationale, reliability, and validity. *Journal of Educational Psychology, 58*, 290–302.

Pervin, L.A. (1968). Performance and satisfaction as a function of individual-environment fit. *Psychological Bulletin, 69*, 56–68.

Provost, J. (1984). *A case book: Applications of the Myers-Briggs Type Indicator in counseling*. Gainesville, FL: Center for Applications of Psychological Type.

Provost, J., & Anchors, S. (1987). *Applications of the Myers-Briggs Type Indicator in higher education*. Palo Alto, CA: Consulting Psychologists Press.

Reynolds, A. (1984). *A graduate housing ecosystem: An international-North American student comparison*. Unpublished master's thesis, The Ohio State University, Columbus.

Rodgers, R. (1974–1988). *Perry level of entering freshmen*. Unpublished research studies. Columbus, OH: The Ohio State University.

Rodgers, R. (1988, September). *Origins of the care voice: Gender or type?* Paper presented at Association for Psychological Type Great Lakes Regional Conference, Indianapolis, IN.

Rodgers, R.F. (1980). Theories underlying student development. In D.G. Creamer (Ed.), *Student development in higher education: Theories, practices, & future directions* (pp. 10–95). Alexandria, VA: American College Personnel Association.

Rodgers, R.F. (1983). Using theory in practice. In T.K. Miller, R.B. Winston, & W.R. Mendenhall (Eds.), *Administration and leadership in student affairs* (pp. 111–144). Muncie, IN: Accelerated Development.

Rodgers, R.F. (1984a, June). *Student development through campus ecology*. Paper presented at Annual Conference on Campus Ecology, Pingree Park, CO.

Rodgers, R.F. (1984b). Theories of adult development: Research status and counseling implications. In S. Brown & R. Lent (Eds.), *Handbook of counseling psychology* (pp. 479–519). New York: Wiley.

Ruhl, D., & Rodgers, R. (in press). The perceived accuracy of the 16 type descriptions of Jung/Myers and Keirsey: A replication of McCarley and Carskadon's (1986) study. *Journal of Psychological Type.*

Sabock, A.F. (1980). *A context evaluation of female athletes' perceptions of study tables, tutoring, academic advising and scheduling, counseling, and social life at The Ohio State University.* Unpublished master's thesis, The Ohio State University, Columbus.

Schroeder, C. (1976). New strategies for structuring residential environments. *Journal of College Student Personnel, 17,* 386–391.

Schroeder, C. (1980a). Designing college environments for students. In F.B. Newton & K.L. Ender (Eds.), *Student development practices* (pp. 52–79). Springfield, IL: Charles C Thomas.

Schroeder, C. (1980b). Territoriality: An imperative for personal development and residence education. In D. DeCoster & P. Mable (Eds.), *Personal education and community development in college residence halls* (pp. 114–132). Alexandria, VA: American College Personnel Association.

Schroeder, C. (1981). Student development through environmental management. In G. Blimling & J. Schuh (Eds.), *Increasing the educational role of residence halls* (pp. 35–49). San Francisco: Jossey-Bass.

Schroeder, C., & Belmonte, A. (1979). The influence of residence environment on pre-pharmacy student achievement and satisfaction. *American Journal of Pharmaceutical Education, 43,* 16–19.

Schroeder, C., & Jackson, S. (1987). Designing residential environments. In J. Provost & S. Anchors (Eds.), *Applications of the Myers-Briggs Type Indicator in higher education* (pp. 65–88). Palo Alto, CA: Consulting Psychologists Press.

Schuh, J.H. (1979). Assessment and redesign in residence halls. In L.A. Huebner (Ed.), *Redesigning campus environments* (pp. 23–36). New Directions for Student Services Series, No. 8. San Francisco: Jossey-Bass.

Stern, G.G. (1970). *People in context.* New York: Wiley.

Straub, C. (1987). Women's development of autonomy and Chickering's theory. *Journal of College Student Personnel, 28,* 198–205.

Straub, C., & Rodgers, R.F. (1986). An exploration of Chickering's theory and women's development. *Journal of College Student Personnel, 27,* 216–224.

Treadway, D.M. (1979). Use of campus-wide ecosystem surveys to monitor a changing institution. In L.A. Huebner (Ed.), *Redesigning campus environments* (pp. 37–49). New Directions for Student Services Series, No. 8. San Francisco: Jossey-Bass.

Vaillant, G.E. (1977). *Adaptation to life.* Boston: Little, Brown.

Walker, L. (1984). Sex differences in the development of moral reasoning: A critical review. *Child Development, 55,* 667–691.

Welfel, E.R., & Davison, M.L. (1986). The development of reflective judgment in the college years: A four year longitudinal study. *Journal of College Student Personnel, 27,* 209–216.

CHAPTER 4

Assessing Development From a Cognitive-Developmental Perspective

Patricia M. King

Many authors (e.g., Bok, 1986; Gamson & Associates, 1984; Hanson, 1982; Mentkowski, 1984; Miller, 1982) have stated convincingly and eloquently that it is important to assess student development. Without assessment, they argue, it is impossible to monitor students' educational or developmental progress, to set realistic and informed program goals, to evaluate the effectiveness of given programs, or to document an institution's success in fulfilling its mission. Using assessment data for such purposes requires that changes be documented. Both education and development imply change toward developing the characteristics and skills associated with mature, educated people, and documenting change requires assessment. As Miller (1982) noted, "In many ways, assessment is the glue that holds development processes together" (p. 11).

There are, of course, many approaches to assessing development, and each approach asks characteristically different sets of questions and makes different sets of assumptions about developmental processes. This chapter focuses on one broad category of assessments, cognitive-developmental assessment, and consists of three sections. The first section presents the major assumptions of the cognitive-developmental perspective and their implications for assessment. The second section explores the benefits and risks of using informal and formal assessment procedures. The third section discusses two major approaches to cognitive-developmental as-

The author wishes to express her thanks to Michael Coomes, Jonathan Dings, and Carney Strange for their helpful comments on an earlier draft of this chapter.

81

sessment, production and recognition tasks, and describes representative instruments for each approach.

MAJOR ASSUMPTIONS OF THE
COGNITIVE-DEVELOPMENTAL PERSPECTIVE

Many of the major assumptions of the cognitive-developmental approach were first explicated by Jean Piaget (1932) and later extended by Lawrence Kohlberg (1969, 1984). Three major assumptions are presented below.

The meaning of experiences is cognitively constructed. At the foundation of the cognitive-developmental approach is the assumption that individuals actively attempt to make sense of what they experience by creating their own interpretations or explanations of their experiences. In other words, a person's interpretations of his or her experiences are assumed to be cognitively constructed. When an explanation is viewed from the perspective of the individual who created it, an internal logic to the explanation may be seen; the interrelated sets of assumptions that underlie this logic are referred to as a "cognitive structure." Most cognitive-developmental theories are attempts to describe these cognitive structures and elucidate the internal logic that they hold.

Cognitive structures evolve. The second major assumption is that cognitive structures are not stable but evolve over time, with earlier structures providing the foundation for later structures. Furthermore, more mature structures are assumed to offer more complex, complete, and adequate ways of interpreting reality. For example, they may allow an individual to consider more information at one time, to accommodate discrepant or contradictory information, and to become increasingly able to critique others' as well as his or her own thought processes. In other words, children are not thought to be merely small adults with less height, less weight, and less reasoning ability. Rather, adult cognition is assumed to reflect qualitative changes in reasoning that are built on earlier structures, but revised when these structures became inadequate. For example, college seniors who say, "I can't believe that when I was a freshman, I thought that professors knew all the answers," are acknowledging the inadequacy of their previous assumptions. They don't simply know more (quantitatively); they think in qualitatively different terms about sources of knowledge and their own role in evaluating the truth of given statements.

Development occurs in interaction with the environment. Third, the cognitive structures that provide this interpretive framework are assumed to evolve as a result of both maturity and interaction with the environment. Although the direction of cognitive changes (i.e., toward greater complexity and adequacy) is assumed to be predictable, the rate of change for any individual is assumed to fluctuate depending on the characteristics of his or her environment, including the amount of stimulation and the balance of challenge and support she or he perceives (Sanford, 1966). (A discussion of this concept appears in Strange & King's chapter 2 of this volume.)

The "cognitive structures" alluded to above are more commonly referred to as "stages." Each stage in a cognitive-developmental theory typically refers to a set of interrelated assumptions (about knowledge, morality, self, etc.) that give individuals a foundation from which to interpret their experiences. The stage concept has provided a relatively easy way for student affairs practitioners to understand readily observed differences between students. Furthermore, the basic assumptions that stage-related characteristics evolve over time and are affected by environmental characteristics are both consistent with a student development perspective (Brown, 1972). These assumptions have allowed practitioners to counsel students and provide programs that take such developmental differences into account (e.g., Loxley & Whiteley, 1986; Welfel, 1982; Whiteley & Associates, 1982; Widick, Knefelkamp, & Parker, 1975; Widick & Simpson, 1978).

Psychosocial theories, by contrast, typically attempt to describe the *types* of developmental tasks students are addressing, such as gaining intellectual competence, becoming more independent from parents, or deciding on a major and career (Chickering, 1969). A cognitive-developmental assessment might use these issues as the *content* of an assessment question, but the assessment objective would be to discover *how* respondents think about (i.e., how they make meaning or interpret) their experiences in addressing these issues. For example, a Dualist (Perry, 1970) typically approaches career decision making differently from a Relativist. Thus, the fairness of group billing (a procedure of billing a group of students for damages when an individual perpetrator cannot be identified) in a residence hall will be judged differently depending on whether an individual holds Preconventional or Conventional level moral judgments (Kohlberg, 1969).

Stage theory: Implications for assessment. In the last two decades, the stage concept has received a great deal of attention (Fischer & Silvern, 1985; Flavell, 1970, 1971, 1982; Flavell & Wohlwill, 1969; Wohlwill, 1973). Rest (1979b) offered a detailed analysis of the stage concept in moral judgment research, many points of which are applicable to cognitive-developmental theories in other domains (e.g., intellectual or identity). He drew several important distinctions between simple and complex developmental stage models. In the more familiar simple-stage model, each individual was assumed to proceed through the specified stages, one stage at a time, with no skipping, no overlapping, and no steps backwards. Using these assumptions, the typical assessment question is: "What stage is a person in?" The only circumstance in which a person could be in more than one stage was if she or he was in transition between stages, in which case the use of assumptions from two adjacent stages would be expected. Stage assessments, therefore, were also assumed to be context-independent, or applicable across a broad range of topics and contexts.

Closer examination of these assumptions about development has shown, however, that the simple-stage model reflects an overly simplified description of cognitive processes, and is inconsistent with many research findings. For example, people don't seem to change from the exclusive use of one set of assumptions to the exclusive use of those of the next adjacent stage; rather, the use of assumptions characteristic of several stages at once often has been found. Stage usage seems to be influenced by a variety of individual factors (e.g., consolidation of existing structures, fatigue, readiness for change) and environmental factors (e.g., whether one is asked to create one's own solution to a problem or to critique someone else's solution, explaining one's beliefs verbally or in writing).

The finding that participant responses vary with test characteristics and test demands has been particularly problematic for simple-stage theory. Some assessment strategies (e.g., asking respondents spontaneously to produce and then defend their own argument about a given issue) impose heavier cognitive demands than others (e.g., paraphrasing someone else's ideas as an indication of comprehension). Therefore, cognitive-developmental assessment is not independent of context: Differences in assessment procedures and content can influence the score an individual earns on a developmental assessment tool.

These results also suggest that it is probably inappropriate to refer to an individual as "being in a stage." Although an individual frequently may reason using the assumptions of a given stage, it would be incorrect to assume that she or he can use only one such set of stage-related assumptions at a time, regardless of the circumstances under which stage scores were assessed.

Because of inadequacies of the simple-stage model such as those listed above, Rest (1979b) proposed an alternative: the complex-stage model. This model requires a shift in the developmental assessment question from "What stage is a person in?" to the following: "To what extent and under what conditions does a person manifest the various types of organizations of thinking?" (p. 63). This approach acknowledges that a person's responses vary depending on situational variables (e.g., test characteristics, task demands, content differences) and assumes that people are *not* single-track (i.e., single-stage) thinkers. Rest presented his position as follows:

> Rather than moving "one step," a subject may advance in several organizations of thinking simultaneously, for example, moving to advanced levels of Stage 3, to moderate levels of Stage 4, and to the earliest levels of Stage 5. It is difficult to talk about movement out of one stage and into the next when there is so little evidence of developmental synchrony of the constituent concepts of the stages. Instead of alternating phases of transition and consolidation (Stage 2 consolidation, then transition to Stage 3, then Stage 3 consolidation, then transition to Stage 4, etc.), the structure of thinking may continue to develop much beyond the onset of the next stages of thinking (for example, becoming able to explain and critique Stage 3 at the same time that Stage 5 statements can be intuitively discriminated from Stage 4 statements). (Rest, 1979b, p. 65)

As Rest noted, this model reflects "a much messier and more complicated picture of development" (1979b, p. 65), but one that is more in line with the empirical evidence and (I would add), common sense. From a complex-stage perspective, assessment of an individual's use of a given stage has become more probabilistic, focusing on the *likelihood* that it will be evidenced, rather than on *whether or not* it is evidenced. In addition, this approach suggests that a person may understand her or his reasoning and subsequent actions most fully not at the point of their fullest development (a single-stage assumption), but after they have been replaced by a more adequate structure. This explains why college seniors often seem so cogent and articulate about the fallacies in their thinking as freshmen (and the troubles that caused), but diffuse or illogical about their current reasoning and plans for the future. Furthermore, the complex-stage perspective suggests that teachers, counselors, or advisors who attempt to match exactly their responses to a student's modal stage may underestimate the student's ability to recognize or understand higher-stage reasoning.

Summary

Cognitive-developmental theories attempt to describe changes in the underlying thought processes people use to understand their experiences. These processes are not assumed to be either stable traits nor skills that simply can be taught. Rather, these processes are at the core of individuals' cognitive functioning and ways of actively constructing meaning in their lives. These constructions develop over time and in response to challenging learning opportunities; less adequate constructions are abandoned and are replaced by more adequate structures. Identifying where individuals are in the process of moving from the immature, simpler, and less adequate structures to the more mature, inclusive, and more adequate structures is the primary task of cognitive-developmental assessment.

INFORMAL AND FORMAL ASSESSMENT:
PURPOSES, BENEFITS, AND RISKS

Assessment data may be collected either formally or informally. As will be explained below, the decision to use formal or informal assessment depends on the specific needs and purposes for conducting the assessment; each type of assessment carries its own set of benefits and risks. (Much has been written on this topic that is beyond the scope of this chapter; for cogent discussions of these distinctions, see Argyris, 1976; and Lenning, 1980.)

The distinctions drawn below between formal and informal assessment should not be confused with the distinctions between qualitative and quantitative (or "naturalistic" and "positivistic") research methodologies (Guba & Lincoln, 1982). Rather, formal and informal assessment procedures may be used within either research perspective; the examples given below apply to both qualitative and quantitative perspectives.

Informal Assessment

The process of generating hunches about students' developmental levels has been referred to as "tuning your ears" (Weathersby & Tarule, 1980) and listening to "developmental clues" (Stonewater & Stonewater, 1983). There are many appropriate uses and contexts for gathering information about students informally, for example, supervising student peer consultants, advisors, resident assistants, or office workers; advising student groups; or having informal conversations with students over lunch or in a television lounge. More specific examples follow.

1. You are the judicial officer conducting a disciplinary hearing involving a student charged with pulling a fire alarm. You ask the student what she thinks happened that was wrong. If the answer is "I didn't do anything wrong; I just

needed an excuse to miss a meeting and I got caught,'' you may suspect that the student is using Preconventional (Stage 2) moral reasoning (Kohlberg, 1969), where an act is considered right if it serves one's own purpose. If the answer is "my friend squealed on me,'' you may suspect that the student is using Conventional level (Stage 3) reasoning, where what is considered wrong is that the friend violated the "friendship pact,'' which includes covering up for each other's indiscretions. Choosing an effective response to either answer will require accurate assessment.

2. You are a staff member having an informal conversation with a student who is complaining about a course he is taking. You decide to try to learn the source of the frustration. He explains that he is earning low grades on his position papers, even though he copied his class notes nearly verbatim into his arguments. This type of response might suggest to you that he assumes that he should justify his point of view by citing (verbatim) the words of experts or authority figures. This would suggest to you that, in this situation, he may hold Reflective Judgment (Kitchener & King, 1981) Stage 2 assumptions for an assignment that requires at least Stage 4 reasoning. Alternatively, the student may be genuinely confused about the instructor's expectations because the instructor teaches from a Myers-Briggs (Myers, 1980) Intuitive-Perceiving perspective and uses abstract tasks for her assignments, whereas the student's dominant modes are Sensing-Judging, with a strong preference for concrete tasks. How you would choose to respond to this student's frustration would depend to a significant degree on how you assessed or analyzed the source of the problem.

Benefits

In both examples, a staff member has a hunch (or makes a probabilistic assessment) about the student's developmental level. There are several advantages to using informal assessments such as these in deciding how to respond to students. First, they allow the staff member/assessor to conduct the assessment within the context of the current relationship or point of contact that already exists with the student. Assessment is thus assumed to be a normal part of staff-student relationships, not an activity performed for someone else's uses and that may or may not enhance the quality of the relationship.

Second, informal assessments allow the staff member to make a judgment based not only on a particular interaction, but on the history of interactions with a student. The staff member may be able to identify patterns in the student's responses, or ways in which this particular problem is unique. This provides a more complete basis for making a judgment.

A third category of major advantages includes some very practical ones: Informal assessments are typically faster and less expensive to conduct. Although these are persuasive elements in an assessment decision, they are not always the most important elements, for reasons discussed next.

Risks

Some important risks accompany the use of informal assessments. The most significant of these is the risk of error. If you are the assessor, one possible source of such error is your own biases, such as a previous negative contact with the student, or the fact that this student may remind you of another person, tempting you to generalize inappropriately from one to the other. Another source of error is your own selective attention to some developmental cues (perhaps those that are consistent with your biases) while overlooking others. Second, your informal assessment may be based on a very limited sampling of behavior, such as when the student is influenced by drugs or alcohol, or a one-time encounter at a judicial hearing.

Third, although it can be argued that some errors may be minimized or overcome by being aware of and trying to compensate for these limitations, a compounding factor is that informal hunches are seldom self-correcting (Parker, 1977) and may escape the notice of even the most conscientious assessor. In other words, if assessors neglect to check the validity of their assessment hunches, they risk basing their decisions on incorrect assessments that result in ineffective practice. For example, in the disciplinary hearing case mentioned above, it probably would not be effective to explain the offense to the student by reference to established social arrangements and agreements for living in a community (a Stage 5 response). The assumptions of this response are incompatible with the assumptions of earlier stages. Therefore, this response would probably not serve as an effective counterargument because it would not be understood in the way it was intended. Such are the perils of inaccurate assessment.

Formal Assessment

Formal approaches to assessment typically are preferred when major decisions or plans will be made based on the assessment findings. A formal approach is also preferred when the accuracy of the assessment is critical, such as when decisions affecting individuals must be made.

Benefits

The advantages of formal assessments are fairly well documented (Argyris & Schon, 1978). They include the potential for being systematically conducted, applicable to specified populations, administered using established procedures, and scored using specified criteria. The most important of these characteristics is accuracy, which is usually inferred from an instrument's indices of reliability and validity. For these reasons, research and evaluation projects that attempt to document the effectiveness of programs usually rely either exclusively on formal assessments, or on a formal approach complemented by the use of informal assessments. Attempts made to document program effectiveness with data that may be construed as idiosyncratic or biased (common criticisms of informal assessments) often generate considerable argument and confusion about the legitimacy of interpretations regarding the success of the specified program.

Risks

Formal assessment, however, is not without its risks. Some student subgroups are skeptical about the fairness of standardized tests (or tests that have been standardized on different subgroups) and are less willing to complete them. Others may be unwilling for political or personal reasons to participate in formal studies. These types of concerns may yield unacceptably low response rates that preclude the researcher from generalizing to the specified population. And worse, this occurrence diminishes the base of information from which decisions can be made. In such cases, carefully collected informal assessment data are clearly more useful.

Another risk of formal assessment is that it may unintentionally serve as an intervention itself, with unknown consequences. For example, when done formatively (i.e., while an intervention is in progress), a formal assessment may be beneficial, causing the participants to reevaluate and reaffirm their agreement to participate fully in the project. A negative effect may result, however, if participants who were beginning to become invested in the project begin to feel like anonymous guinea pigs and subsequently distance themselves from the project. This effect also may be described as pulling a plant up by its roots to see if it is growing; the result is that it then needs to be repotted. In other words, such assessments actually may interfere with the program they were designed to assess.

Some formal assessments, such as those that utilize personal interviews, also tend to be expensive to administer. They tend to be time- and labor-intensive, and often require highly trained staff to collect and score the data. Although interview data yield rich and complex information about student characteristics, the costs associated with such test administration often preclude their widespread use.

Summary

In summary, each approach is useful and should be considered when developmental assessments are needed. A decision to use formal or informal assessment depends on the purposes for which the assessment is being conducted, the risks of low response rates and inaccurate assessments, and the specific situational variables associated with the assessment and evaluation process.

MAJOR APPROACHES TO COGNITIVE-DEVELOPMENTAL ASSESSMENT

This section focuses on specific instruments designed to measure cognitive-developmental theories. Production tasks and recognition tasks represent the two major categories of instruments currently in use, each reflecting the type of task the participant is asked to complete. Different tasks place different cognitive demands on the individuals being tested, which in turn yield different pictures of their developmental status.

Production Tasks

Jean Piaget (1932), a major force in articulating the cognitive-developmental perspective, popularized the clinical interview as a means of eliciting information to determine a subject's structural competencies. This is an example of a production task, in which the individual is required spontaneously to produce a response based on his or her repertoire of skills and cognitive competencies. For example, subjects are typically presented with a problem and are then asked to solve it and explain the solution. Several layers of explanation may be required, such as expressing and justifying the solution, as well as arguing against alternative solutions (Rest, 1979b). These types of tasks (also referred to as response modes) often place heavy cognitive demands on the individual. The thoroughness with which an individual is able to respond to such a series of demands is assumed to depend on the stability and degree of consolidation of the given structure being tapped. For example, some individuals may be able to express a solution, but not be able to argue against alternatives. This example illustrates the difficulty in applying the simple-stage assumption of ''having a structure'' or ''being in a stage'' (discussed earlier). From a complex-stage perspective, this is an example of ''having a structure at different levels.'' Anyone attempting to conduct a developmental assessment should be aware that the choice of a specific task may well affect the resulting assessment of development level, and that individuals can be expected to perform better or score higher on less demanding tasks (e.g., describing a solution) than on more difficult tasks (e.g., explaining why one solution is better than another).

Disadvantages

The disadvantages of production tasks are that they tend to be highly labor-intensive, requiring trained assistants to collect and rate the data, and often are not conducive to group testing. Production tasks are time-consuming as well as expensive. Furthermore, they require subjective classification of subject responses, which is subject to bias, and may be influenced by such extraneous factors as rater fatigue, poor training, or lapses in concentration.

Second, because production tasks typically allow the respondent a great deal of latitude in the focus of the response, the response itself may ramble or may not be focused on the constructs that are of particular interest. In verbal settings, such as interviews, interviewers are typically trained to keep the interview focused; they are not always successful, however. When written formats are used for gathering production task data, this check is not usually available.

Another common concern about production task formats is the difficult challenges they present to respondents. Articulating thoughtful, well-reasoned explanations for beliefs or feelings is a complicated process, and is made more difficult when subjects previously have not given the questions much thought, when the issues are emotionally laden, or when subjects find it hard to capture their ideas or feelings in words. The resulting concern is that this assessment format may lead the rater to underestimate subjects' structural competencies because the tasks are so difficult.

Advantages

The major advantage of production tasks is that they yield rich and complex information about the subject's reasoning capacities, including ways a task is approached, what solutions are tested, whether and why alternative solutions are rejected, and so forth. This approach is often preferred because the assessment reflects the subject's own approach to the problem presented rather than one that has been fitted into categories supplied by the investigator, and thus yields more accurate and more complete assessment data.

Examples of production task instruments—structured interviews. The structured interview has been used as the data collection procedure of choice for the development and refinement of many cognitive-developmental theories, including Kohlberg's (1984) theory of moral development, Perry's (1970) scheme of intellectual and ethical development, Kitchener & King's (1981) Reflective Judgment model, Kegan's (1982) theory of the Evolving Self, Gilligan's (1982) conjectures about women's moral development, Basseches's (1984) model of dialectical thinking, and Belenky, Clinchy, Goldberger, and Tarule's (1986) "women's ways of knowing." Because of the richness and high degree of content or internal validity of the data it yields and the opportunity it provides to clarify ambiguous or incomplete responses, the structured interview remains one of the most common formats used in making cognitive-developmental assessments.

A representative example of a structured interview is Kohlberg's Moral Judgment Interview (MJI). The MJI consists of three parallel forms, each of which contains three moral dilemmas; each dilemma is accompanied by a set of probe questions. The probe questions are designed to elicit subjects' most advanced level of reasoning on two moral issues (law, property, life, contract, affiliation, etc.) for each dilemma. These dilemmas are designed so that two or more moral norms are in conflict. As Gibbs and Widaman (1982) explained:

> . . . most of us feel that we should of course help a friend or save a human life, just as we feel that we should refrain from theft and obey the law. We may even be tempted, if we are asked out of the blue about these values, to say that they are self-evident. We become much more reflective, however, once we experience a value *conflict*. What if the only way we can save a friend's life is by stealing and breaking the law? Then we . . . struggle to achieve and defend an answer to this dilemma. Kohlberg's counterposing of some normative values (e.g., life, affiliation) against others (e.g., law, property) has proven to be an excellent tool for revealing and studying the cognitive structures by which we coordinate and evaluate values—even though we are not ordinarily conscious of those structures. (p. 10)

The famous "Heinz and the Drug" dilemma will illustrate this conflict between the moral issues of life and law. This dilemma reads as follows:

> In Europe a woman was near death from a special kind of cancer. There was one drug that doctors thought might save her. It was a form of radium that a druggist in the same town had recently discovered. The drug was expensive to make, but the druggist was charging ten times what the drug cost to make. He paid $200 for the radium and charges $2000 for a small dose of the drug. The sick woman's husband, Heinz, went to everyone he knew to borrow the money, but he could only get together about $1000, which is half of what it cost. He told the druggist that his wife was dying, and asked him to sell it cheaper and to let him pay later. But the druggist said, "No, I discovered the drug and I'm going to make money from it." So Heinz got desperate and began to think about breaking into the man's store to steal the drug for his wife. (Colby, Kohlberg, Speicher, Hewer, Candee, Gibbs, & Power, 1987, p. 1)

The probe questions for this dilemma are:

1. Should Heinz steal the drug? Why or why not?
2. Is it actually right or wrong for him to steal the drug? Why is it right or wrong?
3. Does Heinz have a duty or obligation to steal the drug? Why or why not?
4. [If subject originally favors stealing, ask:] If Heinz doesn't love his wife, should he steal the drug for her? Why or why not?

   [If subject originally favors not stealing, ask:] Does it make a difference whether or not he loves his wife? Why or why not?
5. Suppose the person dying is not his wife but a stranger. Should Heinz steal the drug for the stranger? Why or why not?
6. [If subject favors stealing the drug for a stranger, ask:] Suppose it's a pet animal he loves. Should Heinz steal to save the pet animal? Why or why not?
7. Is it important for people to do everything they can to save another's life? Why or why not?
8. It is against the law for Heinz to steal. Does that make it morally wrong? Why or why not?
9. In general should people try to do everything they can to obey the law? Why or why not? How does this apply to what Heinz should do? (Colby et al., 1987, pp. 1–2)

A three-part rating procedure is then employed. In the first part, subjects' responses are classified by issue. For example, if a subject answers that Heinz should steal the drug, life is classified as the chosen issue and law as the non-chosen issue. Next, the responses are classified by moral norm and element.

> For example, a response that Heinz should steal the drug "because a good husband should care about his wife" would be coded as applying a "duty" element (since "a good husband should . . ." implies a role obligation) to an affiliation norm (relations between husband and wife) on the chosen issue (life). To give another example, a subject who responds to question 2 by stating that, even if Heinz doesn't love her, he should still steal it because "he has a basic responsibility to save a human life" would provide a case of the same "duty" element (albeit at a different stage) applied to the *life* norm of the life issue. (Gibbs & Widaman, 1982, p. 11)

The second part of the rating process is stage assessment. Here, the rater must match the responses for each dilemma with appropriate stage-related criterion judgments from the rating manual. The third step is the calculation of stage scores from these ratings, both overall and by issue. For a more complete description of the rating process and its rationale, see Colby and Kohlberg (1987) and Colby et al. (1987).

Examples of production task instruments—incomplete sentence stem. Several cognitive developmental researchers have chosen to use a written format for assessment purposes in which the subject is presented with an incomplete sentence stem that she or he is then instructed to complete. For example, Loevinger uses such stems as "Raising a family . . .," "The thing I like about myself is . . .," and "When I am criticized . . ." to elicit information about ego development status (Loevinger & Wessler, 1970, p. 142). The responses are then evaluated by trained raters and an assessment code is assigned. This approach has been used extensively to measure Loevinger's (1976) theory of ego development (Loevinger & Wessler) and Harvey, Hunt, and Schroder's (1961) conceptual level model. Sentence stems were also included in one of the earliest attempts to measure development along Perry's (1970) scheme (Knefelkamp, 1974; Widick, 1975).

Examples of production task instruments—short essay questions. Short essay questions are a fuller version of the incomplete sentence stem format. They typically consist of a short paragraph that either describes a situation to which the subject is instructed to respond in a short essay, or extended instructions for structuring such an essay. Instruments that use this format include the "Knewi" (Knefelkamp, 1974; Widick, 1975) and its successor, the Measure of Intellectual Development or "MID" (Moore, 1982). Both were designed to measure development along Perry's (1970) scheme. (The "Knewi" originally consisted of five sentence stems and two short essay questions; the MID consists of the original essay questions plus a third). The Paragraph Completion Method (Hunt, Butler, Noy, & Reese, 1977) also uses this format to measure conceptual level (Harvey et al., 1961).

An exemplary model of this approach is Gibbs and Widaman's (1982) Social Reflection Questionnaire. This is a more structured version of Kohlberg's Moral Judgment Interview that retains the issue-norm-element scoring system, but simplifies the scoring by omitting the need for the classification phase of rating. It also makes group administration feasible by eliminating the need for individual follow-up questions in that the classification system and the follow-up questions are built directly into the structure of the requested essay responses.

The Measure of Epistemological Reflection (MER) was designed by Baxter Magolda and Porterfield (1985) to measure the first five positions of Perry's (1970) scheme of intellectual and ethical development. (For a detailed description of the development of the MER and a copy of the scoring manual and training procedures, see Baxter Magolda and Porterfield, 1988.) The MER addresses six content domains specific to the learning process in the college environment: decision making in an educational context; role of the learner in the learning process; role of the instructor in the learning process; role of peers in the learning process; evaluation in the learning process; and nature of knowledge, truth, and reality.

In administering the MER, an introductory statement is first given, followed by a separate series of probe questions for each domain. The probe questions are designed to elicit details and reasons for the response. The questions for the *decision-making domain* are given below.

> Think about the last time you had to make a major decision about your education in which you had a number of alternatives (e.g., which college to attend, college major, career choice, etc.). What was the nature of the decision?
> What alternatives were available to you?
> How did you feel about these alternatives?
> How did you go about choosing from the alternatives?
> What things were the most important considerations in your choice? Please give details.
> (Baxter Magolda & Porterfield, 1988, p. 103)

The questions for the *role of instructor* domain are:

During the course of your studies, you have probably had instructors with different teaching methods. As you think back to instructors you have had, describe the method of instruction which had the most beneficial effect on you. What made that teaching method beneficial? Please be specific and use examples. Were there aspects of that teaching method which were not beneficial? If so, please talk about some of the aspects and why they were not beneficial. What are the most important things you learned from the instructor's method of teaching? Please describe the type of relationship with an instructor that would help you to learn best and explain why. (Baxter Magolda & Porterfield, 1988, p. 151)

Scoring the MER follows the approach suggested by Gibbs and Widaman (1982), described earlier. Identification of the content areas (or "issues") is given in the instrument format, and the rating manual is organized according to these areas.

The manual is based on reasoning structures, or consistent ways respondents justify their thinking. Each position in each domain contains a number of reasoning structures which serve as the basic unit for response interpretation. Interpretation, or rating, is a matter of reading an entire domain response, deciding what reasoning structure or basic justification the response represents, and then finding the reasoning structure in the manual that best matches the response. The position in which the reasoning structure is located in the manual is the one assigned for that domain. (Baxter Magolda & Porterfield, 1988, p. 23)

After the scores are assigned for each domain, two total protocol ratings are calculated, one based on the modal position evident in the protocol, and one based on the average rating across domains.

Recognition Tasks

In recognition tasks, the subject typically is presented with a series of response options rather than being asked to generate responses spontaneously at the time of testing. There are many variations on the responses subjects may be asked to make. For example, using a set of prototypic statements, Rest (1976) identified four such possibilities: (a) a preference task, where subjects are asked to evaluate each statement on a specified criterion, such as persuasiveness or importance; (b) comprehension-recapitulation, where subjects are asked to paraphrase a statement to demonstrate understanding; (c) comprehension-by-matching, where subjects select statements that match a given statement for meaning; and (d) recall, where subjects are asked to recall statements at a later time as a measure of comprehension.

Disadvantages

Recognition tasks are not usually appropriate for theory development or a researcher's search for new ways of defining or describing characteristics of thinking (Rest, 1976). Thus, if subjects are asked to select the statements that most closely reflect their own thinking, and none fit exactly, they may be forced to choose the statements that fit "least worst." The risk here is attributing characteristics to subjects' thinking that are at best approximations and furthermore may be inaccurate. Also, there is no guarantee that statements designed to convey a given stage property actually do so, and subjects may impose a meaning on a given statement that differs greatly from what was intended (Lawrence, 1977).

Advantages

A major advantage of using recognition tasks is that they allow the researcher to focus subjects' attention on the specific features of interest. This in turn provides a greater degree of standardization across respondents.

Second, the difficulty level of recognition tasks is not as high as for production tasks. For example, students often can recognize which of several given options is better on a multiple choice test, but have difficulty constructing such a response in an essay test. Voters, too, often prefer one candidate's explanations over another's, but have difficulty presenting such an argument and articulating its advantages when asked to do so "from scratch." Several studies have shown that ". . . a person can recognize and discriminate and thus prefer an idea before he can paraphrase it or before he can spontaneously produce the idea in response to a story dilemma" (Rest, 1976, p. 202).

The third set of advantages is perhaps the most obvious: Recognition tasks have the practical advantage of being less expensive and faster to administer and score. Both factors make these tests amenable to group and large-scale administration, which is difficult if not impossible for most production tasks.

Examples of recognition task instruments. Few instruments exist that are designed to measure cognitive-developmental phenomena using a recognition task format. The most well-known and well-researched of these is the Defining Issues Test (DIT), which is discussed below. Several other instruments are in earlier "stages" of development and use a variety of formats. For example, in the intellectual development domain, three instruments have been widely disseminated. King (1983) designed the Reflective Judgment Questionnaire to measure Reflective Judgment level (Kitchener & King, 1981), using a format similar to that used in the DIT. This instrument is now under revision.

Two recognition measures of William Perry's (1970) scheme have been proposed. The Scale of Intellectual Development (Erwin, 1983) consists of 119 statements (e.g., "If I were having personal problems, I would want a counselor to tell me what to do") to which subjects respond using a 4-point Likert scale. The instrument is scored using only four categories: Dualism, Relativism, Commitment, and Empathy. This rather reductionistic approach to scoring may limit the validity and thus the usefulness of this measure, especially given Perry's (1981) concerns about differentiating Multiplicity and Relativism.

A second recent Perry measure was designed by Moore (1987). The Learning Environment Preferences provides a series of five incomplete sentence stems regarding the learning environment. These are: "My ideal learning environment would: . . ."; "In my ideal learning environment, the teacher would: . . ."; "In my ideal learning environment, as a student I would: . . ."; "In my ideal learning environment, the classroom atmosphere and activities would: . . ."; and "Evaluation procedures in my ideal learning environment would: . . . ." Respondents evaluate 13 prototypic statements for each sentence stem using a rating and ranking procedure very similar to that used on the DIT, which is discussed next.

The Defining Issues Test (Rest, 1979a) was designed as a measure of moral judgment based on Kohlberg's moral development theory. It has been administered to thousands of subjects and translated into several languages. Research using the DIT has been summarized in two major volumes (Rest, 1979b, 1986b). The scoring procedures have been refined and updated in light of the research; these are described in detail in the test manual (Rest, 1986a).

The DIT consists of seven moral dilemmas (including "Heinz and the Drug," discussed earlier); each dilemma is followed by a list of 12 stage-prototypic statements. These statements list possible issues a person might take into account in responding to the dilemma. For example, on the Heinz dilemma, this list includes the following statements:

1. Are a community's laws going to be upheld?
2. Isn't it only natural for a loving husband to care so much for his wife that he'd steal?
3. Should the druggist's rights to his invention be respected?
4. What values are going to be the basis for governing how people act toward each other?

The list of options also includes items designed to check on how seriously the subject is taking the test. (See Rest, 1979a, 1986a for details.)

Using a 5-point scale, respondents are asked to indicate how important each statement would be if they were making a decision about the dilemma. In other words, their cognitive task is to evaluate what the important considerations are in a moral dilemma, and then to rank their top four choices in order of importance.

Although the test can be scored to yield stage responses (e.g., a subject's modal stage), Rest recommends using the "P score." This indicates the proportion of time a respondent used in ranking as most important those statements that reflect a principled moral orientation (Stages 5 and 6).

CONCLUSION

Cognitive-development assessments measuring students' growth and educational achievements may be used for a variety of purposes in higher education. These include: (a) helping students understand themselves in developmental terms; (b) providing baseline data from which to initiate or change programs; (c) identifying what types of experiences are associated with development; and (d) selecting the design and delivery of developmentally appropriate services, classes, and programs. Regardless of the type of approach (formal or informal) or the type of task (production or recognition) used, a practitioner or researcher who uses cognitive-developmental assessment data for these purposes increases the likelihood that the services and programs offered will facilitate student development, the goal toward which our educational efforts are aimed.

REFERENCES

Argyris, C. (1976). Theories of action that inhibit individual learning. *American Psychologist, 31*, 638–654.

Argyris, C., & Schon, D.A. (1978). *Organizational learning: A theory of action perspective.* Reading, MA: Addison-Wesley.

Baxter Magolda, M.B., & Porterfield, W.D. (1985). A new approach to assessing intellectual development on the Perry scheme. *Journal of College Student Personnel, 26*, 343–351.

Baxter Magolda, M.B., & Porterfield, W.D. (1988). *Assessing intellectual development: The link between theory and practice.* Alexandria, VA: American College Personnel Association.

Basseches, M. (1984). *Dialectical thinking and adult development.* Norwood, NJ: Ablex.

Belenky, M.F., Clinchy, B.M., Goldberger, N.R., & Tarule, J.M. (1986). *Women's ways of knowing: The development of self, voice and mind.* New York: Basic Books.

Bok, D. (1986, November/December). Toward higher learning. *Change,* pp. 18–27.

Brown, R.D. (1972). *Student development in tomorrow's higher education: A return to the academy.* (Student Personnel Monograph Series No. 16.) Washington, DC: American College Personnel Association.

Chickering, A.W. (1969). *Education and identity.* San Francisco: Jossey-Bass.

Colby, A., & Kohlberg, L. (1987). *The measurement of moral judgment, Volume I: Theoretical foundations and research validation.* New York: Cambridge University Press.

Colby, A., Kohlberg, L., Speicher, B., Hewer, A., Candee, D., Gibbs, J., & Power, C. (1987). *The measurement of moral judgment, Volume II: Standard issue scoring manual.* New York: Cambridge University Press.

Erwin, T.D. (1983). The scale of intellectual development: Measuring Perry's scheme. *Journal of College Student Personnel, 24*, 6–12.

Fischer, K.W., & Silvern, L. (1985). Stages and individual differences in cognitive development. *Annual Review of Psychology, 36*, 613–647.

Flavell, J.H. (1970). Cognitive changes in adulthood. In B.L.R. Goulet & P.B. Baltes (Eds.), *Theory and research in life-span developmental psychology* (pp. 247–253). New York: Academic Press.

Flavell, J.H. (1971). Stage-related properties of cognitive development. *Cognitive Psychology, 2*, 421–453.

Flavell, J.H. (1982). Structures, stages, and sequences in cognitive development. In W.A. Collins (Ed.), *Minnesota Symposium on Child Development: Vol. 15. The concept of development* (pp. 1–28). Hillsdale, NJ: Erlbaum.

Flavell, J.H., & Wohlwill, J.F. (1969). Formal and functional aspects of cognitive development. In D. Elkind & J. Flavell (Eds.), *Studies in cognitive development: Essays in honor of J. Piaget* (pp. 67–120). New York: Oxford University Press.

Gamson, Z.F., & Associates. (1984). *Liberating education.* San Francisco: Jossey-Bass.

Gibbs, J.C., & Widaman, K.F. (1982). *Social intelligence: Measuring the development of sociomoral reflection.* Englewood Cliffs, NJ: Prentice-Hall.

Gilligan, C. (1982). *In a different voice: Psychological theory and women's development.* Cambridge, MA: Harvard University Press.

Guba, E.G., & Lincoln, Y.S. (1982). *Effective evaluation: Improving the usefulness of evaluation results through responsive and naturalistic approaches.* San Francisco: Jossey-Bass.

Hanson, G.R. (1982). Critical issues in the assessment of student development. In G.R. Hanson (Ed.), *Measuring student development* (pp. 47–63). (New Directions for Student Services, No. 20.) San Francisco: Jossey-Bass.

Harvey, O.J., Hunt, D.E., & Schroder, H.M. (1961). *Conceptual systems and personality organization.* New York: Wiley.

Hunt, D.E., Butler, L.F., Noy, J.E., & Reese, M.E. (1977). *Assessing conceptual level by the Paragraph Completion Method.* Toronto: Ontario Institute for Studies in Education.

Kegan, R.G. (1982). *The evolving self.* Cambridge, MA: Harvard University Press.

King, P.M. (1983). *Reflective judgment questionnaire* (Tech. Rep. No. 1). Bowling Green, OH: Bowling Green State University.

Kitchener, K.S., & King, P.M. (1981). Reflective judgment: Concepts of justification and their relationship to age and education. *Journal of Applied Developmental Psychology, 2,* 89–116.

Knefelkamp, L.L. (1974). *Developmental instruction: Fostering intellectual and personal growth of college students.* Unpublished doctoral dissertation, University of Minnesota, Minneapolis.

Kohlberg, L. (1969). Stage and sequence: The cognitive-developmental approach to socialization. In D. Goslin (Ed.), *Handbook of socialization theory and research* (pp. 347–480). Chicago: Rand McNally.

Kohlberg, L. (1984). *The psychology of moral development: The nature and validation of moral stages.* San Francisco: Harper & Row.

Lawrence, J.A. (1977). *Review and rationale for moral judgment process research using the Defining Issues Test and the stimulated recall techniques.* Unpublished manuscript, University of Minnesota, Minneapolis.

Lenning, O.T. (1980). Assessment and evaluation. In U. Delworth, G.R. Hanson, & Associates (Eds.), *Student services: A handbook for the profession* (pp. 232–266). San Francisco: Jossey-Bass.

Loevinger, J. (1976). *Ego development: Conceptions and theories.* San Francisco: Jossey-Bass.

Loevinger, J., & Wessler, R. (1970). *Measuring ego development.* San Francisco: Jossey-Bass.

Loxley, J.C., & Whiteley, J.M. (1986). *Character development in college students: Volume II. The curriculum and longitudinal results.* Schenectady, NY: Character Research Press.

Mentkowski, M. (1984). *The college as an enabling institution.* Milwaukee: Alverno College Publications.

Miller, T.K. (1982). Student development assessment: A rationale. In G.R. Hanson (Ed.), *Measuring student development* (pp. 5–15). (New Directions for Student Services, No. 20). San Francisco: Jossey-Bass.

Moore, W.S. (1982). *The measure of intellectual development: A brief review.* Unpublished paper. Farmville, VA: Center for Applications of Developmental Instruction.

Moore, W.S. (1987). *The learning environment preferences: Establishing preliminary reliability and validity for an objective measure of the Perry scheme of intellectual and ethical development.* Unpublished doctoral dissertation, University of Maryland, College Park.

Myers, I.B. (1980). *Gifts differing.* Palo Alto, CA: Consulting Psychologists Press.

Parker, C. (1977). On modeling reality. *Journal of College Student Personnel, 18,* 419–425.

Perry, W., Jr. (1970). *Intellectual and ethical development in the college years: A scheme.* New York: Holt, Rinehart & Winston.

Perry, W. (1981). Cognitive and ethical growth: The making of meaning. In A. Chickering & Associates (Eds.), *The modern American college* (pp. 76–116). San Francisco: Jossey-Bass.

Piaget, J. (1932). *The moral judgment of the child.* London: Kegan Paul.

Rest, J.R. (1976). New approaches in the assessment of moral judgment. In T. Lickona (Ed.), *Moral development and behavior: Theory, research and social issues* (pp. 198–218). New York: Holt, Rinehart & Winston.

Rest, J.R. (1979a). *Revised manual for the Defining Issues Test.* Minneapolis: Moral Research Projects.

Rest, J.R. (1979b). *Development in judging moral issues.* Minneapolis: University of Minnesota.

Rest, J.R. (1986a). *Manual for the Defining Issues Test* (3rd ed.). Minneapolis: Center for the Study of Ethical Development, University of Minnesota.

Rest, J.R. (1986b). *Moral development: Advances in research and theory.* New York: Praeger.

Sanford, N. (1966). *Self and society: Social change and individual development.* New York: Atherton.

Stonewater, B.B., & Stonewater, J.K. (1983). Developmental clues: An aid for the practitioner. *NASPA Journal, 21,* 52–59.

Weathersby, R., & Tarule, J. (1980). Adult development: Implications for higher education. *AAHE-ERIC Higher Education Research Report, Number 4* (pp. 42–51). Washington, DC: American Association for Higher Education.

Welfel, E.R. (1982). The development of reflective judgment: Implications for career counseling. *Personnel and Guidance Journal, 61,* 17–21.

Whiteley, J.M., & Associates. (1982). *Character development in college students: Volume 1.* Schenectady, NY: Character Research Press.

Widick, C. (1975). *An evaluation of developmental instruction in a university setting.* Unpublished doctoral dissertation, University of Minnesota, Minneapolis.

Widick, C., Knefelkamp, L., & Parker, C.A. (1975). The counselor as developmental instructor. *Counselor Education and Supervision, 14,* 286–296.

Widick, C., & Simpson, D. (1978). Development concepts in college instruction. In C.A. Parker (Ed.), *Encouraging development in college students* (pp. 27–59). Minneapolis: University of Minnesota Press.

Wohlwill, J. (1973). *The study of behavioral development.* New York: Academic Press.

CHAPTER 5

Assessing Development From a Psychosocial Perspective

Theodore K. (Ted) Miller and Roger B. Winston, Jr.

THE CONTEXT OF PSYCHOSOCIAL DEVELOPMENT

Student affairs practitioners generally believe that there is far more to the higher education experience than academic and intellectual development alone. Most educators, administrators, and student affairs practitioners, however, experience some difficulty defining or describing the true nature of "nonacademic" development. They agree that students learn factual information about the humanities, the physical and behavioral sciences, and other academic disciplines. They concur that nearly all students learn to think critically; to identify, use, and evaluate sources; to solve methodological and technical problems; and to communicate ideas more effectively. In fact, if evaluation procedures reflect that these kinds of academic and intellectual changes have not occurred, those responsible for providing higher education experiences say that they have failed in their educational missions. These same individuals, however, are usually much less concerned about the possible shortcomings of the educational experience or lack of concrete evidence when it comes to the "personal development" of students.

Most higher education leaders accept the fundamental presuppositions that people can change and that *educators and educational environments can facilitate that change.*

Observations of college students from entry through graduation confirm that students do change as a direct result of the higher education experience (Astin, 1977; Feldman & Newcomb, 1969; Pace, 1979). Chickering (Chickering & Associates, 1981), among others, sought to support and gain official recognition of that change when he proposed that we should use human development as the unifying, overarching educational purpose of colleges and universities "to encourage and enable intentional developmental change in students throughout the life cycle" (p. 2). And, much of that intentional change is

99

reflected in holistic, personal development as well as academic development. Katz, for instance, identified some of the nonacademic developmental changes resulting from the college experience as: (a) decline in authoritarianism, (b) growth in autonomy, (c) increased self-esteem, (d) increased capacities for relatedness, (e) increased political sophistication, (f) increased freedom to express impulses, and (g) increased capacity for appreciating aesthetics (Katz, cited in Pace, 1979). These changes may or may not reflect the primary developmental outcomes desired by those responsible for higher education. As Caple (1987) noted, when discussing the change process in developmental theory and the hypothesis that second-order (beta) change is unpredictable, "educators must become much more open to unpredictable conflict and change" (p. 11).

The Hazen Foundation Report (1968) pointed out that colleges are a major social agent in promoting personal development and that students mature and develop beyond what they learn in the classroom. Students' interactions with teachers; encounters with college leaders; involvement in friendship groups; acquisition of values from the student culture; and exposure to climates of flexibility or rigidity that permeate the college environments as well as the colleges' operative educational goals all have an immense impact on the evolution of students' self and world views, on their confidence and altruism, and on their achievement of personal identify and mature intimacy. By the very fact that colleges intend to inform students' minds, these institutions become intimately involved in the development of the whole person, of which intellectual faculties are but a part. As Chickering and Associates (1981) noted, every college and university in the country (whether public or private, 2-year or 4-year) is in the business of shaping human lives, lives that reflect much more than academic learning. The key issue is not so much whether the higher education experience promotes growth and development beyond the intellectual domain alone, for there is consensus that it does, but rather what forms that development takes and how it can be identified and assessed.

Personal, nonintellective development has been conceptualized in various forms by developmental theorists. Most typically, this view of development, which emphasizes the whole person as opposed to cognitive components only, has been referred to as psychosocial development. Whereas cognitive-developmental theory is concerned primarily with the processes involved in thinking and the making of meaning from life experiences, psychosocial-developmental theory is concerned more with the content of individuals' personal preoccupations, social interactions, and ego development. From the psychosocial perspective, young adults, whether college students or not, seek to resolve their child-parent relationships in a search for independence (Cohen, 1985; Coons, 1971; Erikson, 1963), to establish a sense of identity and self-worth (Chickering, 1969; Erikson, 1968), and to form concepts about themselves as separate adult persons (Chickering, 1969; Kegan, 1982). College students also tend to develop increasingly mature patterns of interpersonal behaviors, coping styles, career orientations, value systems, and life-styles that will influence their future. The college experience also provides many opportunities for students to gain increased understandings about themselves as developing human beings (Astin, 1985) and to learn such important life skills as personal assessment, goal setting, and conducting interpersonal relationships (Gazda, Childers, & Brooks, 1987; Miller & Prince, 1976).

The higher education experience alone, however, is not the only factor impinging on students' development. Another important variable is their cultural heritage, which influences the directions psychosocial development takes. In many ways an individual's culture defines what is appropriate behavior and when and under what conditions it is appropriate to exhibit certain behaviors. For instance, although most young adults are very interested in establishing personal liaisons, often with members of the opposite sex, social and cultural values and mores influence the way such interests are manifested. In some instances there is nearly complete freedom to pursue social relationships without limitations, whereas in others there are clearly established rules to be followed, as can be seen in the traditional Latin custom of chaperoning. These cultural impingements are present in all of us, even though they are often unrecognized in daily life activities. Sometimes they are gender-related. For instance, in some cultures there exist what seem to be double standards to which members adhere without challenge. A young man, for example, may be free or even encouraged to pursue liaisons aggressively with women of questionable virtue from a lower social class, but be expected to act circumspectly and follow well-established social protocols in relations with the young women of his own social class. Young women, on the other hand, may be viewed with disdain if they aggressively pursue a liaison with a man. In some cultures it may be expected that children will vacate the home on a rather permanent basis during their late teenage years—this tends to be true in middle-class America—whereas in other cultures, such as those that predominate in the Virgin Islands where the extended family is more highly emphasized, parents may expect children to reside in the family home well into the adult years, perhaps even after marriage. These cultural imperatives influence the way individuals grow and develop, and reflect the influence of the "social" in psychosocial development.

Psychosocial development, in effect, is concerned with those personal, psychologically oriented aspects of self and the relationships that exist between the self and society. Conceptually, this type of development is significantly influenced by the interactions that take place between individuals and their environments. Person-environment interaction theory focuses on the ways that individuals influence their environments and the way environments influence individuals (See chapter 6 by Huebner and Lawson in this volume). Without this important interaction, psychosocial development would not occur, because it is the stimuli and challenges that result from these interactions that bring about change or growth.

DEVELOPMENTAL PRINCIPLES AND TERMS

Several fundamental developmental principles that reappear throughout the literature on human development are of particular importance for an understanding of the dynamic nature and process of psychosocial development.

1. *Psychosocial development is continuous in nature*, and normal maturation leads to developmental changes regardless of the environment, but not independent of it. Growth tendencies are modified by individual life experiences, and those experiences influence whether change is optimal, minimal, or somewhere in between.

2. *Psychosocial development is cumulative in nature*, and life experiences tend to represent "building blocks." In effect, a person's past experiences influence significantly what his or her future will be like. Some developmental tasks must be accomplished or mastered before advancing to other, more complicated tasks, for there are additive and interlocking processes involved.

3. *Psychosocial development progresses along a continuum from simpler to more complex behavior.* Simple, more elemental behavior must be mastered before more complex behavior can be attained, assuming that the simpler behavior is relevant to the more complex behavior. Throughout life human beings progress along a series of developmental continua, accomplishing increasingly formidable and complex learning.

4. *Psychosocial development tends to be orderly and stage-related.* A developmental stage represents a time period or interval in an individual's life when biological, psychological, or sociological forces interact in ways that promote discomfort, conflict, tension, challenge, differentiation, or crisis that requires response. The developmental stage concept was initially popularized by Erikson (1950) when he postulated an "eight ages of man" ego development model that identified patterns of behavior and essential learning common to most individuals as they moved through life stages. Although it has been argued that this model is too mechanistic (Caple, 1987), it continues to have great utility for understanding the general nature of the common processes of human development. As Winston (1987) noted, individual development may seem somewhat chaotic in the short term; however, patterns almost always become evident from the long-range perspective. There is considerable evidence to support the contention that college students as a group share common challenges and that development is coherent and predictable (Chickering, 1969; Chickering & Havighurst, 1981; Erwin & Kelly, 1985; Heath, 1968; Hood, Riahinejad, & White, 1985; Polkosnik & Winston, 1989; Riahinejad & Hood, 1984; White & Hood, 1989).

5. *Psychosocial development is reflected in developmental tasks.* Developmental tasks are the best available organization of psychosocial development and represent experiences essential to the full development of the individual. A framework of developmental tasks proves useful to higher education professionals because such tasks cover important components of human development, give a comprehensive and orderly view of the life cycle, and can be stated in terms of behaviors useful for assessment purposes.

Developmental stages and tasks are of particular import to those who would assess psychosocial development for they represent a somewhat concrete content of development that can be identified, observed, and measured. In light of this, we shall examine them in more detail as a foundation for the discussion of assessment strategies.

From Erikson's (1950) perspective, psychosocial development is viewed as an *epigenetic* process where ego growth involves a progressive differentiation of interrelated characteristics, each of which has a time of special ascendancy crucial to further development. As a result, different qualities of ego strength tend to arise during distinct life stages, a process that continues throughout the full life cycle (Stevens, 1983). Although Erikson (1950) hypothesized that all human beings experience relatively similar internal changes that conflict with societal expectations and cause *developmental crises* or *turning points*, there is no way to be certain that a given individual will experience a particular developmental crisis at a predetermined chronological point in life. In fact, authorities tend to differ on when a particular developmental change is most likely to occur in a person's life and, to some extent, why.

Probably the main reason for the disagreements is the fact that human development does not occur at precisely the same chronological age for all people. As Montagu (1981) warned, beware of the "age-stage dilemma" when considering human development. Even though there is strong evidence that individuals experience common developmental tasks and progress through similar developmental processes and stages, the individual differences involved make it impossible to predict with even reasonable accuracy when a particular individual will face or deal with a particular developmental task, crisis, or stage.

Several authorities have postulated a late adolescence, youth, or young adult stage between adolescence and early adulthood. Sanford (1962) for instance, proposed such a distinctive stage, as did Keniston (1970). Chickering (1969) maintained that the increasing complexity of the world society—the fact that approximately 50% of the college age population is enrolled in college because of increased demand for skilled and specialized personnel—has created a new developmental period. The developmental age spanning the years from 18 to 25 must be studied separately from other developmental stages because the tasks of this period are related to, but are substantially different from, those of both adolescence and adulthood. Calling this developmental stage "the young adult," Chickering (1969, pp. 8–19) postulated seven major developmental tasks that he called developmental vectors.

1. *Achieving competence.* Competence involves the development of intellectual, physical and manual, and social and interpersonal competence. It involves also a sense of confidence in one's ability to cope with circumstances and to achieve successfully what one sets out to do.

2. *Managing emotions.* The young adult's first task is to become aware of feelings and to trust them more, to recognize that they provide information relevant to contemplated behavior or to decisions about future plans. As a larger range of feelings are fully expressed, new and more useful patterns of expression and control can be achieved.

3. *Becoming autonomous.* Mature independence requires both emotional and instrumental independence and the recognition of one's interdependencies. To be emotionally independent is to be free of continual and pressing needs for reassurance or approval. Instrumental independence has two components, the ability to carry on activities and to cope with problems without seeking help, and the ability to be

mobile in relation to one's needs. Interdependency is recognizing that loving and being loved are complementary, or that one cannot receive benefits of a social structure without contributing to it.

4. *Establishing identity*. Identity is confidence in one's ability to maintain inner sameness and continuity. It involves clarifying one's conceptions concerning physical needs, characteristics, and personal appearance, and clarifying one's sexual identification and sex-appropriate roles and behaviors.

5. *Freeing interpersonal relationships*. Relationships should shift toward greater trust, independence, and individuality. They should become less anxious, less defensive, less burdened by inappropriate past reactions, and more friendly, more spontaneous, more warm, and more respectful. Developing tolerance for a wide range of persons is a significant aspect of this task.

6. *Clarifying purpose*. Development of purpose requires formulating plans and priorities that integrate avocational and recreational interests, vocational plans, and life-style considerations.

7. *Developing integrity*. Developing integrity is defined as "the clarification of a personally valid set of beliefs that have some internal consistency and provide a guide for behavior." Such development involves the humanizing of values, the personalizing of values, and the development of congruence. Humanizing of values describes the shift from a literal belief in the absoluteness of rules to a more relative view. Personalizing of values occurs as an individual first examines and then selects values. The development of congruence is the achievement of behavior consistent with an individual's personalized values.

According to Chickering (1969), these seven areas represent the common core of development during the young adult college years and are variously termed growth trends, developmental tasks, stages of development, needs and problem areas, or student typologies.

A developmental task represents an interrelated set of behaviors and attitudes that one's culture specifies should be exhibited at approximately the same chronological time in life by a given age cohort in a designated environmental context such as the higher education setting. Successful accomplishment or achievement of a developmental task enables the individual to acquire the experiential base needed to accomplish future developmental tasks. Failure to meet successfully the challenges inherent in a given developmental task results in social disapproval and may hinder further growth in that area of development or can lead to maladaptive adjustment (Havighurst, 1953, 1972; Kitchener, 1982; Mines, 1982). From the psychosocial-developmental perspective, young adult college students are engaged in a series of developmental tasks that reflect change in their lives. Numerous psychosocial theorists and research authorities have used the developmental task as a common theoretical construct. Theorists have postulated a variety of behavioral expectations common to young adult college students and other adults throughout the life cycle.

Havighurst (1953, p. 2), an early proponent of the developmental task concept, presented the best recognized and most commonly used definition of the term to date: "A developmental task is a task which arises at or about a certain period in the life of an individual, successful achievement of which leads to happiness and to success with later tasks, while failure leads to unhappiness in the individual, disapproval by society and difficulty with later tasks.''

Some developmental tasks reflect intellectual change in areas such as logical reasoning and concepts of knowledge. Although these aspects often interact when an individual seeks to solve a problem, they seem to function as separate developmental dimensions (Kitchener & Kitchener, 1981). Some tasks are social in nature and lead to learning ways of relating more effectively to peers, professors, and parents whereas other tasks are concerned with intrapersonal development, resulting in increased self-knowledge and reformulated self-concepts. Still other developmental tasks are concerned with increased effectiveness when dealing with cultural aspects of the environment. The student who engages in and learns from these tasks becomes a person with new skills and abilities who is capable of learning from future life experiences and assuming increased social responsibilities (Oetting, 1967).

Most young adult college students are in the unique position of being, at one and the same time, at the end of adolescence and the beginning of early adulthood. As a result, their developmental tasks overlap both stages. ''Many will enter college without having completed the developmental tasks of adolescence, while others will be ready to embark on those associated with the older group'' (Kitchener, 1982, p. 39). It is important that those concerned with facilitating the development of young adult college students come to understand their unique developmental characteristics and use strategies and tools to help them assess their current developmental needs and status so that developmental plans may be established and implemented.

In sum, knowledge of the processes of development as well as the tasks that must be mastered in those processes are significant for student development educators. Because development is *continuous*, practitioners need to know what behaviors must be mastered and in what order for optimum development to result. Because development is *cumulative*, actions to promote further development must be based on an understanding of the experiences and learning individuals have had to date. Because development *progresses* from the simpler to the more complex, it is important to know the individual's present level of development. Because development is *orderly* and stage-related, it is essential that practitioners be able to make logical connections between their observations of students' behavior and the developmental stages in which the students presently function. Because healthy development reflects the successful achievement of developmental tasks, it is imperative that student development educators understand the importance of the tasks and aid students to accomplish them as their developmental needs dictate. Therefore, in order to help college students effectively attain a maximal level of personal development, facilitators need the ability to assess behaviors that individual students have previously acquired.

PSYCHOSOCIAL COMMONALITIES AND DIFFERENCES IN STUDENTS

Although the primary focus of the discussion to this point has been on traditional, young adult college students, it is important to recognize the psychosocial developmental differences that exist between and among other student populations on today's college campuses. Many persons not representative of the more traditional, 17- to 23-year-old, single, and White Anglo-Saxon student population are taking advantage of higher education each year. Increasing numbers of Native Americans, Blacks, Hispanics, and Asian Americans attend American colleges and universities as do older, nontraditional students, many of whom are entering for the first time or returning to higher education after years of employment or child rearing. In addition, this country now accepts thousands of international students each year who come from all corners of the globe to study here. When considering psychosocial development, it is important to be cognizant of the cultural differences among these various populations, as well as to recognize the unique developmental needs of female students. Although all human beings have much in common when it comes to psychosocial development, a number of special considerations must be recognized if accurate and valid assessment is to become a reality.

Ethnic Minority Students

Because sociocultural influences are important considerations when attempting to understand and assess psychosocial development, it is paramount that student development educators incorporate such factors into their conceptualizations. Sedlacek (1987) presented an excellent compendium of research concerning Black students on predominantly White campuses when he reviewed his own and others' research of the past two decades. His collaborative research efforts identified eight noncognitive variables critical to the success of Black students in higher education (Sedlacek & Brooks, 1976; Tracey & Sedlacek, 1985, 1987; White & Sedlacek, 1986). Most of these variables can be readily identified as characteristic of psychosocial development, and each has aspects unique to Black students when compared with others. Reflecting on the use of the Noncognitive Questionnaire, Sedlacek (1987) identified these important variables as (a) positive self-concept or confidence, (b) realistic self-appraisal, (c) management of racism, (d) demonstrated community service, (e) preference for long-range goals over immediate needs gratification, (f) availability of a strong support person, (g) successful leadership experience, and (h) nontraditionally acquired knowledge. Although most would argue that these or related factors are relevant in the educational lives of all students, it is important to note that they were identified as being of special importance to the success of Black college students attending predominantly White institutions in the 1970s and 1980s.

In a study that examined the psychosocial development of students attending traditionally Black institutions, Jordan-Cox (1987) found gender differences in a Black student sample not apparent in most studies with White student samples. She discovered that Black female students evidenced advanced levels of psychosocial development when compared to their male counterparts in the areas of interpersonal relationships, autonomy, and life purpose. The latter two variables, however, seemed to be affected by the type of collegiate environment involved. Jordon-Cox also found, using a cross-sectional design, that although students who attended different

.nstitutions were at different levels of development on 75% of the variables upon entrance, they differed on only 25% of the variables by their senior years. These findings suggest that the psychosocial development of students attending tradition- ally Black institutions is affected positively by the college experience.

Another study focused attention on college students' socialization. Nettles and Johnson (1987) found that whereas socialization of White students seems to be primarily related to the cultivation of peer group relationships in college, satisfaction with the institution and academic integration are more significant to the socialization of Black students. These researchers also found that socioeconomic status did not seem to be the significant factor in the peer group relationships of Black men that it was for Black women and Whites of both genders. Some observers (Fleming, 1981) have noted that many Blacks on predominantly White campuses experience isolation, which results in feelings of loneliness and alienation and negatively affects the capacity to establish and maintain interpersonal relationships on campus. Pounds (1987) did an excellent job of identifying many of the unique needs of Black students involved in a predominantly White college environment. It seems clear that, al- though Black students possess similar developmental needs and have many devel- opmental experiences in common with White students, those who assess psychosocial development must be cautious in regard to their assumptions about students and the generalizations drawn from their measurements.

Obviously, Black students do not represent the only minority group in colleges today, although it may well be the largest single minority group. Increased numbers of Asian-American and Hispanic students are matriculating and, although somewhat less common for many reasons, Native American students are also in attendance. Because ethnic and cultural influences are important to psychosocial development, these factors must be taken into account when assessing students from these pop- ulations.

Asian-Americans, as Chew and Ogi (1987) pointed out, tend to possess certain cultural values that influence their psychosocial development. These authors noted, for instance, that women traditionally have been viewed more as commodities than as independent, rational thinkers in some Asian cultures. In addition, values such as filial piety reflected in total devotion to the family—along with comparatively exaggerated degrees of humility, restraint of emotional expression, and sense of obligation—have been emphasized in traditional Asian cultures. These factors sometimes make it difficult for Asian-Americans to become integrated into the higher education community along with their non-Asian student counterparts.

The Hispanic population in the United States has grown rapidly in recent years, and increasing numbers of students with a Spanish-language heritage are attending college (U.S. Department of Commerce, 1985). Most Hispanic students possess an abiding loyalty to their families and communities and generally identify them- selves nationally with their family's country of origin (e.g., Mexico, Puerto Rico, Cuba). Nevertheless, many recognize a Hispanic culture in the United States based on socioeconomic class (Grossman, 1984). Quevedo-Garcia (1987) suggested that one of the major developmental challenges most Hispanic students face is the dissonance resulting from the need to establish their personal identity within the framework of the Hispanic heritage as well as within the more dominant American culture. He noted that many Hispanic students face a choice between *assimilation*, relinquishing their cultural identity, or *integration*, becoming an integral part of the larger society while maintaining their cultural identity.

American Indians, or Native Americans, represent a relatively small minority of college students in American colleges and the most likely minority population to delay entrance into college after completing secondary education (Astin, 1982). As with other minority groups, the Native Americans' culture seems to be highly influential in the way development unfolds. From this perspective, the Native American comes from a culture in which a high level of mistrust exists toward non-Indians (LaFromboise & Dixon, 1981). As a result, many Native American students do not trust the establishment represented by the college or university. Unless or until this mistrust can be negated or proved invalid, students from this minority population will have great difficulty establishing relationships on campus or identifying with some aspects of the college community. LaCounte (1987) presented a comprehensive picture of Native American college students and the unique cultural issues they face.

Many different cultures and ethnic groups are represented in higher education today. Nevertheless, considerable evidence shows that minority student development is consistent with the basic patterns of majority student development while in college, although the peculiarities associated with race and culture do impinge upon the way that development is manifested (Stikes, 1984).

Gender Differences

The vast majority of psychosocial development research has focused on the nature of male development, largely as a result of the fact that male samples were being studied. As Evans (1985) noted, women's development when recognized by early developmental researchers tended to be viewed from a narrow perspective and was often judged as being abnormal because it did not adhere to male patterns. As a result of more recent research focusing on the developmental processes women experience, certain gender differences have been noted that deserve attention. For instance, those proposing to initiate programs of psychosocial-developmental assessment may benefit from Gilligan's (1982) observations and findings:

> From the different dynamics of separation and attachment in their gender identity formation through the divergence of identity and intimacy that marks their experience in the adolescent years, male and female voices typically speak of the importance of different truths, the former of the role of separation as it defines and empowers the self, the latter of the ongoing process of attachment that creates and sustains the human community. (p. 156)

In effect, Gilligan found that from the perspective of a woman's development, identity is viewed in a context of relationship and judged by a standard of responsibility, whereas for men, identity is viewed in a context of separation and judged by a standard of logic or intelligence. Men, more often than women, fear that intimacy may entail entrapment or betrayal, whereas women feel more threatened by competitive success and the isolation that may be its consequence (Gilligan, 1982). Other researchers have identified differences between the developmental processes men and women experience. For instance, one study determined that women tend to experience greater variations in the order of developmental task completion (Stewart, 1977), and another found that women tend to establish their careers from a passive perspective whereas men decide from a more active perspective (Hennig & Jardim, 1977). Straub (1987) concluded that for many women, the developmental task of freeing interpersonal relationships precedes the developmental task of autonomy, with the former having a significant impact on the latter's development. Likewise, there is evidence that men and women view their worlds differently in that men make clear distinctions between career and marriage or parenthood whereas women see the three as clearly interconnected (Tittle, 1982). Rodgers, in chapter 3 of this volume, reviews other related studies.

Nontraditional Students

Each life stage tends to reflect certain qualities, characteristics, and learning that have their ascendancy during that particular stage of development. Erikson (1968) referred to this development phenomenon as an epigenetic process, and Havighurst (1972) noted likewise that a given developmental task typically arises during a certain period or stage of an individual's life. On the basis of this thinking it is possible to hypothesize that substantive developmental differences exist between and among individuals at various points throughout their life spans as they experience different life stages. This thinking has led to increased attention in recent years to adults as they progress through different life stages (Chickering & Havighurst, 1981; Gould, 1978; Knox, 1977; Levinson & Associates, 1978; McCoy, 1977; Montagu, 1981; Neugarten, 1968). Examples of developmental tasks identified as common to older, nontraditional students include the development of intimacy, generativity, and integrity (Erikson, 1950, 1963); leaving home, getting into the world, settling down, becoming one's own person, and restabilizing (Levinson & Associates); selecting a mate, parenting, establishing a permanent home, reexamining work, reassessing personal priorities and values, and increasing community involvement (McCoy, 1977); and assuming civic responsibilities, revising career plans, adjusting to biological change, and preparing for retirement (Chickering & Havighurst, 1981).

This older adult group, represented by increasing numbers of adult learners or nontraditional college students over the age of 25 years (Brodzinski, 1980), reflects a population that is experiencing considerably different developmental needs and tasks than those of students of traditional college age. Because these nontraditional students are at different developmental levels, it is important that psychosocial assessment strategies and instrumentation be geared to the special characteristics and life patterns of these different age cohorts.

International Students

Foreign students represent a small, but important, college student population that deserves recognition as a special and unique student subculture. Nearly 350,000 foreign students are now studying in American colleges and universities annually (Bulthuis, 1986), the majority of whom come from 15 countries (Barber, 1985). These students are especially vulnerable to and challenged by the higher education environment they experience in the United States. Not only do their cultural and ethnic backgrounds influence their developmental experiences, as is true with any student, but they are faced with learning to function in a largely alien environment and communicating in a language in which they are only marginally proficient. Lee, Abd-Ella, and Burks (1981) found that most problems associated with interpersonal relationships, social adjustment, and housing are directly related to a lack of a command of the English language. This confirmed earlier findings by Spaulding and Flack (1976) that international students who have oral and written problems with English tend to have academic and social adjustment problems as well.

These students, who stand with their feet in two different cultures, experience the difficulty of contradictory challenges and the ensuing personal conflict in trying to select the most appropriate response. Because psychosocial development incorporates social and cultural impingements within its process, foreign students face compounded conflicts and crises as they strive to maneuver through the maze that is higher education and try to learn to function in an alien culture as well. In effect, the developmental tasks of international students include not only those common to all college students of their age and stage, but the uniquely pressing ones necessary to manage successfully as a stranger in a foreign land. If "development occurs within the person and in interaction with the environment" as theory hypothesizes, and if "each change in one person reverberates throughout many, virtually infinite, systems with which we live and act" (Ivey, 1986, p. 293), then foreign students' personal development must be viewed from unique multicultural perspective. It is therefore extremely important that student development assessors be aware of these important impingements for foreign students and take special consideration when seeking to assess their development.

THEORETICAL AND METHODOLOGICAL ISSUES

A number of serious theoretical and methodological issues are associated with the measurement of psychosocial development. Principal among these are: (a) complexity of psychosocial-developmental processes, (b) definition of content domains, (c) significance of the environmental context, and (d) measurement formats.

Complexity of Psychosocial-Developmental Processes

The very nature of psychosocial development makes assessment difficult. Many theorists agree that development is multidimensional (Chickering, 1969; Drum, 1980; Hanson, 1982; Heath, 1968). For example, people do not concentrate exclusively on developing more mature interpersonal relationships while putting "on hold" intellectual, autonomy, and career development. Development is holistic. Persons may concentrate on a particular aspect of development at any given time, but all aspects of personality are involved and cannot be segregated and segmented. Likewise, as noted earlier in this chapter, a given behavior may have a totally different meaning or significance depending on the context or environment in which it occurs. Psychosocial development must be viewed as a system; a change in any part of that system affects or has implications for all other parts of the system. Chickering (Chickering & Associates, 1981, p. 776) recognized this when he wrote: "By seriously addressing one of two key dimensions [for example, personality and cognitive development] we will not only serve . . . [students'] ego and moral development, we are likely to increase their intellectual development, their inter-personal competence, their capacity for intimacy, and the development of their humanitarian concerns."

The complex interaction of psychosocial and intellectual processes has been recognized by a number of researchers (Kitchener, 1982; Mines, 1982, 1985; Pol-kosnik & Winston, 1989; Stonewater & Daniels, 1983). Mines (1985) suggested a kind of "push-pull" relationship between cognitive and psychosocial develop-ment. For example, in the development of interdependence, an aspect of Chick-ering's (1969) Becoming Autonomous vector, "An increase in [cognitive] complexity is implied by being able to process inter-relationship issues and the relevant com-promises and benefits necessary to relate interdependently without becoming de-pendent or counterdependent" (Mines, 1985, p. 104). Polkosnik and Winston found that the degree of relationships among psychosocial dimensions, as well as the relationship between complexity of intellectual reasoning and psychosocial devel-opment dimensions, is fluid and changes substantially even over the course of one academic term. The relationships are dynamic and interrelated.

Because of the dynamic features of development, measurement is particularly difficult. As with most psychological measurement, the best that can be achieved is a "snapshot" of a relatively small part of an individual at a particular point in time. To extend the photography analogy, present assessment techniques allow only for a relatively clear picture of a person's ear, nose, or eye on Thursday; we cannot get a complete picture of the face, much less the entire body. We are left to infer or to construct the missing features based on a knowledge of the theory.

Measurement specialists must also deal with the paradox of consistency. As Hanson (1982) noted, unless there is a certain degree of consistency in behavior (or evident patterns), meaningful measurement is impossible because, otherwise, we would have only a random collection of behaviors, attitudes, or thoughts. On the other hand, if people are conceived of as being totally consistent, then there is no room for change or development. "A central issue in the assessment of student development is measuring those thoughts and behaviors that form patterns that are sufficiently stable to suggest important psychological constructs while at the same time having sufficient sensitivity built into the instrument to detect significant change when it does occur" (p. 54). Selecting the key constructs and conceptualizing the change process are dictated by competing and incomplete theories of student development. Their use, therefore, will give only incomplete pictures of students developmental lives.

Definition of the Content Domains

The developmental tasks or behaviors selected for measurement are dependent on some particular theory. Without a coherent theory to provide structure for viewing experience, construction of a measurement tool is difficult, if not impossible. Bates, Reese, and Lipsitt (1980) indicated that psychosocial development must take into account diverse influences that determine or shape individuals' development: (a) normative age-related influences, (b) normative history-graded influences, and (c) non-normative life influences. Normative age-graded influences are demands caused by biological maturation, such as puberty and subsequent sexual develop- ment, and social expectations such as the age at which children begin their formal education or enter college.

History-graded influences are generation-specific and are the result of historical events such as the depression, the Vietnam War, or periods of general social liberalism or conservatism. For the current generation of college students the general conservative movement of the political system in the United States in the 1980s is a historical fact that affects how they view the world and the challenges presented to them. The emergence of AIDS as a devastating disease is another historical influence that seems to be having a substantial effect on young adults' sexual practices and attitudes. Social trends and historical events have differential impacts on each generation of college students.

Non-normative influences are the unpredictable and individualized events that tend to overwhelm or radically redirect individuals' responses to other develop- mental influences. Examples of non-normative influences may be the death of a parent or spouse, an illness or accident that impairs normal functioning, or traumatic events that have long-term debilitating effects, such as rape or physical abuse. These influences are highly significant, but are unique to the individual. As Kitchener (1982, p. 38) noted, "When events such as these happen, they can influence how an individual tackles the tasks that are normally expected of his or her age group. These events can provide an impetus for further social-cognitive development and for tackling normative age-related tasks with new vigor, or they can lead to stag- nation and regression."

Kitchener also pointed out that some normative environmental influences unique to being a college student are not shared by members of the age cohort who do not attend college. For example, developing academic competencies (such as note taking, writing formal papers, and test taking skills) are required of college students, but are not required of individuals who do not attend college. An adequate psy- chosocial-developmental portrait of an individual must take into account all of these influences.

Psychosocial measurement instruments can reasonably account for age-graded, normative history-graded, and environmental influences; however, they usually cannot account for non-normative influences. Because these unique individual experiences can dramatically shape an individual's development, the personal interview is probably the most viable means of collecting data. A "true picture" of an individual's developmental status can be obtained only through an integration of normative and ideographic data.

Significance of the Environmental Context

Because measuring an individual's psychosocial development is dependent on a particular social or cultural context for meaning, a given behavior or attitude may have very different meaning or significance depending on the context. From a measurement perspective, then, a behaviorally oriented approach must be placed in a specific context and will therefore be limited somewhat in its general applicability. Because most colleges and universities are basically middle class in terms of social structure, dominant attitudes and customs, and values orientations, an instrument designed to measure college students' psychosocial development must adopt that perspective. Consequently, this middle-class perspective will be appropriate for the vast majority of college students, but it may give a misleading or inaccurate picture of students who come from different backgrounds and desire to maintain the value orientations of their cultures. This is particularly evident for minority students, but is also true to a lesser extent for majority students who come from lower and lower-middle socioeconomic class families.

An understanding of the demands or challenges inherent in the environment is necessary to define the psychosocial behavioral domain. For example, most colleges and universities value the development of autonomous student action and goal-oriented behavior. These values are evident in institutional policies about the selection of academic majors at particular points in a college student's career. By the same token, students who enter college with the conception that their primary purpose for being there is to allow them to get a "good-paying job" upon graduation—an attitude often emphasized in the families of students with limited financial resources—are unlikely to appreciate the goals of general education and learning for its own sake. As a result, these students may be overly concerned about grades and exhibit a rigid focus on meeting the minimum degree requirements, and therefore will be unlikely to exhibit high levels of involvement in general education.

Another measurement issue related to the environmental context is the need to account for both environmental and personality influences concurrently and to account for the interaction of the social and the psychological. For example, Lynch (1987, pp. 23–24) noted in regard to Chickering's vector of Managing Emotions, "Feeling types, especially EFs [Extraverted Feeling on the Myers-Briggs Type Indicator], have more practice in expressing themselves verbally and in relying on their subjective values. . . . [On the other hand,] since Thinking types do not frequently express their feelings, but rather attend more to logic and objectivity, their emotions may emerge or even explode unexpectedly." Psychosocial measurement instruments must be flexible enough to accommodate a wide range of "normal personality characteristics" and the unique ways different personality types interact with their environments and express their emotions and thoughts.

Measurement Formats

As Mines (1982, 1985) noted, measurement of psychosocial development presents a significant problem to the would-be instrument developer because development, by definition, involves a process that is dynamic and changing. As a consequence, the question becomes one of whether to focus on assessing the quality and direction of the process or to focus on the content or subject matter through which the process can be observed as it unfolds. At present, no methodology exists that can assess both the process *and* the content simultaneously; we must therefore infer one after measuring the other. As noted earlier, psychosocial development is an extremely complex process. Three basic measurement formats may be used to assess psychosocial development, each of which focuses principally on either process or content. These are: (a) production formats, (b) preference and comprehensive formats, and (c) specific behavior descriptions.

Open-ended and semistructured interviews and sentence completion are examples of production formats. The Reflective Judgment Interview (Kitchener & King, 1981), Measure of Epistemological Reflection (Baxter Magolda & Porterfield, 1988), and the Sentence Completion Test (Loevinger & Wessler, 1970) are examples of the production format. The production format gives students stimulus material (for example, an obvious dilemma, specific questions about their classroom experience, or ambiguous sentence stems) and then allows for freedom of expression in response. This format, however, requires the use of expert judges who must receive extensive training for scoring, thereby making it expensive to use and sometimes difficult to interpret.

Preference and comprehensive formats present stimulus material and then ask the student to respond using a Likert-type scale or to select one response from among several alternatives. Rest's (1976) Defining Issues Test for the assessment of moral development on the Kohlberg scheme is the best known format of this type. This objective-scoring format has the advantage of being relatively inexpensive and easy to score, but does not permit access to the reasoning the student used in making the particular selection.

The third format focuses on identifying specific behaviors that the student has exhibited in the recent past. This format has been the one most often used to assess psychosocial development from a developmental task frame of reference. The specific behaviors format generally asks students whether a statement about behavior is true of them (using a true-false response format) or how frequently they engage in a particular behavior (using a Likert-type response format). The basis of this approach is grounded in the assumption that a student who exhibits certain behaviors has reached a certain level or stage of development in a task or content area. Although this approach allows for objective scoring, making it relatively inexpensive and easy to use, it says little about the "process fundamental to an individual's progress in task resolution" (Mines, 1985, p. 105). This approach also has another limitation in that it requires students to recall their behavior accurately and to make reports about their behavior honestly, even when that behavior may not be perceived as being "socially approved." How accurately students can recall and objectively report their behavior is sometimes questionable because doing so requires considerable skill in self-analysis and introspection—skills college students possess in widely varying degrees and that are themselves indicative of developmental status.

INSTRUMENTS FOR ASSESSING PSYCHOSOCIAL DEVELOPMENT

Two major efforts, centered at the University of Georgia and the University of Iowa, have been made to develop instruments to assess psychosocial development of college students based on Chickering's (1969) conceptualizations in *Education and Identity*. In this section, we will briefly summarize the scales and the reliability and validity of the known instruments.

Student Developmental Task Inventory

The first phase of the creation of the Student Developmental Task Inventory (SDTI) was begun by Prince (1973) and was based on spontaneous statements of problems and concerns by high school seniors and college students. These statements were refined and classified by a panel of experts using Chickering's (1969) vectors as categories. Following extensive data collections, the final instrument was constructed based on the techniques of scalogram analysis. Following a Delphi study of student affairs professionals and college faculty members, the results of the two studies were used to construct the Student Developmental Task Inventory (Prince, Miller, & Winston, 1974) for use primarily as a counseling tool. A second, revised edition of the SDTI, known as the SDTI-2 (Winston, Miller, & Prince, 1979), was composed of three developmental tasks, each further defined by three subtasks: Developing Autonomy Task (includes Emotional Autonomy, Instrumental Autonomy, and Interdependence Subtasks), Developing Purpose Task (includes Appropriate Educational Plans, Mature Career Plans, and Mature Lifestyle Plans Subtasks), and Developing Mature Interpersonal Relationships Task (includes Intimate Relationships with Opposite Sex, Mature Relationships with Peers, and Tolerance Subtasks). Greater attention to the use of the SDTI-2 as a potential research tool was incorporated into the revision, with norms for the three tasks.

Student Developmental Task and Lifestyle Inventory

A major reevaluation and revision of the SDTI-2 was begun in 1984. Several motivations contributed to continued work: (a) additional research called into question the scale structure of the SDTI-2 (Stonewater, 1987; Winston & Polkosnik, 1986), (b) objections about the exclusive emphasis on heterosexual relationships in the Mature Interpersonal Relationships Tasks were raised and reflected an increased awareness and acceptance of homosexual life-styles in the college community, and (c) experience with the instrument suggested a need to address several areas of students' lives unaddressed by the SDTI-2 (namely, participation in cultural activities, attention to health and wellness issues, and identification of response bias in the instrument).

The revised instrument, which is now entitled the Student Developmental Task and Lifestyle Inventory [SDTLI] (Winston, Miller, & Prince, 1987), is substantially different from its predecessors. It is composed of three developmental tasks: the Establishing and Clarifying Purpose Task, the Developing Mature Interpersonal Relationships Task, and the Academic Autonomy Task, which for the purposes of the inventory are defined as "an interrelated set of behaviors and attitudes which the American culture specifies should be exhibited at approximately the same time by a given age cohort in a designated context" (Winston & Miller, 1987, p. 8). Two of the tasks are further defined by subtasks, which are more specific components of the larger task. The SDTLI also has three scales—Salubrious Lifestyle, Intimacy, and Response Bias—that measure the degree to which students report exhibiting certain behaviors or holding certain attitudes. Tasks are distinguished from scales in that tasks are differentially affected by participation in the higher education environment (that is, seniors show higher levels of achievement than do freshmen), whereas scales may not be affected directly by participation in the college environment.

SDTLI task and scale descriptions. The *Establishing and Clarifying Purpose Task* is made up of five subtasks. High achievement on the subtasks is characterized by the following: (a) *Educational Involvement*—Students have well-defined and thoroughly explored educational goals and plans and are active, self-directed learners; (b) *Career Planning*—Students have synthesized knowledge about themselves and the world of work into appropriate career plans, making an emotional commitment as well as taking steps designed to enhance career goal achievement; (c) *Lifestyle Planning*—Students have established a personal direction to their lives and made plans for their future that take into account personal, ethical, and religious values, future family plans, and vocational and educational objectives; (d) *Cultural Participation*—Students exhibit a wide range of cultural interests and are active participants in traditional cultural events; and (e) *Life Management*—Students structure their lives and manipulate their environment to satisfy daily needs, meet personal responsibilities, manage personal finances appropriately, and meet academic demands satisfactorily (Winston & Miller, 1987).

The *Developing Mature Interpersonal Relationships Task* is composed of three subtasks: (a) *Peer Relationships*—Students have developed relationships with peers characterized by independence, frankness, and trust; they appreciate individual differences among friends and acquaintances and feel reduced pressure to conform to group norms or to conceal disagreements; (b) *Tolerance*—In relationships with persons from different cultures, races, and backgrounds, students show high levels of respect and acceptance and have a general attitude of openness to and appreciation of differences; and (c) *Emotional Autonomy*—Students high on this subtask are free from the need for continuous reassurance and approval from others and have minimal dependence on parents for direction in decision making.

High achievement on the *Academic Autonomy Task* is characterized by students who have the capacity to deal well with ambiguity and to monitor and control their behavior in ways that allow them to attain personal goals and fulfill responsibilities.

High scorers devise and execute effective study plans and schedules, perform academically at levels they deem to be consistent with their abilities, and are self-disciplined and require a minimal amount of direction from others.

The *Salubrious Lifestyle Scale* measures the degree to which a student's lifestyle is consistent with or promotes good health and wellness practices. A high score includes eating well-balanced, nutritious meals, maintaining an appropriate body weight, planning for and getting sufficient amounts of sleep and physical exercise, using effective stress reduction techniques, and evaluating physical appearance positively.

The *Intimacy Scale* is presently classified as "experimental" and was designed to be appropriate for all students who are currently involved, or have been involved within the past 12 months, in an intimate relationship regardless of sexual orientation. Students scoring high on this scale have established a relationship with another person based on high levels of mutual respect, honesty, and trust. Intimacy involves the uninhibited expression of feelings, values, attitudes, wants, and needs to one's partner. Both partners can be themselves, without feeling the need to create a facade, and do not "play games" with each other. Intimacy involves the capacity to love and care for another and to be loved and cared for by another, as well as testing one's ability and desire to make long-term commitments.

The *Response Bias Scale* indicates whether the student is attempting to project an inflated or unrealistically favorable self-portrait. (The purpose of this scale is to identify students who either did not pay careful attention when completing the SDTLI or who are attempting to "fake good" when completing it. The RB Scale should not, however, be viewed either as a personality measure or as an indicator of pathology.)

Reliability and validity of the SDTLI. Space does not permit a complete summary of reliability and validity studies. In summary, the SDTLI alpha coefficients ranged from .90 for the Purpose Task to .70 for the Academic Autonomy Task, with the subtasks having somewhat lower coefficients ranging from .80 for the Career Planning Subtask to .55 for the Tolerance and Emotional Autonomy subtasks. Two-week test-retest coefficients ranged from .87 to .78, and 4-week coefficients ranged from .85 to .70. Validity was estimated in several ways, including correlations with selected scales from established instruments including the Career Development Inventory (Super, Thompson, Lindeman, Jordaan, & Myers, 1981), College Student Questionnaire (Peterson, 1968), Omnibus Personality Inventory (Heist & Yonge, 1968), and other instruments based on Chickering's constructs, including the Iowa Developing Autonomy Inventory (Jackson & Hood, 1986a), Erwin Identity Scale (Erwin, 1978), and the Mines-Jensen Interpersonal Relationships Inventory (Hood & Mines, 1986). Intercorrelations of tasks and subtasks revealed that the Establishing and Clarifying Purpose and Mature Interpersonal Relationships tasks are relatively independent of each other and that their subtasks correlate more highly with their assigned tasks than to any other task or scale. The Academic Autonomy Task, however, was moderately correlated with the other two tasks, which suggests that it is not totally independent (Winston & Miller, 1987).

Iowa Student Development Inventories

Faculty, staff, and students at the University of Iowa began some years ago to develop instruments based on Chickering's vectors. The Iowa instruments have recently become available (Hood, 1986) to researchers and evaluators. The instruments include six inventories to measure all of the vectors, except Developing Integrity. Brief descriptions of the inventories and abbreviated summaries of their reliability and validity studies follow.

Iowa Developing Competency Inventory

Based on Chickering's (1969) assertion that there are three types of competencies that undergraduates need to develop—intellectual, physical and manual skills, and interpersonal—Jackson and Hood (1986b) created an instrument with three scales. The Self-Confidence (SC) Scale is composed of 30 items dealing with interactions with authority figures, friends, and classmates, and ease of communicating with others. The Competency in Math (CM) Scale is composed of 20 items that deal with confidence in the ability to perform in mathematics or the enjoyment of mathematics. The Competency in Writing (CW) Scale is composed of 20 items that deal with confidence in writing abilities or the enjoyment of writing. Coefficient alphas were found to be .92 for SC, .96 for CM, and .92 for CW; the scales correlate with the total inventory .78, .66, and .60, respectively. No validity studies have been reported to date.

Iowa Managing Emotions Inventory

The Iowa Managing Emotions Inventory addresses both the awareness of emotions and the integration of emotions. "These concepts included (1) the recognition of emotions, (2) the exploration of these emotions, and (3) insights into emotions" (Hood & Jackson, 1986, p. 1–1). Five categories of emotions were selected for inclusion in the inventory: happiness, attraction, anger, depression, and frustration. Twelve items for each of the emotions were ultimately included in the inventory. Considerable attention was paid to response set in order to control for social desirability and acquaintance. Coefficient alpha reliability for the Depression Scale was .85, for Anger, .79, for Frustration, .81, for Happiness, .80, and for Attraction, .76. No validity studies have been reported.

Iowa Developing Autonomy Inventory

Various aspects of autonomy as described by Chickering were included in the Iowa Developing Autonomy Inventory (Jackson & Hood, 1986a). Items for measuring emotional independence from parents and from peers were included, as were items measuring instrumental autonomy (including management of time, money, school and work experiences, and mobility) and items measuring interdependence (including interdependencies between self and others, between self and the community, and between self and the larger society). The inventory is made up of 90 items, with six 15-item scales: Mobility, Time Management, Money Management, Interdependence, Emotional Independence Regarding Peers, and Emotional Independence Regarding Parents. Coefficient alpha reliabilities and correlations with the total inventory were reported as: .87 and .75, .85 and .69, .81 and .70, .80 and .60, .77 and .69, and .88 and .73 for the six scales, respectively. No validity studies are currently available.

Erwin Identity Scale

Chickering (1969) specified two aspects of identity—"conceptions concerning body and appearance, and clarification of sexual identification. For Chickering, the changing, growing, physical body and self-probing questions about self become partially focused on one's presentation of self" (Hood, 1986, p. 4–1). Erwin (1978) suggested a third component of identity that he termed "personal confidence" or self-assurance. The Erwin Identity Scale is composed of 58 items that are grouped into three subscales: Confidence, Sexual Identity, and Conceptions about Body and Appearance. Confidence measures the "assuredness of one's self and in one's capabilities. Confidence includes a conscious self-reliance while recognizing the necessary dependence on outside sources. This recognition is an awareness and faith in one's own capabilities yet a realization that there are limits to these processes" (Hood, 1986, p. 4–1). Sexual Identity addresses the clarification, understanding, and acceptance of one's sexual feelings. A high score on this scale indicates the student recognizes his or her sexual feelings as natural and does not feel guilty because of them. Higher scorers are also able to control their sexual feelings. The Conceptions about Body and Appearance Scale includes an acceptance of one's body in comparison to others, as well as dressing in ways that balance personal preference, the desires of others, and situational expectations.

Reliability estimates have ranged from .74 to .90 (Erwin & Delworth, 1982; Hood, 1986). Evidence of convergent validity has been reported by Erwin and Schmidt (1982). These studies have found moderately high relationships between Confidence and Sexual Identity and measures of personal integration, lack of anxiety, internal locus of control, and personal commitment. In a longitudinal study of college students Erwin (1982) found scores to increase on Confidence, but to decrease on Conceptions about Body and Appearance during the freshman year. In a 4-year longitudinal study Erwin and Kelly (1985) reported that seniors had gained in Confidence and had a wider range of scores than did freshmen.

Mines-Jensen Interpersonal Relationship Inventory

Chickering's (1969) Freeing Interpersonal Relationships vector is measured by the Mines-Jensen Interpersonal Relationship Inventory. This inventory is composed of 42 items and has two scales: Tolerance, defined as "an increasing openness and acceptance of diversity which expands one's sensitivities and increases the range of alternatives for satisfying exchanges and friendships," and Quality of Relationships, defined as a "shift in relationships with friends from either extreme dependence or independence, toward a state of interdependence. It is characterized by greater trust and stability" (Hood & Mines, 1986, p. 5–1). Reliabilities have ranged from .65 to .87, depending on the sample and version of the inventory used. Longitudinal studies of a group of students at the University of Iowa showed that there were increases in scores on both scales during the freshman year and from the freshman year to the senior year (Hood & Mines, 1986).

Developing Purposes Inventory

The Developing Purposes Inventory was developed by Barratt to measure Chickering's vector of Developing Purpose. It contains 45 items and has three scales: Avocational-Recreational, Vocational Interest, and Style of Life. The Avocational-Recreational Scale measures the development of a pattern of activities and openness to new activities within the context of vocational plans, social demands, and personal interests; in other words, how they fit into one's total life plan. The scales' alpha coefficients for various samples ranged from .39 to .84; 3-month test-retest reliability was reported as .61.

The Vocational Interest Scale was designed to measure the degree of commitment to vocational choice. "It is not limited to the selection of a career or major but focuses on the degree of sophistication and personal investment made in vocational activities" (Barratt & Hood, 1986, p. 6–2). Test-retest reliabilities for 3 months were found to be around .55; coefficient alphas ranged from .68 to .80. The Style of Life Scale is intended to measure "the maturity of the relationship between the student and the community, significant others, and self. Goal setting to achieve a consistency in these relationships . . ." is also part of this scale (Barratt & Hood, p. 6–2). Alpha coefficients for the Vocational Interest Scale were reported to range from .69 to .87, and 3-month test-retest reliability was found to be .82. Validity studies have been confined primarily to correlation with demographic, behavioral, and attitudinal data.

MEASUREMENT ISSUES OF THE FUTURE

Applications of psychosocial-developmental theory to both the study of college students and the programming strategies and interventions to which they are exposed have been increasingly apparent in recent years. The theoretical conceptualizations, model building, and research initiated in the 1960s and 1970s have had observable impact upon students and their institutions during the 1980s. It is, however, time to review our understandings and renew our efforts to increase knowledge about the psychosocial development of college students from a current world perspective. We need, for instance, to initiate several longitudinal studies of comparable size and duration as that conducted by Chickering (1969) to confirm his vectors or to determine how college student's psychosocial development has changed over the past 25 years. It would be reasonable to expect there to be substantial differences, given the social and cultural changes that have occurred during that time span, especially concerning the greater importance of women's roles in society. We have evidence (Straub, 1987; White & Hood, 1989; Winston & Miller, 1987) that Chickering's vector structure may need reformulation to reflect more adequately both current social conditions and our greater understanding of intellectual development processes.

The increase in the number of minority and post-age-25 college students on many campuses is another change from the 1960s that must be researched more extensively. We need to understand better the developmental processes of older, nontraditional students and how the college-going experience affects (or can affect) their development. Given the cultural diversity of students in colleges today, we must investigate more thoroughly how different entry variables interact with the college environment to affect psychosocial development differentially. We know that it is unrealistic to view all college students through the same perceptual lens, but we have yet to devise effective models and methods to ensure that students' individual differences will be truly recognized and addressed.

We are in need of well-conceived, sophisticated studies designed to investigate the complex interactions among intellectual, psychosocial, and moral developmental processes. Isolated studies of these processes give an incomplete, and sometimes misleading, picture of students' lives. Investigation of how different educational environments affect or influence development is also needed. Measurement techniques and instruments are needed that will provide a simultaneous measure of developmental processes and identification of salient environmental features. In order for that to be feasible, more sensitive and rigorously constructed instruments are needed. Even though considerable strides have been made in instrument construction in the past two decades, the field still suffers from an acute shortage of psychometrically reliable and valid instruments to measure psychosocial-developmental constructs.

That increased emphasis on the assessment of psychosocial development in college students is desirable is not in doubt. That our current technology is adequate to accomplish effectively these important assessment processes, however, is in doubt. What is presently needed are a series of second-generation research projects to further test psychosocial development theory and to create measurement tools and methodologies to carry us into the 21st century.

REFERENCES

Astin, A.W. (1977). *Four critical years*. San Francisco: Jossey-Bass.
Astin, A.W. (1982). *Minorities in American higher education: Recent trends, current prospects, and recommendations*. San Francisco: Jossey-Bass.
Astin, A.W. (1985). *Achieving educational excellence: A critical assessment of priorities and practices in higher education*. San Francisco: Jossey-Bass.
Barber, E.G. (Ed.). (1985). *Foreign student flows*. New York: Institute of International Education.
Barratt, W.R., & Hood, A.B. (1986). Assessing development of purpose. In A.B. Hood (Ed.), *The Iowa student development inventories* (p. 6–2). Iowa City, IA: Hitech Press.
Bates, P.B., Reese, H.W., & Lipsitt, L.P. (1980). Life-span developmental psychology. In M.R. Rosenzweig & L.W. Porter (Eds.), *Annual Review of Psychology* (pp. 65–110). Palo Alto, CA: Annual Reviews.

Baxter Magolda, M.B., & Porterfield, W.D. (1988). *Assessing intellectual development: The link between theory and practice.* Alexandria, VA: American College Personnel Association.

Brodzinski, F.R. (1980). Adult learners—the new majority: A demographic reality. In F.R. Brodzinski (Ed.), *Providing student services for the adult learner* (pp. 1–6). (New Directions for Student Services, No. 11.) San Francisco: Jossey-Bass.

Bulthuis, J.D. (1986). The foreign student today: A profile. In K.R. Pyle (Ed.), *Guiding the development of foreign students* (pp. 19–28). (New Directions for Student Services, No. 36.) San Francisco: Jossey-Bass

Caple, R.B. (1987). The change process in developmental theory: A self-organization paradigm, part 1. *Journal of College Student Personnel, 28,* 4–11.

Chew, C.A., & Ogi, A.Y. (1987). Asian American college student perspective. In D.J. Wright (Ed.), *Responding to the needs of today's minority students* (pp. 39–48). (New Directions in Student Services, No. 38.) San Francisco: Jossey-Bass.

Chickering, A. W. (1969). *Education and identity.* San Francisco: Jossey-Bass.

Chickering, A.W., & Associates. (1981). *The modern American college.* San Francisco: Jossey-Bass.

Chickering, A.W., & Havighurst, R.J. (1981). The life cycle. In A.W. Chickering, & Associates, *The modern American college* (pp. 16–50). San Francisco: Jossey-Bass.

Cohen, R.D. (Ed.). (1985). *Working with parents of college students.* (New Directions for Student Services, No. 32.) San Francisco: Jossey-Bass.

Coons, F.W. (1971). The developmental tasks of college students. In S.C. Feinstein, P.L. Glovacchini, & A.A. Miller (Eds.), *Adolescent psychiatry: Developmental and clinical studies, Vol. 1* (pp. 257–273). New York: Basic Books.

Drum, D. (1980). Understanding student development. In W. Morrill & J.C. Hurst (Eds.), *Dimensions of intervention for student development* (pp. 14–38). New York: Wiley.

Erikson, E.H. (1950). *Childhood and society.* New York: Norton.

Erikson, E.H. (1963). *Childhood and society* (2nd ed.). New York: Norton.

Erikson, E.H. (1968). *Identity: Youth and crisis.* New York: Norton.

Erwin, T.D. (1978). The validation of the Erwin Identity Scale. (Doctoral dissertation, University of Iowa, 1978). *Dissertation Abstracts International, 39,* 4818A.

Erwin, T.D. (1982). Academic status as related to development of identity. *Journal of Psychology, 110,* 163–169.

Erwin, T.D., & Delworth, U. (1982). Formulating environmental constructs that affect students' identity. *National Association of Student Personnel Administrators Journal, 20,* 47–55.

Erwin, T.D., & Kelly, K. (1985). Changes in students' self-confidence in college. *Journal of College Student Personnel, 26,* 395–400.

Erwin, T.D., & Schmidt, M.R. (1982). The convergent validity of the Erwin Identity Scale. *Educational and Psychological Measurement, 41,* 1307–1310.

Evans, N.J. (Ed.). (1985). *Facilitating the development of women.* (New Directions for Student Services, No. 29.) San Francisco: Jossey-Bass.

Feldman, K.A., & Newcomb, T.M. (1969). *The impact of college on students: An analysis of four decades of research.* San Francisco: Jossey-Bass.

Fleming, J. (1981). Special needs of Blacks and other minorities. In A. Chickering (Ed.), *The modern American college* (pp. 279–295). San Francisco: Jossey-Bass.

Gazda, G.M., Childers, W.C., & Brooks, D.K., Jr. (1987). *Foundations of counseling and human services.* New York: McGraw-Hill.

Gilligan, C. (1982). *In a different voice: Psychological theory and women's development*. Cambridge, MA: Harvard University Press.

Gould, R.L. (1978). *Transformations: Growth and change in adult life*. New York: Simon & Schuster.

Grossman, H. (1984). *Educating Hispanic students*. Springfield, IL: Charles C Thomas.

Hanson, G.R. (1982). Critical issues in the assessment of student development. In G.R. Hanson (Ed.), *Measuring student development* (pp. 47–63). (New Directions for Student Services, No. 20.) San Francisco: Jossey-Bass.

Havighurst, R.J. (1953). *Human development and education*. New York: Longmans, Green.

Havighurst, R.J. (1972). *Developmental tasks and education* (3rd ed.). New York: David McKay.

Hazen Foundation. (1968). *The student in higher education*. New Haven, CT: Author.

Heath, D.H. (1968). *Growing up in college*. San Francisco: Jossey-Bass.

Heist, P., & Yonge, G. (1968). *Omnibus personality inventory* (Form F). New York: Psychological Corporation.

Hennig, M., & Jardim, A. (1977). *The managerial woman*. New York: Doubleday.

Hood, A.B. (Ed.). (1986). *The Iowa student development inventories*. Iowa City, IA: Hitech Press.

Hood, A.B., & Jackson, L.M. (1986). The Iowa managing emotions inventory. In A.B. Hood (Ed.), *The Iowa student development inventories* (pp. 1–4). Iowa City, IA: Hitech Press.

Hood, A.B., & Mines, R.A. (1986). Mines-Jensen interpersonal relationships inventory. In A.B. Hood (Ed.), *The Iowa student development inventories* (pp. 1–5). Iowa City, IA: Hitech Press.

Hood, A.B., Riahinejad, A.R., & White, D.B. (1985). Changes in ego identity during the college years. *Journal of College Student Personnel, 27*, 107–113.

Ivey, A.E. (1986). *Developmental therapy: Theory into practice*. San Francisco: Jossey-Bass.

Jackson, L.M., & Hood, A.B. (1986a). The Iowa developing autonomy inventory. In A.B. Hood (Ed.), *The Iowa student development inventories* (pp. 1–4). Iowa City, IA: Hitech Press.

Jackson, L.M., & Hood, A.B. (1986b). The Iowa developing competency inventory. In A.B. Hood (Ed.), *The Iowa student development inventories* (pp. 1–7). Iowa City, IA: Hitech Press.

Jordan-Cox, C.A. (1987). Psychosocial development of students in traditionally Black institutions. *Journal of College Student Personnel, 28*, 504–511.

Kegan, R. (1982). *The evolving self*. Cambridge, MA: Harvard University Press.

Keniston, K. (1970). Youth: A ''new'' stage of life. *American Scholar, 39*, 631–654.

Kitchener, K.S. (1982). Human development and the college campus: Sequences and tasks. In G.R. Hanson (Ed.), *Measuring student development* (pp. 17–46). (New Directions for Student Services, No. 20.) San Francisco: Jossey-Bass.

Kitchener, K.S., & King, P.M. (1981). Reflective judgment: Concepts of justification and their relationship to age and education. *Journal of Applied Developmental Psychology, 2*, 89–116.

Kitchener, K.S., & Kitchener, R.F. (1981). The development of natural rationality: Can formal operations account for it? In J.S. Meacham & N.R. Santilli (Eds.), *Social development in youth: Structure and content* (pp. 160–181). Basel, Switzerland: Karger.

Knox, A.B. (1977). *Adult development and learning: A handbook on individual growth and competence in the adult years for education and the helping professions.* San Francisco: Jossey-Bass.

LaCounte, D.W. (1987). American Indian students in college. In D.J. Wright (Ed.), *Responding to the needs of today's minority students* (pp. 65–80). (New Directions in Student Services, No. 38.) San Francisco: Jossey-Bass.

LaFromboise, T.D., & Dixon, D.N. (1981). American Indian perception of trustworthiness in a counseling interview. *Journal of Counseling Psychology, 28,* 135–139.

Lee, M.J., Abd-Ella, M., & Burks, L.A. (1981). *Needs of foreign students from developing nations at U.S. colleges and universities.* Washington, DC: National Association for Foreign Student Affairs.

Levinson, D.J., & Associates. (1978). *The seasons of a man's life.* New York: Knopf.

Loevinger, J., & Wessler, R. (1970). *Measuring ego development I: Construction and use of a sentence completion test.* San Francisco: Jossey-Bass.

Lynch, A.Q. (1987). Type development and student development. In J.A. Provost & S. Anchors (Eds.), *Applications of the Myers-Briggs Type Indicator in higher education* (pp. 5–29). Palo Alto, CA: Consulting Psychologists Press.

McCoy, V.R. (1977). *Lifelong learning: The adult years.* Washington, DC: Adult Education Association.

Miller, T.K., & Prince, J.S. (1976). *The future of student affairs: A guide to student development for tomorrow's higher education.* San Francisco: Jossey-Bass.

Mines, R.A. (1982). Student development assessment techniques. In G.R. Hanson (Ed.), *Measuring student development* (pp. 65–92). (New Directions for Student Services, No. 20.) San Francisco: Jossey-Bass.

Mines, R.A. (1985). Measurement issues in evaluating student development programs. *Journal of College Student Personnel, 26,* 101–106.

Montagu, A. (1981). *Growing young.* New York: McGraw-Hill.

Nettles, M.T., & Johnson, N.A. (1987). Race, sex, and other factors as determinants of college students' socialization. *Journal of College Student Personnel, 28,* 512–524.

Neugarten, B. (1968). *Middle age and aging.* Chicago: University of Chicago Press.

Oetting, F.R. (1967). A developmental definition of counseling psychology. *Journal of Counseling Psychology, 14,* 382–385.

Pace, C.R. (1979). *Measuring outcomes of college: Fifty years of findings and recommendations for the future.* San Francisco: Jossey-Bass.

Peterson, R.E. (1968). *College student questionnaire* (rev. ed.). Princeton, NJ: Educational Testing Service.

Polkosnik, M.C., & Winston, R.B., Jr. (1989). Relationships between students' intellectual and psychosocial development: An exploratory investigation. *Journal of College Student Development, 30,* 10–19.

Pounds, A.W. (1987). Black students' needs on predominantly white campuses. In D.J. Wright (Ed.), *Responding to the needs of today's minority students* (pp. 23–38). (New Directions in Student Services, No. 38.) San Francisco: Jossey-Bass.

Prince, J.S. (1973). *Identification and analysis of selected developmental tasks of college students.* Unpublished doctoral dissertation, University of Georgia, Athens.

Prince, J.S., Miller, T.K., & Winston, R.B., Jr. (1974). *Student developmental task inventory.* Athens, GA: Student Development Associates.

Quevedo-Garcia, E.L. (1987). Facilitating the development of Hispanic college students. In D.J. Wright (Ed.), *Responding to the needs of today's minority students* (pp. 49–64). (New Directions in Student Services, No. 38.) San Francisco: Jossey-Bass.

Rest, J.R. (1976). New approaches in the assessment of moral development. In T. Lickona (Ed.), *Moral development and behavior* (pp. 198–218). New York: Holt, Rinehart & Winston.

Riahinejad, A.R., & Hood, A.B. (1984). The development of interpersonal relationships in college. *Journal of College Student Personnel, 25*, 498–502.

Sanford, N. (1962). Developmental status of the entering freshman. In N. Sanford (Ed.), *The American college* (pp. 253–282). New York: Wiley.

Sedlacek, W.E. (1987). Black students on white campuses: 20 years of research. *Journal of College Student Personnel, 28*, 484–495.

Sedlacek, W.E., & Brooks, G.C., Jr. (1976). *Racism in American education: A model for change.* Chicago: Nelson-Hall.

Spaulding, S., & Flack, M.J. (1976). *The world's students in the United States: A review and evaluation of research on foreign students.* New York: Praeger.

Stevens, R. (1983). *Erik Erikson: An introduction.* New York: St. Martin's Press.

Stewart, W.R. (1977). *A psychological study of the formation of the early adult life structure in women.* Unpublished doctoral dissertation, Columbia University, New York.

Stikes, C.S. (1984). *Black students in higher education.* Carbondale, IL: Southern Illinois University Press.

Stonewater, B.B. (1987). The second edition of the Student Developmental Task Inventory and sex differences: A factor analysis. *Journal of College Student Personnel, 28*, 365–369.

Stonewater, J., & Daniels, M.H. (1983). Psychosocial and cognitive development in a career decision making course. *Journal of College Student Personnel, 24*, 403–410.

Straub, C.A. (1987). Women's development of autonomy and Chickering's theory. *Journal of College Student Personnel, 28*, 198–204.

Super, D.E., Thompson, A.S., Lindeman, R.H., Jordaan, J.P., & Myers, R.A. (1981). *The career development inventory* (College and University Form). Palo Alto, CA: Consulting Psychologists Press.

Tittle, C.K. (1982). Career, marriage, and family: Values in adult roles and guidance. *Personnel and Guidance Journal, 61*, 154–158.

Tracey, T.J., & Sedlacek, W.E. (1985). The relationship of noncognitive variables to academic success: A longitudinal comparison by race. *Journal of College Student Personnel, 26*, 405–410.

Tracey, T.J., & Sedlacek, W.E. (1987). Prediction of graduation using non-cognitive variables by race. *Measurement and Evaluation in Counseling and Development, 19*, 177–184.

U.S. Department of Commerce. Bureau of the Census. (1985). *Persons of Spanish origin in the United States: March 1982.* (Series P–20, No. 396.) Washington, DC: U.S. Government Printing Office.

White, D.B., & Hood, A.B. (1989). An assessment of the validity of Chickering's theory of student development. *Journal of College Student Development, 30*, 354–361.

White, T.J., & Sedlacek, W.E. (1986). Noncognitive predictors of grades and retention for specially admitted students. *Journal of College Admissions, 3*, 20–23.

Winston, R.B., Jr. (1987). A theory of change in search of data. *Journal of College Student Personnel, 28*, 17–18.

Winston, R.B., Jr., & Miller, T.K. (1987). *Student developmental task and lifestyle inventory manual.* Athens, GA: Student Development Associates.

Winston, R.B., Jr., Miller, T.K., & Prince, J.S. (1979). *Student developmental task inventory* (rev., 2nd ed.). Athens, GA: Student Development Associates.

Winston, R.B., Jr., Miller, T.K., & Prince, J.S. (1987). *Student developmental task and lifestyle inventory*. Athens, GA: Student Development Associates.

Winston, R.B., Jr., & Polkosnik, M.C. (1986). Student Developmental Task Inventory (2nd ed.): Summary of selected findings. *Journal of College Student Personnel, 27,* 548–559.

CHAPTER 6

Understanding and Assessing College Environments

Lois A. Huebner and Jane M. Lawson

There is nothing so complex as a simple idea. Kurt Lewin (1936) had a simple idea. He proposed that behavior is the function of the person and the environment $[B = f(P \times E)]$. Practitioners and researchers were captivated by this idea because it suggested the paradigm of matching persons with environments and environments with persons. That is, they believed that by defining the salient person and environment variables, persons could be matched with the appropriate environment to foster growth and development.

In 1972, Kaiser applied Lewin's paradigm to the college experience. He offered an intriguing conceptualization: "A transactional relationship exists between college students and their campus environment: that is, the students shape their environment and are shaped by it . . . [thus] the campus [can and] should be intentionally designed to offer opportunities, incentives, and reinforcements for growth and development" (p. 8). Since then, student development practitioners and researchers have attempted to interpret this simple idea and to make Kaiser's vision of an intentionally and scientifically designed college environment operative; that is, to ensure that college environments exert a positive and intentional influence on students.

Scholars and researchers have been accumulating data on students, on campus environments, and on the ways in which persons and environments relate and change in respect to one another (Chickering, 1969; Chickering & Associates, 1981; Feldman & Newcomb, 1969). Practitioners have attempted to match environments within the university to certain kinds of students and to help faculty design instructional strategies to meet students' developmental levels. In Lewin's terms, this research relates to the Person (P), to the Environment (E), and to the Function (F)—the interaction of P and E—and to a variety of outcomes (B).

This chapter will review the literature focusing on the environmental and the interactional components of Lewin's paradigm as it relates to the college experience.

127

We will verify that Lewin's and Kaiser's simple ideas are enormously and frustratingly complex, so much so that they have nearly eluded effective implementation.

COMPONENTS OF THE INTERACTION:
STUDENTS, FACULTY, AND THE COLLEGE ENVIRONMENT

What is the nature of the educational experience for students? An educational experience can be exhilarating and challenging, demoralizing and frustrating, competitive or cooperative. What accounts for this diversity of experience? The students? The faculty? The facilities? The curriculum? All of these are significant contributors to the quality and diversity of the educational experience, as is the interaction among them. These interactions, and other factors as well, account for each individual's unique educational experience.

Students

Students come to the university with diverse characteristics. Their range of intellectual ability is great. They represent both the "best and the brightest" as well as the academically mediocre. Some reports (Hodgkinson, 1985) suggest that by the year 2000 college students will come from the top three fourths of their high school graduating class as opposed to the top quartile or top half as was true 25 years ago. Students' economic status also varies. Many students work two or three jobs to pay tuition, and others worry about keeping scholarships. Still others have tuition and living expenses paid by parents. Students increasingly are older; some have parental responsibilities that compete for time and energy. Students come with a variety of educational values. They come with different ways of thinking about and perceiving the world and of making decisions. They have diverse learning styles and varied preferences for structure, clarity, diversity, and complexity. In summary, we can describe today's students in numerous ways: by demographics, cognitive style, personality type, developmental level, or learning styles.

Environments

Into what environments do these diverse students come? Institutions of higher education can be described along a number of dimensions: their selectivity, graduation rates, faculty, libraries, social climate, and size. Data support the fact that most students choose institutions that match their needs, styles, values, or interests (Holland, 1961; Nafziger, Holland, Helms, & McPartland, 1974; Osipow, Ashby, & Wall, 1966). However, many students choose universities that do not seem to be a good "fit" for them. For example, some "new" (nontraditional) students are entering fairly old (traditional) universities that have not changed in response to these new students, and according to Bloom, should not change (Bloom, 1988).

There are other ways to define college environments as well. Salient dimensions include physical facilities and physical environmental characteristics; the curriculum and co-curriculum; the human element, including faculty, administrators, and students; and the social/psychological climate and university philosophy. Typically, a university will provide a number of distinct subenvironments defined by these dimensions. We will briefly explore some of the variability and diversity across these conditions.

As noted above, environments and subenvironments can be defined by physical characteristics. A typical campus may offer a variety of physical spaces including lecture halls, seminar rooms, laboratories, surgical suites, play and recreation areas, athletic fields, grassy spaces, benches along walkways, weight rooms, bars, music rooms, old buildings with movable furniture, and high-rise residence halls. Physical space also can be defined by factors of architecture, ambient temperature, spatial configuration, colors, texture, density, and so on.

Environments and subenvironments can be defined by the tasks presented to students such as facts to memorize, essays to write, experiments to perform, and human interactions to negotiate. Some tasks require good social skills; some require manual dexterity. After-class activities present a different set of tasks, including volunteer work where compassion and the ability to care for those who are hurting are needed; leadership offices where the ability to negotiate, compromise, and think clearly are required; dating relationships where sociability and assertiveness are valued; and residence hall living where aggression and dominance may be required in order to fit in.

Universities differ in terms of their overall climate. Even within a given university, the environment is not homogeneous. Subunits may have different "personalities." The social climate of residence halls and classrooms has been studied extensively because of its influence on students' growth and development (e.g., Moos, 1979, 1976; Pace, 1964; Walberg, 1969). We know much less of the influence of social clubs, volunteer experiences, and other extracurricular activities.

Environments and subenvironments also may be defined by the people who inhabit them (the "human aggregate"). Thus, total universities, academic departments, bars, athletic teams, and newspapers are influenced by the types of individuals who are members of the setting, including students, faculty, and administrators. In this sense, aggregated individual characteristics (e.g., Myers-Briggs type or Holland Code type) or group identity features (the combined effects of artistic or competitive or religious people) also constitute a dimension of the environment with which individuals may interact.

Development Occurs in a Context

All of this complexity and diversity makes defining and understanding what happens in a university an overwhelming task. The question posed by acknowledging this interactional complexity is the same question inherent in Lewin's paradigm: What features of the environment promote development, such as enhancing academic and psychosocial performance, and aiding in retention, for what kinds of students, and at what points in their lives?

A review of theories and research on student development reminds us that a number of relevant environmental characteristics and salient elements of the person-environment interaction have been identified as facilitating or hindering students' development and performance. Based on our review (Huebner, 1983), six constructs recur repeatedly in the literature. These constructs include five environmental dimensions: heterogeneity/homogeneity, support-challenge balance, social support, social climate, and the physical environment. A sixth construct, person-environment congruence, is explicitly interactional.

ENVIRONMENTAL FACTORS, DEFINITIONS, AND FINDINGS

Heterogeneity/Homogeneity

Although seldom explicitly defined, this concept is a measure of internal consistency or variability along some dimensions in the population or within an environment. Thus, populations become more heterogeneous as their members reflect increasing diversity on one or more attributes, such as choice of major, learning style, or age. An environment would be more homogeneous if it had fewer distinctly different subenvironments, if the same requirements, support, and reinforcements were present for all members at all times, or if the population were relatively homogeneous.

The concept of heterogeneity/homogeneity also has empirical linkages with the notion of person-environment fit. The most significant finding is that students not only select environments with which they share basic similarities, but also tend to change or reinforce aspects of themselves so that they continue to be congruent with the environment. This fact is amplified in homogeneous settings. Thus incongruent students in cohesive and homogeneous settings are more likely to change in the direction of the majority, whereas congruent students are likely to maintain or accentuate their behavior and beliefs (Moos, 1984). Moos (1979) referred to this tendency as "progressive conformity."

Overall, students report more satisfaction in colleges with heterogeneous profiles (Holland, 1968; Walsh, 1973). This may be because a heterogeneous organization is more diverse and provides a greater possibility of finding friends and exerts less pressure to change (Moos, 1979). On the other hand, cohesive committed settings create special problems for divergent or deviant students who cannot or do not wish to conform. Nonconforming students are likely to feel a good deal of pressure to conform and to experience a lack of support for their perceptions, goals, or preferences.

Support/Challenge Balance

Many student development theorists and practitioners refer to the concepts of support and challenge, although they define these concepts in somewhat different ways. Generally, however, support refers to making available to students experiences or relationships that aid them in managing stress (e.g., Blocher, 1974) or structuring experiences so that they provide a degree of familiarity, or are "negotiable" with current abilities and resources. Support emerges as a function of receiving personal attention, caring, empathy, and warmth from others. A student may experience support when living with someone who shares similar values, life-style, or choice of major or career. Enrolling in classes that require academic tasks compatible with a student's skills, conceptual level, or learning preferences also may serve as a support.

Challenge, on the other hand, refers to the presence of stress-producing (and potentially growth-producing) elements in the learning situation. These elements include novelty, intensity, complexity, ambiguity, abstractness, diversity, and rapid change. Challenge also may reflect a "mismatch" between the demands of the environment and an individual's present coping behaviors.

The literature suggests that support is facilitative of a number of the goals of the undergraduate experience, and, when combined with an appropriate degree of challenge (e.g., Blocher, 1978; Rodgers, 1984; Widick, Knefelkamp, & Parker, 1975), often promotes development. Thus, a certain amount of challenge is deemed necessary for growth and development. Environments that are too challenging, however, tend to be perceived as overwhelming and may produce illness (Moos, 1979, 1976), exit from the environment (Schroeder, 1976; Schroeder, Warner, & Malone, 1980), dissatisfaction (Bauer, 1975; Holland, 1968), greater stress and strain (Huebner, 1975; Tracey & Sherry, 1984), or difficulty in learning (Moos, 1979; Widick et al., 1975; Widick & Simpson, 1978). For example, coed units may be especially stressful (thus challenging) for freshmen due to divergent influences that create internal conflicts (Moos, 1979).

The necessity of designing environments that have an optimal balance of support and challenge seems well documented in the literature but again points to the complexity of Lewin's simple idea. What one student might perceive as supportive another may perceive as challenging and vice versa.

Social Support

The third concept, social support, lacks an agreed-upon conceptual definition. However, it has a broad meaning of friendship, social ties, and social integration plus the availability of emotional and tangible resources. Pace (1984) noted that in all types of colleges, the single most important contributor to student satisfaction was an environment perceived as friendly, supportive, and helpful. Data from studies in health psychology, stress management, person-environment interaction, and social climate lend credence to the notion that social support is useful in directly promoting: (a) normal development, emotional adjustment, and a sense of well-being (Cohen & Wills, 1985; Gottlieb, 1983; Hirsch, 1980; Moos, 1979; Pilisuk & Froland, 1978); (b) longevity/mortality (Berkman & Syme, 1979; Cohen, 1988); (c) protection from illness (Cohen, 1988; Joseph, 1980; Seeman & Syme, 1987); (d) recovery from illness (Holmes, Joffe, Ketcham, & Sheehy, 1961; Moos, 1979); and (e) a buffer effect to mediate the adverse effects of various stresses (Kaplan, Cassel, & Gore, 1977; Moos, 1979; Norbeck & Tilden, 1983). One of the most interesting and consistent findings among these studies is that an emphasis on achievement or competition without social support or cohesion tends to produce physical symptoms, dissatisfaction, and strain (Moos, 1979; Moos & Van Dort, 1979).

Although it is not clear precisely how social support functions, either directly or in a buffering capacity, several models have been proposed. Cohen, in his 1988 review, suggested that social integration is the primary cause of "main effect" of social support. Similarly, he posited that perceived availability of support is the primary cause of stress-buffering effects, that is, the protection from the potentially pathogenic influence of stressful events. Pearson (1986) also offered several hypotheses about the mechanisms involved in social support. Noting the interactional nature of social support, she elaborated on an idea, earlier promoted by Gottlieb (1983), that access to social support depends on many reciprocal factors including ethnicity and social class, values and beliefs, expectations about helpers and helping, ability to reciprocate, self-disclosure, and social competence.

Social Climate

Moos (1979) has been the leading researcher in defining this concept, which, according to his research, includes three major components: (a) relationship dimensions—the way people affiliate and provide mutual support for one another; (b) personal development or goal orientation dimensions—the opportunities available for personal growth in specific areas related to the purpose of the setting, maturation, and the development of self-esteem; and (c) system maintenance and system change dimensions—the extent to which the environment is orderly and clear in its expectations, maintains control, and is responsive to change.

According to Moos, relationship dimensions, which include involvement, support, genuineness, and friendship, facilitate student satisfaction, well-being, and social and interpersonal growth. On the other hand, goal-related dimensions that include competition, achievement, independence, and task orientation are associated with students' productivity and academic development and achievement.

Moos summarized a complicated literature by noting that achievement gains on traditional academic measures are most likely when classes offer a combination of warmth and supportive relationships, an emphasis on specific academic tasks and accomplishments, and a reasonably clear, orderly, well-structured milieu. Such classes score high on social climate dimensions labeled "supportive task" and "supportive competition," combining affective concern for students as people with an emphasis on working hard for academic rewards in a coherent, organized context.

Similar findings occur in studies of social climate with living groups. Freshmen in relationship-oriented living groups focused their attention on social concerns, had more social interests, and scored higher on impulse expression, but their academic performance was lower than expected. On the other hand, freshmen in independent (goal-oriented) living groups had a higher academic orientation and GPA than would be expected, but reported less dating, less involvement in student activities, less religious involvement, and lower academic aspirations (Moos, 1979).

Social climate dimensions, like dimensions of social support, also have been related to psychological maladjustment, psychosomatic complaints, and depression

(Holahan & Moos, 1981, 1982). Researchers have identified social climate characteristics that make an environment "high risk" for producing physical symptoms (Moos & Van Dort, 1979).

The Physical Environment

A number of dimensions of the physical, architectural, and built environment have been related to student outcomes of interest in the educational community. Among the numerous research findings in this area, some of the most compelling relate to issues of density, environmental complexity, stimulation provided by the environment, personal control over the environment, and use of territoriality mechanisms.

A number of researchers have demonstrated that the architectural and organizational properties of high-rise living spaces tend to result in lower satisfaction, higher rates of attrition, and more vandalism (Holahan & Wilcox, 1978). Highrises also were rated lower on the social climate dimensions of involvement, emotional support, order and organization, and influence, but higher on independence (Wilcox & Holahan, 1976). These same characteristics also differentiated higher floors from lower floors of a high-rise residence hall. Smaller, low-rise halls have been described as more cheerful, friendly, relaxing, spacious, and warm in comparison to larger, high-rise dorms (Bickman, Teger, Gabriele, McLaughlin, Berger, & Sunaday, 1973).

Length of corridors (and hence, number of inhabitants) has also proven to influence student feelings and behavior, with long (vs. short) corridors being associated with lower satisfaction with college, and more negative feelings toward other students in the residence hall neighborhood, less time spent socializing and studying in the hall, more residence-related problems, and more reported difficulty in controlling interactions with others (Baum, Aiello, & Colesnick, 1978). Similarly, 10-person suites (as compared with a large hall) were seen by students as much more involving, supportive, student-controlled, and innovative (Moos, 1979). In general, it seems that cohesive and satisfying social environments are more likely to develop in smaller groups (Ford, 1975; Moos, 1976).

Density effects also can be seen when students are assigned to "triples" (three students to a room). Students assigned to triples reported less perceived privacy and control when compared to students in doubles. They were less satisfied with their privacy, their rooms, and their roommates, felt less in control of their space, decor, sleep, and sharing of personal belongings, and spent less time in their rooms. In one study, students in triples obtained lower grades; in another, adequacy of interpersonal adjustment and academic performance were inversely related. The authors interpreted this latter finding as indicating that so much time and effort went into making interpersonal adjustments that less time was left for academic pursuits (Baron, Mandel, Adams, & Griffen, 1976; Glassman, Burkhart, Grant, & Vallery, 1974).

Moos (1979) indicated that the architectural feature with the "most pervasive relationship to social climate" is the proportion of single rooms. Living groups with a larger proportion of single rooms were more oriented toward competition and less toward supportive achievement, independence, intellectuality, or relationships.

Several interventions have sought to help students gain control over their living environment through programs to increase adaptive displays of territoriality. Student "personalization" of rooms has been associated with decreased attrition from school (Hansen & Altman, 1976; Vinsel, Brown, Altman, & Foss, 1980) and from the residence halls (Schroeder, 1976), less damage, higher room occupancy, and increased academic achievement (Schroeder, 1976). In addition, early establishment of territories by roommates was associated with their stable functioning (Altman & Haythorn, 1967). West, Warner, and Schroeder (1979) noted that residence hall floors having group rooms that students could personalize and control had a greater emphasis on emotional support, academic achievement, and intellectuality.

In summary, this fifth concept—physical environment—clearly represents the environmental side of the $B = f(P \times E)$ equation, and indicates that the environment itself has a powerful influence on behavior. Although the physical environment is perhaps the least directly influenced by person variables, individuals do, of course, formally and informally change the environment to better fit their needs (as in rearranging chairs in classrooms or wearing paths through the grass).

PERSON-ENVIRONMENT INTERACTION: DEFINITIONS AND FINDINGS

Congruence is perhaps the most widely used and most powerful concept in the person-environment literature and the only truly interactional variable we will address in this review. The basic notion is that outcomes for individuals and for environments will be best when there is an "optimal mismatch" between certain salient characteristics of the person and commensurate or related characteristics of the environment. This optimal mismatch allows for comfort, psychological safety, ability to complete the task (because of the matching), and also for some change or "growth" (because of the lack of congruence).

Studies of person-environment congruence are legion and have used a bewildering variety of concepts and measures for person and environment. In general, "good" person-environment fit has been related to stimulation of achievement (Jackson, 1985; Schroeder & Jackson, 1987); better performance (Amidon & Flanders, 1961; Bauer, 1975; Beach, 1960; Grimes & Allinsmith, 1961; McKeachie, 1961; Pervin, 1968; Smelser, 1961); increased satisfaction (Holland, 1968; Pervin, 1967; Pervin & Rubin, 1967; Pervin & Smith, 1968); and successful coping behavior (Walsh & Lewis, 1972; Walsh & Russell, 1969). "Poor" person-environment fit has been related to dissatisfaction (Bauer, 1975; Holland, 1968); greater stress and strain (Huebner, 1975; Tracey & Sherry, 1984); and higher rates of psychological disorder (Moos, 1976). Some studies, however, have found that low person-environment congruence (i.e., low need-press congruence as defined by Stern, 1970) stimulates achievement (Kirkland, 1967; Lauterbach & Vielhaber, 1966; Pace, 1964).

In applications of particular interest to those who function in an ac₂ concepts such as conceptual level (Hunt, 1975), ego development (Lo Weathersby, 1981), and level of cognitive development (Widick & Si ......) have been used to describe relevant student attributes and to identify and describe academic environments and tasks in which such students would perform better or develop toward desired goals. Thus, for example, students at lower conceptual levels have been found to profit more from structured teaching approaches, whereas students at higher conceptual levels have been found to profit from lower structure and to be less affected by variations in structure (Hunt, 1966; Moos, 1979).

Developmental theorists advocate creating teaching environments and practices that are congruent with the developmental levels of students, but which also use minor discrepancies between the students' actual experience in a learning situation and their current beliefs and preferences in order to help the students move to a more advanced developmental level (i.e., the optimal mismatch). Researchers using Perry's scheme of intellectual development, for example, report that when students are matched to teaching techniques that correspond to their developmental level (including the growth-stimulating optimal incongruence), they demonstrate superior substantive mastery and developmental progress when compared with students in traditional classes (Stephenson & Hunt, 1977; Widick, Knefelkamp, & Parker, 1975).

Researchers have identified specific teaching practices that facilitate learning and progress for students at various developmental levels. For example, dualistic students are identified as needing direct experience (Sprinthall, 1973) and structure (Hunt, 1971; Jacob, 1957). Incorporating these elements provides needed support or congruence. For these students, challenge or a degree of incongruence can be provided by presenting materials and exercises with a relativistic perspective, such as presenting content with conflicting points of view. On the other hand, relativistic students need and find support in latitude to direct their own learning (Mann, Arnold, Binder, Cytrnbaum, Newan, Ringwald, Ringwald, & Rosenwein, 1970), a wide range of alternatives, and the opportunity to experiment without failure. For these students, challenge involves confrontation that requires them to focus on intellectual and personal commitment (e.g., drawing conclusions), indirect experience, and an extensive degree of freedom. Both dualistic and relativistic groups were seen to profit from and find support in a trusting, personal atmosphere (Widick et al., 1975).

ISSUES IN ASSESSING THE ENVIRONMENT

No consensus exists about whether to define the environment as "real," existing independently of observation, or "ideal," existing only in terms of perceptions. There also is a lack of consensus about whether the environment is best understood as "objective," transcending any one individual's perception, or "subjective," private and nongeneralizable beyond oneself.

This conceptual dilemma is translated into differing opinions about how to measure the environment: by perceptions or by direct measures of behaviors, physical characteristics, and observable events. Barker (1968), Craik (1971), and Sommer (1969) argued for a "real" and "objective" approach, whereas Lewin (1936), Magnusson (1971), Pace (1969), Pervin (1967), and Stern (1970) advocated the "ideal" view.

Over the years a number of methods for defining and measuring persons, environments, and their interactions have been developed. These generally can be classified through a modification of Menne's scheme (1967), which includes demographic, perceptual, and behavioral types of measures. In this modification, methods and instruments can be classified as perceptual (i.e., ideal), objective (i.e., real), or multimethod.

Perceptual methods are the best developed and most frequently used methods in university studies. Assessments consist of individuals' responding to a series of descriptive statements that yield global characterizations of the setting along various scales or factors. Individual responses generally are aggregated to arrive at consensual perceptions, although individual (subjective) scores also may be calculated.

Objective methods make use of three primary approaches to assessment: demographic, behavioral, or physical. Demographic approaches are primarily descriptive, and in the university environment traditionally are concerned with environmental variables such as institutional size, student ability level, faculty descriptors, library holdings, and so forth. Objective methods also may include measurement of human aggregate characteristics, such as the number of students with various MBTI profiles or Holland codes (Huebner, 1989a).

The behavioral approach may use several different assessment techniques: direct observation of behavior, self-report, and interviewing. Physical environmental measures generally consist of observation and measurement of various "real" features of a physical environment, including the natural and built environments, temperature, density, and so forth. This methodology also is concerned with observing and discovering how the environment is used and adapted. These approaches have not been defined specifically with respect to the campus setting or used much in campus-based research.

Multimethod approaches attempt to combine elements of several different approaches in one instrument. Pragmatic (generally non-theory based) techniques typically fall into the multimethod category.

Reviews of a wide variety of assessment techniques are available (Huebner, 1989b; Walsh, 1973). Because of limited space, we will confine our review here to measures of the major constructs we identified earlier.

Measuring Heterogeneity/Homogeneity

There is no single accepted way of measuring heterogeneity/homogeneity. Demographic measures such as age, socioeconomic status, ethnic origin, educational background, and personality attributes can be used to gain some indication of the degree of internal variability or consistency in the population. Researchers have used devices such as the MBTI type table to organize information about the MBTI scores of individuals within a setting that reveals the extent of variability within the group. The Environmental Assessment Technique (Astin & Holland, 1961) also can be used to indicate the extent to which the environment resembles primarily one vocational type or a mixture of types, a concept Holland labeled "differentiation." Because of the variety of constructs along which a heterogeneity/homogeneity continuum can be constructed, the possibilities for measurement are varied and numerous.

Measuring the Support/Challenge Balance

Because challenge and support are related to congruence and to heterogeneity, knowledge about a setting's status with respect to those variables will provide a good deal of insight about the degree of support and challenge students experience. The greater the incongruence between the setting and an individual student or student group, the greater is the challenge and the less the support. Likewise, the greater the diversity within a group, the greater is the challenge and the less the support.

Schroeder (1976) and Kalsbeek, Rodgers, Marshall, Denny, and Nicholls (1982) identified a number of other variables that may be indicators of challenge in a residence hall setting: high density due to long, narrow, double-loaded corridors; small cell-like rooms that must accommodate diverse functions; lack of privacy; heterogeneity between roommates and among floormates; developmental level of residents, built-in furniture, size and complexity of the setting, and size and complexity of the university. On the other hand, support can be gauged from variables such as the presence of student and professional staff and low student/staff ratios, and the presence of upper-class role models. Based on other studies reviewed earlier in this chapter, we also presume that support could occur in such variables as clear rules and procedures, open channels of communication, and ability to personalize one's own space. Some of these variables are measurable using Moos's measures of social climate, which are discussed later.

Kalsbeek et al. (1982) and Schroeder (1976) used the Myers-Briggs Type Indicator to arrange various combinations of student personality types in a suite-mate setting along a support/challenge continuum. They identified identical matches on all four MBTI processes as a "pure" or "compatible" matching strategy and concluded that such a maximally supportive strategy may be the best arrangement when the residence hall is especially challenging in other respects or when students are new and unintegrated or in developmental transition. What they label the "dominant" or "complimentary" strategy (matching on the most preferred process, with other processes different) was the next most supportive and was identified as perhaps ideal for most situations. More challenging would be the "auxiliary" strategy, in which individuals would have their second most preferred process in common, and the "external" strategy, in which the only element in common would be the preferred process for dealing with the external world. MBTI scores can thus be used to assess one element of the degree of support and challenge in a residence hall setting. Additional information on these matching strategies is presented in Schroeder and Jackson (1987).

Somewhat similar effects can be attained by aggregating students in rooms, suites, floors, or halls according to academic major or interests (e.g., active on football team or desire to speak French in the residence hall), or by allowing students to self-select.

Recently, Jacobsen and her colleagues (Jacobsen, Hurst, & Collins, 1985) devised a scale to measure the support substructure of a university, along with opportunity and reward substructures as defined by Blocher (1978). This Student Affairs Inventory consists of 50 items in Likert-type format. It measures whether various features are "currently present" or "preferred."

Measuring Social Support

Researchers have defined social support in various ways. In part because of the multitude of definitions, a plethora of unrelated assessment devices exists. In most cases, researchers have developed their own instruments for particular studies, designed to measure particular conceptions of social support. However, several potentially useful standardized, multidimensional instruments have been developed recently. Several of these scales, plus a number of others, have been given a careful psychometric review by Heitzmann and Kaplan (1988).

The Norbeck Social Support Questionnaire (Norbeck, Lindsey, & Carrieri, 1981) focuses on interpersonal transactions and includes subscales named: Total Functional Support, Total Network, and Total Loss. Brandt and Weinert's Personal Resource Questionnaire (1981) is divided into two parts. Part 1 provides descriptive information about individuals' social resources and satisfaction with those resources. Part 2 contains a 25-item scale using a Likert-type format, based on a model of the relational functions of social support. Part 2 includes six subscales: Intimacy, Social Integration, Nurturance, Worth, Assistance, and Self-Help.

The Inventory of Socially Supportive Behaviors (Barrera, Sandler, & Ramsey, 1981) is a 40-item questionnaire that focuses on social processes. Respondents use a Likert-type format to indicate the frequency with which they have received various types of help from others. The Interpersonal Network Questionnaire (Pearson, 1983) includes three scales developed from 31 items: Mutuality, Network Size, and Frequency of Contact. It is designed to aid in network analysis and is built around constructs describing social network morphology.

Counseling Center staff at the University of Utah modified the Arizona Social Support Interview Schedule (Barrera, 1980) for use in a large-scale epidemiological study. The new instrument, The Social Support Questionnaire (Ostrow, Paul, Oritt, & Dark, 1981), measures total network support size, type of support received, as well as the type of support individuals seek during particularly stressful events. In addition, the instrument measures conflictive network size, general availability of support, and satisfaction with support.

Social support also can be measured via the Family Relationship Index (FRI) [derived from the Family Environment Scale (FES) (Moos, 1974; Moos & Moos,

1981)] and the Work Relationships Index (WRI) [derived from the Work Environment Scale (WES), (Moos & Insel, 1974)]. The FES measures family social climate using 10 subscales. The FRI is based on three subscales that pertain to the "relationship" domain of the FES. These three subscales are Cohesion, measuring the degree to which family members are helpful and supportive of one another; Expressiveness, measuring the extent to which family members are openly encouraged to express their feelings directly; and Conflict, measuring the extent to which open expression of anger, aggression, and conflict are characteristic of the family.

The WES assesses individual perceptions of the work environment on 10 subscales. The WRI is based on three subscales that compose the relationship domain. These subscales are Peer Cohesion, measuring the extent to which co-workers are friendly and supportive; Staff Support, measuring the extent to which management is supportive of workers and encourages workers to be supportive of each other; and Involvement, the extent to which workers are concerned with and committed to their jobs.

Assessing Social Climate

Moos and his colleagues developed a series of parallel social climate scales. Particularly relevant to students' development are the University Residence Environment Scale (URES) (Moos & Gerst, 1974) and the Classroom Environment Scale (CES) (Moos & Trickett, 1974). The rationale underlying these scales is that "the consensus of individuals characterizing an environment constitutes a measure of the social climate of that environment" (Moos & Van Dort, 1979, p. 33). Each of these scales purports to describe the consensually perceived "personality" of the environment. This is accomplished by asking respondents to describe their usual patterns of behavior in the environment and their subjective impressions of the environment. Each instrument measures dimensions of personal development or goal orientation, relationships, and system maintenance/system change. Specific subscales that pertain to each of these dimensions vary from instrument to instrument.

The URES consists of 100 items that fall into 10 subscales, each of which measures the emphasis on one dimension of living-group climate. In the URES, the relationship dimension is represented by the Involvement and Emotional Support subscales. The subscales assess the extent to which students and staff support and help one another and the extent to which students are involved in their residence hall. Personal growth/development dimensions are represented by the Independence and Traditional Social Orientation subscales, which measure the emphasis on personal and social maturation, and by the Competition, Academic Achievement, and Intellectuality subscales, which measure emphasis on different aspects of academic growth. The three subscales of Order and Organization, Student Influence, and Innovation assess the system maintenance/system change dimension, tapping information about the structure of the hall organization and about the processes and likelihood of organizational change.

The Classroom Environment Scale (CES) consists of 90 items that form nine scales. Relationship dimensions are measured by three subscales: Involvement, Affiliation, and Teacher Support. Involvement reflects the extent to which students become involved in the class, Affiliation measures student friendship and the extent of mutual help and support, and Teacher Support measures the extent to which teachers are supportive of students. Two scales, Task Orientation and Competition, measure the personal growth/goal orientation dimensions. Task Orientation and Competition assess the emphasis on completion of planned materials and sticking to the subject matter, and the emphasis on competition and the difficulty of achieving good grades. System maintenance and change dimensions are measured by four subscales: Order and Organization, Rule Clarification, and Teacher Control, which reflect the emphasis on keeping the classroom functioning in an orderly, clear, and coherent manner, and Innovation, which assesses the degree of variety, novelty, and change in the classroom setting.

In addition to Form R of the URES and CES, which measure student perceptions of the actual environment, Moos and his colleagues developed Form E, which measures expectations of the classroom environment, and Form I, which measures the individuals' ideal living environment.

Measuring the Physical Environment

Much of the research on the effects of physical environmental properties has come from academic areas unconnected to student development—for example, environmental psychology, architecture, and archaeology (See Craik, 1973; Rapoport, 1982; Sommer, 1972; Steele, 1973). Few instruments or methodologies have been developed for or adapted to the college campus as a whole. The residence hall environment, however, is one area that has received serious study.

The impact of campus residence environments has been studied primarily by direct observation, and conceptually through several constructs: density, complexity, stimulation, and privacy, for example. These have been measured, or, more accurately, inferred through the presence or absence of various features of the "built environment" such as high-rise/low-rise dorms, suites versus floors, triples versus doubles versus singles, and "hard architecture"—built-in furniture, institutional decor, and so forth (Sommer, 1974). Thus halls with more floors and more students have been identified as more dense, complex, and stimulating. Although little effort has been made to differentiate these concepts from one another, it should be possible, following the examples of Galle, Gove, and McPherson (1972), to measure several of their different dimensions to discover how each relates to various outcomes.

Student use of territoriality mechanisms also has been assessed through observation—for example, by noting the use of personal items in rooms and hallways for decoration or to "mark" personal space, and the use of paint to define space. Other assessment strategies include observation of: (a) the way space is used for individual or group activities, play, or work, and (b) opportunities for privacy and the use of behavioral mechanisms for regulating privacy (e.g., verbal and paraverbal behavior, nonverbal behavior, environmentally oriented behaviors of personal space and territoriality, and culture-specific norms and rules) (Vinsel, Brown, Altman, & Foss, 1980). Outcomes in the realm of the physical environment also have been assessed primarily through observation; these include marks of vandalism or adaptive use.

Banning (1988) summarized the use of "behavioral traces" (Bechtel & Zeisel, 1987) to understand how students use the college environment. Specifically, these "traces" can be studied through: (a) by-products of use, such as erosion (e.g., paths through the grass), leftovers (e.g., garbage), and missing traces (e.g., evidence that space is not used); (b) adaptation for use, such as renovation, expansion, and informal changes; (c) displays of self, such as "markings" (signs) or affiliation messages (group t-shirts); and, (d) public messages, such as official signs and symbols or graffiti.

One of the few structured measuring devices for assessing the physical environment of residence halls was developed by Altman and his colleagues (Vinsel et al., 1980). They developed an 18-item Privacy Regulation Scale that assesses techniques students use to seek out or avoid contact with other students. They also developed a standardized method of content analysis of room decorations using eight categories. Decorations were scored in terms of area (size), number of items, diversity, and commitment (involvement with the university community).

Moos (1979) also developed a residence hall information form that focuses on the architectural and organizational characteristics of living groups. It includes questions about the number of rooms in a unit, percentage of single rooms, library or study areas, recreational facilities, dining facilities, as well as various organizational characteristics such as frequency of house meetings, educational programs, intramural activities, student influence, and decision making.

ASSESSING THE PERSON-ENVIRONMENT INTERACTION

Measuring Congruence

Conceptually, congruence is defined as the relationship between the status of two or more variables, namely person dimensions and environment dimensions. Problems in measuring congruence include the fact that many measures are static and give readings on variables at only one point in time, typically at the beginning or end of an intervention or a semester. In addition, measures attempt to isolate one dimension of an organic, holistic process, which may be necessary for the "scientific method," but in the end yield artificially mechanistic information. These criticisms aside, several methodologies for measuring congruence are worth examining.

One standard device for measuring congruence has made use of Stern's need/press concept (Stern, 1970). In this scheme, need and press are defined as commensurate dimensions of a single situation. Personal needs can be measured through the Activities Index (Pace & Stern, 1958), which consists of 300 "like/dislike" items and results in a profile of scores on 30 need scales. Environmental press can be measured through any one of several instruments based on a common format, each consisting of 300 items measuring 30 kinds of press, each of which is parallel to an analogous need scale. The environment is defined as collectively perceived and is measured by activities that are perceived to occur there. Relevant to campuses are the College Characteristics Index (Pace & Stern, 1958), the Organizational Climate Index (Stern, 1970), and the Evening College Characteristics Index (Stern, 1970).

According to Holland's conceptualization of person and environment types, persons have been measured by their choice of occupation or major (hypothesized to be related to a variety of personality variables) using the Vocational Preference Inventory (Holland, 1965) or the Self-Directed Search (Holland, 1971). These instruments yield 3-point Holland codes for each person. The environment in this scheme has been conceptualized according to the predominant vocational or academic major choices of the members of the setting, which may be measured by the Environmental Assessment Technique (Astin & Holland, 1961) or by ascertaining the dominant Holland code types for members of the community. Individuals may then be identified according to their degree of congruence with the dominant themes of the aggregate for that setting.

In a similar vein, personality measures such as the Myers-Briggs Type Indicator (Myers, 1962, 1976) have been used to measure individual preferences (in this case using four bipolar scales reflecting Jungian personality constructs) and also to measure the "press" of the human aggregate (environment), which is defined according to the predominant preferences of members of the community.

An additional method of measuring congruence is to look at "ideal" and "real" perceptions of the environment. For example, Pervin's Transactional Analysis of Personality and Environment (Pervin & Rubin, 1967) asks students to make both ideal and real ratings for concepts of self, college, faculty, administration, and students on 52 scales using an 11-point semantic differential. In this case, students define both person and environment on one measure. Congruence can be defined either for the group or for an individual. Students also provide satisfaction ratings on this same instrument. The Institutional Goals Inventory (Educational Testing Service, 1972) also can be used to yield ratings of both the currently perceived (real) and ideal environments. In fact, any number of instruments that give ratings of perceptions of the environment can be modified also to yield ideal ratings along the same dimensions. Comparisons of individual ideal versus real discrepancies or discrepancies between consensual real and consensual ideal environments (by subgroups) can then be used to identify the amount of congruence or incongruence.

As noted earlier, in academic settings researchers have achieved some success in measuring students' intellectual attributes using concepts such as ego development, moral development, cognitive development, or conceptual level and measuring degrees to which these match the tasks and attributes of various classroom environments. Other chapters in this book elaborate in some detail on the measurement of these intellectual variables.

Summary

There is little doubt that researchers in the student development area, as well as those in psychology and other disciplines, have made a substantial investment in defining salient dimensions of the Lewinian paradigm. Interventions using these concepts, however, lag far behind. Journals are not filled with accounts of outcomes for successful and intentional manipulation of the $B = f(P \times E)$ paradigm. Why not? The following factors seem to contribute to this failure:

1. We still do not know the most salient and powerful environmental variables or the most salient and powerful person (individual difference) variables to study or to manipulate in any given setting. Is this a deficiency of our theory or a testimony to its complexity?

2. The concept of interaction has not been satisfactorily defined in a way that does justice to human complexity and environmental richness. Concepts and measures tend to be static, related to single dimensions, and often do not take into account the influences of perceptions or other cognitive variables, motivations, values, attitudes, prior history and experience, groups, community or family, learning or adaptation in the interaction, and so on. These concepts and measures are far too simple (and simplistic) to account for much of the variance in behavior or other outcomes of interest. Yet, to the extent that models and paradigms have approached adequate complexity, they become unwieldy and impossible to implement.

3. We are still struggling with the problem of outcomes that matter and are measurable. What does "development" mean and how do we know when it has occurred? How do we measure changes in areas such as learning or belongingness? Although studies have looked at changes in retention, GPA, and vandalism, for example, it is not clear if we have an agreement on what the desired developmental educational outcomes are (or, what outcomes for what people), how to measure them meaningfully, and how to relate them to outcomes that may be of interest to administrators, trustees, or legislators.

4. Of the important variables we have identified, many cannot be controlled reliably because they are outside the typical range of influence of student affairs personnel (e.g., faculty teaching styles), or would be too costly to change (e.g., residence hall, student union, or other campus architectural features). These are problems of politics, technique, finances, and other practical matters.

5. Our resources are limited, and the reality is that most of our work time is spent "fighting fires," managing administrative details, and responding to requests from students, administrators, or faculty. Study and change of the sort called for in the "ecological" approach requires time to conceptualize, plan, generate support, implement, monitor, and evaluate. Few university staff realistically have that kind of time on an ongoing basis. Thus, interventions tend to be "one-shot" endeavors or are relatively simplistic and hastily carried out. The compelling vision of intentionally designed developmental and preventive interventions spelled out in Morrill, Oetting, and Hurst's (1974) "Cube" model has not become a reality—at least not on the scale predicted.

6. Perhaps the most compelling difficulty is the very complexity that makes the $B = f(P \times E)$ paradigm accurate and appealing. Literally scores of person variables "make a difference" and are affected by and in turn also affect scores of variables related to human, physical, and organizational environments. And these variables

change (some more, some less) over time as individuals and systems learn, adapt, and evolve. The set of interactions is infinite. It is not surprising that, without a guiding, unifying theory, and with only rudimentary measuring devices, we stumble in our attempts to find a way to understand and harness the power of the student-environment interaction.

Despite these difficulties, the Lewinian formulation still seems to have considerable merit. It is consistent with the most realistic, accurate, and appropriately complex understanding we have about how human beings function. Any other approach, although perhaps more easily understood or applied, will be less satisfying and less powerful. So how do we make this basic "simple" and yet extraordinarily complex view useful in our role as student development practitioners?

GOING BEYOND THE $B = f(P \times E)$ PARADIGM

David Hunt (Hunt, 1987) offered one approach to helping practitioners manage the complexity of the person-environment interaction. He spent 10 years working with teachers to help them match instructional approaches to students' conceptual level (Harvey, Hunt, & Schroder, 1961). From an analysis of his research we can draw the following conclusions:

1. Matching environments to persons can produce desired development or change. For example, grouping students homogeneously according to conceptual level and having teachers provide the appropriate amount of structure can facilitate learning and increase complexity of thought (Hunt, 1976).

2. Using a simple matching model does not explain the complexity of the *P-E* interaction. For example, when good teachers were not told the conceptual level of students or were not given specific instructional strategies, they seemed to adapt their instructional style intuitively and "match in the moment" (Hunt, 1976).

3. A person's ability to "match in the moment" is affected by his or her personal theories and involves two skills: reading—the ability to read and assess students' needs; and flexing—the ability to adapt or create an environment that responds (Hunt, 1976).

4. Practitioners may at times be hindered by their personal theories that may be narrow, constricted, and subject to "student pull"—the tendency to attend only to those student characteristics that fit practitioners' constructs or to label students in ways that inhibit the ability to "match in the moment" (Hunt, 1976).

To elicit practitioners' personal theories about the three components of the Lewinian paradigm, Hunt designed several Role Construct Repertory (REP) tests. The purpose of these exercises is to increase practitioners' awareness of their personal theories and to examine and expand them. For example, thinking about students as "dumb" or "not too bright" can leave a faculty member protesting that these kinds of students simply should not be admitted to college. Examining these students' characteristics in light of Perry's theory, however, might instead lead the faculty member to understand that these students think dualistically about the nature of knowledge. Broadening the faculty member's personal theories to include these new constructs frees her to explore the kinds of teaching strategies that might be effective in working with students at this developmental level; thus, the faculty member is more likely to adapt her teaching style to accommodate such students. In a similar way, when they assess environments and their effects on the *P-E* fit, practitioners' views of the environment may be static and constricted. Hunt's REP test of environments could be used to broaden constructs of the environment. For example, a residence hall floor may get a reputation for attracting troublemakers. The resident advisor (RA) may view this environment as overwhelming, out of control, and perhaps even dangerous. Describing the environment in these terms affects the RA's attitude toward interacting with students on the floor. He may begin to isolate himself, becoming self-protective to defend against what he perceives to be a hostile environment. Using the REP test to draw out the RA's personal theories and expand his constructs about environments can lead him to define the environment in different terms, or in other words, self-correct his personal theories. This redefinition can change the way he responds to the members of the environment, which in turn can change the overall tone of the environment.

Thus, one answer to the question of how to make the $B = f(P \times E)$ paradigm manageable in our role as student development practitioners is to focus on the practitioner as a key variable in the $B = f(P \times E)$ paradigm. How the practitioner defines the $B = f(P \times E)$ variables may exert as much influence on the outcomes of the interaction as would the influence of a formal approach to match persons and environments.

Student development practitioners may uncover their personal theories when they participate in a consultative relationship similar to that developed by Parker and Lawson (1978). This consultation model, initially developed to help faculty adapt their teaching to meet student learning needs, also could be adapted to help student development practitioners respond more easily to a whole range of student developmental needs.

REFERENCES

Altman, I., & Haythorn, W.W. (1967). The ecology of isolated groups. *Behavioral Science, 12*, 169–182.

Amidon, E., & Flanders, N.A. (1961). The effects of direct and indirect teacher influence on dependent-prone students learning geometry. *Journal of Educational Psychology, 52*, 286–291.

Astin, A.W., & Holland, J. (1961). The environmental assessment technique: A way to measure college environments. *Journal of Educational Psychology, 52*, 308–316.

Banning, J.H. (1988). Behavioral traces: A concept for campus ecologists. *The Campus Ecologist, 6*(2).

Barker, R.G. (1968). *Ecological psychology: Concepts and methods for studying the environment of human behavior.* Stanford, CA: Stanford University Press.

Baron, R., Mandel, D., Adams, C., & Griffen, L. (1976). Effects of social density in university residential environments. *Journal of Personality and Social Psychology, 34*, 434–446.

Barrera, M. (1980, May). *The development and application of two approaches to assessing social support.* Paper presented at the Annual Convention of the Western Psychological Association, Honolulu.

Barrera, M., Sandler, I.N., & Ramsey, T.B. (1981). Preliminary development of a scale of social support: Studies on college students. *American Journal of Community Psychology, 9,* 435–447.

Bauer, G.E. (1975). *Performance and satisfaction as a function of person environment fit.* Unpublished doctoral dissertation, University of Missouri, Columbia.

Baum, A., Aiello, J., & Colesnick, L. (1978). Crowding and personal control: Social density and the development of learned helplessness. *Journal of Personality and Social Psychology, 36,* 1000–1011.

Beach, L.R. (1960). Sociability and academic achievement in various types of learning situations. *Journal of Educational Psychology, 51,* 208–212.

Bechtel, R., & Zeisel, J. (1987). Observation: The world under a glass. In R. Bechtel, R. Marans, & W. Michelson (Eds.), *Introduction: Environmental design research.* New York: Van Nostrand Reinhold.

Berkman, L.F., & Syme, L. (1979). Social networks, host resistance and mortality: A nine-year follow-up of Alameda County residents. *American Journal of Epidemiology, 109,* 186–204.

Bickman, L., Teger, A., Gabriele, T., McLaughlin, C., Berger, M., & Sunaday, E. (1973). Dormitory density and helping behavior. *Environment and Behavior, 5,* 465–490.

Blocher, D.H. (1974). Toward an ecology of student development. *Personnel and Guidance Journal, 52,* 360–365.

Blocher, D.H. (1978). Campus learning environments and the ecology of student development. In J.H. Banning (Ed.), *Campus ecology: A perspective for student affairs* (pp. 17–23). Cincinnati, OH: National Association of Student Personnel Administrators.

Bloom, A. (1988). *The closing of the American mind.* New York: Touchstone.

Brandt, P.A., & Weinert, C. (1981). The PRQ: A social support measure. *Nursing Research, 5,* 277–280.

Chickering, A.W. (1969). *Education and identity.* San Francisco: Jossey-Bass.

Chickering, A.W., & Associates. (1981). *The modern American college.* San Francisco: Jossey-Bass.

Cohen, S. (1988). Psychosocial models of the role of social support in the etiology of physical disease. *Health Psychology, 7*(3), 269–297.

Cohen, S., & Wills, T.A. (1985). Stress, social support, and the buffering hypotheses. *Psychological Bulletin, 98,* 310–357.

Craik, K.H. (1971). The assessment of places. In P. McReynolds (Ed.), *Advances in psychological assessment* (pp. 40–62). Palo Alto, CA: Science and Behavioral Books.

Craik, K.H. (1973). Environmental psychology. In P.H. Mussen & M.R. Rossenzweis (Eds.), *Annual review of psychology, 24,* 403–422.

Educational Testing Service. (1972). *The institutional goals inventory.* Princeton, NJ: Author.

Feldman, K.A., & Newcomb, T.M. (1969). *The impact of college on students.* San Francisco: Jossey-Bass.

Ford, J. (1975). *Paradigms and fairy tales.* London: Routledge & Kegan Paul.

Galle, O.R., Gove, W.R., & McPherson, J.M. (1972). Population density and pathology: What are the relations for man? *Science, 176,* 23–30.

Glassman, J.B., Burkhart, B.R., Grant, R.D., & Vallery, G.G. (1974). *Density, expectation, and extended task performance: An experiment in the natural setting.* Unpublished manuscript.

Gottlieb, B.H. (1983). Social support as a focus for integrative research in psychology. *American Psychologist, 38,* 278–287.

Grimes, J.W., & Allinsmith, W. (1961). Compulsivity, anxiety and school achievement. *Merrill-Palmer Quarterly, 7,* 247–271.

Hansen, W., & Altman, I. (1976). Decorating personal spaces: A descriptive analysis. *Environment and Behavior, 8,* 491–504.

Harvey, O.J., Hunt, D.E., & Schroder, H.M. (1961). *Conceptual systems and personality organization.* New York: Wiley.

Heitzmann, C.A., & Kaplan, R.M. (1988). Assessment of methods for measuring social support. *Health Psychology, 7*(1), 75–109.

Hirsch, B.J. (1980). Natural support systems and coping with major life changes. *American Journal of Psychology, 8*(2), 159–172.

Hodgkinson, H.L. (1985). *All one system: Demographics of education, kindergarten through graduate school.* Washington, DC: The Institute for Educational Leadership.

Holahan, C.J., & Moos, R.H. (1981). Social support and psychological distress: A longitudinal analysis. *Journal of Abnormal Psychology, 90*(4), 365–370.

Holahan, C.J., & Moos, R.H. (1982). Social support and adjustment: Predictive benefits of social climate indices. *American Journal of Community Psychology, 10*(4), 403–414.

Holahan, C., & Wilcox, B. (1978). Residential satisfaction and friendship formation in high and low-rise student housing: An interactional analysis. *Journal of Educational Psychology, 70,* 237–241.

Holland, J.L. (1961). Creative and academic performance among talented adolescents. *Journal of Educational Psychology, 52,* 136–147.

Holland, J.L. (1965). *Manual for the Vocational Preference Inventory* (6th rev.). Palo Alto, CA: Consulting Psychologists Press.

Holland, J.L. (1968). Explorations of a theory of vocational choice: VI. A longitudinal study using a sample of typical college students. *Journal of Applied Psychology, 52,* 136–147.

Holland, J.L. (1971). *The self-directed search.* Palo Alto, CA: Consulting Psychologists Press.

Holmes, T.H., Joffe, J.R., Ketcham, J.W., & Sheehy, T.F. (1961). Experimental study of prognosis. *Journal of Psychosomatic Research, 5,* 235–252.

Huebner, L.A. (1975). *An ecological assessment: Person-environment fit.* Unpublished doctoral dissertation, Colorado State University, Fort Collins.

Huebner, L.A. (1983, June). *The status of theory in campus ecology.* Paper presented at the First Annual Campus Ecology Symposium, Pingree Park, CO.

Huebner, L.A. (1989a). Progress in the ecological approach. In U. Delworth & G. Hanson, *Student services: A handbook for the profession* (2nd ed.) (pp. 165–208). San Francisco: Jossey-Bass.

Huebner, L.A. (1989b). *Research and assessment from an ecological perspective: Mental health and development.* Unpublished manuscript, Saint Louis University, St. Louis, MO.

Hunt, D.E. (1966). A conceptual systems change model and its application to education. In O.J. Harvey (Ed.), *Experience, structure, and adaptability* (pp. 277–302). New York: Springer.

Hunt, D.E. (1971). *Matching models in education.* Toronto: Ontario Institute for Studies in Education.

Hunt, D.E. (1975). Person-environment interaction: A challenge found wanting before it was tried. *Review of Educational Research, 45,* 209–210.

Hunt, D.E. (1976). Teachers' adaptation: "Reading" and "flexing" to students. *Journal of Teacher Education, 27,* 268–275.

Hunt, D.E. (1987). *Beginning with ourselves: In practice, theory, and human affairs.* Cambridge, MA: Brookline Books.

Jackson, G.S. (1985). *The impact of roommates on development: A causal analysis of the effects of roommate personality congruence, satisfaction, and initial developmental status, on end-of-quarter developmental status and grade point average.* Unpublished doctoral dissertation, Auburn University, Auburn, AL.

Jacob, P. (1957). *Changing values in college: An exploratory study of the impact of college teaching.* New York: Harper.

Jacobsen, J.K., Hurst, J.C., & Collins, J.R. (1985, June). *An assessment of critical factors in measuring the quality of learning environments.* Paper presented at the Third Campus Ecology Symposium, Pingree Park, CO.

Joseph, J. (1980). *Social affiliation, risk fact status, and coronary heart disease: A cross-sectional study of Japanese-American men.* Unpublished doctoral dissertation, University of California-Berkeley.

Kaiser, L.R. (1972). *The ecosystem model: Designing campus environments.* Boulder, CO: Western Interstate Commission on Higher Education.

Kalsbeek, D., Rodgers, R., Marshall, D., Denny, D., & Nicholls, G. (1982). Balancing challenge and support: A study of degrees of similarity in suitemate personality type and perceived differences in challenge and support in a residence hall environment. *Journal of College Student Personnel, 23*(5), 434–442.

Kaplan, B.H., Cassel, J.C., & Gore, S.S. (1977). Social support and health. *Medical Care, 15,* 47–58.

Kirkland, M.C. (1967). An investigation of the characteristic needs, beta presses, and certain resultant behaviors of selected Auburn University freshmen. *Dissertation Abstracts,* 8272B.

Lauterbach, C.G., & Vielhaber, D.P. (1966). Need-press and expectation-press indices as predictors of college achievement. *Educational and Psychological Measurement, 26,* 1965–1972.

Lewin, K. (1936). *Principles of topological psychology.* New York: McGraw-Hill.

Loevinger, J. (1976). *Ego development: Conceptions and theories.* San Francisco: Jossey-Bass.

Magnusson, D. (1971). An analysis of situational dimensions. *Perceptual and Motor Skills, 32,* 851–867.

Mann, R.D., Arnold, S.M., Binder, J.L., Cytrnbaum, S., Newan, B.M., Ringwald, B.E., Ringwald, J.W., & Rosenwein, R. (1970). *The college classroom: Conflict, change and learning.* New York: Wiley.

McKeachie, W.J. (1961). Motivation, teaching methods, and college learning. In M.R. Jones (Ed.), *Nebraska symposium on motivation* (pp. 111–142). Lincoln: University of Nebraska Press.

Menne, J.W. (1967). Techniques for evaluating the college environment. *Journal of Educational Measurement, 4,* 219–225.

Moos, R.H. (1974). Systems for the assessment and classification of human environments: An overview. In R.H. Moos & P. Insel (Eds.), *Issues in social ecology* (pp. 5–27). Palo Alto, CA: National Press.

Moos, R.H. (1976). *The human context: Environmental determinants of behavior.* New York: Wiley-Interscience.

Moos, R.H. (1979). *Evaluating educational environments: Procedures, measures, findings, and policy implementations.* San Francisco: Jossey-Bass.

Moos, R.H. (1984). Context and coping: Toward a unifying conceptual framework. *American Journal of Community Psychology, 12,* 5–23.

Moos, R.H., & Gerst, M. (1974). *University residence environment scale manual.* Palo Alto, CA: Consulting Psychologists Press.

Moos, R.H., & Insel, P. (1974). *Issues in social ecology.* Palo Alto, CA: National Press.

Moos, R.H., & Moos, B. (1981). *Family environment scale manual.* Palo Alto, CA: Consulting Psychologists Press.

Moos, R.H., & Trickett, E.J. (1974). *Manual: Classroom environment scale.* Palo Alto, CA: Consulting Psychologists Press.

Moos, R.H., & Van Dort, B. (1979). Student physical symptoms and the social climate of college living groups. *American Journal of Community Psychology, 7*(1), 31–45.

Morrill, W.H., Oetting, E.R., & Hurst, J.C. (1974). Dimensions of counselor functioning. *Personnel and Guidance Journal, 52*(6), 354–360.

Myers, I. (1962). *Myers-Briggs Type Indicator: Manual.* Princeton, NJ: Educational Testing Service.

Myers, I. (1976). *Introduction to type.* Gainesville, FL: Center for Application of Psychological Type.

Nafziger, D.H., Holland, J.L., Helms, S.T., & McPartland, J.M. (1974). Applying an occupational classification to the work histories of young men and women. *Journal of Vocational Behavior, 5*, 331–345.

Norbeck, J.S., Lindsey, A.M., & Carrieri, V.L. (1981). The development of an instrument to measure social support. *Nursing Research, 30*, 264–269.

Norbeck, J.S., & Tilden, V.P. (1983). Life stress, social support and emotional disequilibrium in complications of pregnancy: A prospective, multivariant study. *Journal of Health and Social Behavior, 24*, 30–45.

Osipow, S.H., Ashby, J.D., & Wall, H.W. (1966). Personality types and vocational choice: A test of Holland's theory. *Personnel and Guidance Journal, 45*, 37–42.

Ostrow, E., Paul, S.C., Oritt, E., & Dark, V. (1981). *Utah social network rating scale.* Unpublished manuscript, University of Utah, Counseling Center, Salt Lake City.

Pace, C.R. (1964). *The influence of academic and student subcultures in college and university environments.* USOE Cooperative Research Project 1083. Los Angeles: University of California.

Pace, C.R. (1969). *College and university environment scales technical manual* (2nd ed.). Princeton, NJ: Educational Testing Service.

Pace, C.R. (1984). *Measuring the quality of college student experiences.* Los Angeles: Higher Education Research Institute, The University of California.

Pace, C.R., & Stern, G. (1958). An approach to the measurement of psychological characteristics of college environments. *Journal of Educational Psychology, 49*, 269–277.

Parker, C.A., & Lawson, J.M. (1978). From theory to practice to theory: Consulting with college faculty. *Personnel and Guidance Journal, 56*, 424–427.

Pearson, J.E. (1983). *The relationship between social support and Type A behavior pattern on appraisal accuracy.* Unpublished doctoral dissertation, Catholic University of America, Washington, DC.

Pearson, J.E. (1986). The definition and measurement of social support. *Journal of Counseling and Development, 64*, 390–395.

Pervin, L.A. (1967). A twenty-college study of student × college interaction using TAPE: Rationale, reliability, and validity. *Journal of Educational Psychology, 58*(5), 290–302.

Pervin, L.A. (1968). Performance and satisfaction as a function of individual-environment fit. *Psychological Bulletin, 69*(1), 56–58.

Pervin, L.A., & Rubin, D.B. (1967). Student dissatisfaction with college and the college dropout: A transactional approach. *Journal of Social Psychology, 72*, 285–295.

Pervin, L.A., & Smith, S.H. (1968). Further test of the relationship between satisfaction and perceived self-environment similarity. *Perceptual and Motor Skills, 26*, 835–838.

Pilisuk, M., & Froland, C. (1978). Kinship, social networks, social support and health. *Social Science and Medicine, 12*, 273–280.

Rapoport, A. (1982). *The meaning of the built environment: A non-verbal communication.* Beverly Hills, CA: Sage.

Rodgers, R.F. (1984, June). *Student development through campus ecology.* Paper presented at the Second Annual Campus Ecology Symposium, Pingree Park, CO.

Schroeder, C.C. (1976). New strategies for structuring residential environments. *Journal of College Student Personnel, 17*, 386–390.

Schroeder, C., & Jackson, C.S. (1987). Designing residential environments. In J. Provost & S. Anchors (Eds.), *Applications of the Myers-Briggs Type Indicator in higher education* (pp. 65–68). Palo Alto, CA: Consulting Psychologists Press.

Schroeder, C.C., Warner, R., & Malone, D. (1980). Effects of assignment to living units by personality type on environmental perceptions and student development. *Journal of College Student Personnel, 21*, 443–448.

Seeman, T.E., & Syme, S.L. (1987). Social networks and coronary artery disease: A comparison of the structure and function of social relations as predictors of disease. *Psychosomatic Medicine, 49*, 340–353.

Smelser, W.T. (1961). Dominance as a factor in achievement and perception in cooperative problem solving interactions. *Journal of Abnormal and Social Psychology, 62*, 535–542.

Sommer, R. (1969). *Personal space: The behavioral basis of design.* Englewood Cliffs, NJ: Prentice-Hall.

Sommer, R. (1972). *Design awareness.* San Francisco: Rinehart.

Sommer, R. (1974). *Tight spaces: Hard architecture and how to improve it.* New York: Prentice-Hall.

Sprinthall, N. (1973). A curriculum for schools: Counselors as teachers for psychological growth. *The School Counselor, 20*, 361–369.

Steele, F.I. (1973). *Physical setting and organizational development.* Reading, MA: Addison-Wesley.

Stephenson, B., & Hunt, C. (1977). Intellectual and ethical development: A dualistic curriculum intervention for college students. *The Counseling Psychologist, 6*(4), 39–41.

Stern, G.G. (1970). *People in context: Measuring person-environment congruence in education and industry.* New York: Wiley.

Tracey, T.J., & Sherry, P. (1984). College student distress as a function of person-environment fit. *Journal of College Student Personnel, 29*, 436–442.

Vinsel, A., Brown, B., Altman, I., & Foss, C. (1980). Privacy regulation, territorial displays, and effectiveness of individual functioning. *Journal of Personality and Social Psychology, 39*, 1104–1115.

Walberg, H.J. (1969). Predicting class learning: An approach to the class as a social system. *American Educational Research Journal, 6*, 529–542.

Walsh, W.B. (1973). *Theories of person-environment interaction: Implications for the college student.* Iowa City, IA: American College Testing Program.

Walsh, W.B., & Lewis, R.O. (1972). Consistent, inconsistent, and undecided career preferences and personality. *Journal of Vocational Behavior, 2*, 174–181.

Walsh, W.B., & Russell, J.H., III. (1969). College major choice and personal adjustment. *Personnel and Guidance Journal, 47*, 685–688.

Weathersby, R.P. (1981). Ego development. In A.W. Chickering & Associates, *The modern American college* (pp. 51–75). San Francisco: Jossey-Bass.

West, N.C., Warner, R.W., Jr., & Schroeder, C.C. (1979). The group room: An aid to student development. *Journal of College and University Student Housing, 9*(1), 20–24.

Widick, C.C., Knefelkamp, L.L., & Parker, C.A. (1975). The counselor as developmental instructor. *Counselor Education and Supervision, 14*, 286–296.

Widick, C., & Simpson, D. (1978). Developmental concepts in college instruction. In C.A. Parker (Ed.), *Encouraging development in college students* (pp. 27–59). Minneapolis: University of Minnesota Press.

Wilcox, B.L., & Holahan, C.J. (1976). Social ecology of the megadorm in university student housing. *Journal of Educational Psychology, 68*(4), 453–458.

PART III

APPLICATIONS OF DEVELOPMENTAL THEORY

CHAPTER 7

An Integration of Campus Ecology and Student Development: The Olentangy Project

Robert F. (Bob) Rodgers

To integrate student development and campus ecology in the practice of student affairs, Rodgers (see Chapter 3) recommended the following to student affairs practitioners:

1. Use person-environment interaction as the basic general paradigm for your work and then integrate developmental and other relevant theories into it;
2. Person-environment interaction models serve as reminders to assess three things, not just one or two of the following: (a) the *students*, (b) their *environment*, and (c) the degree of congruence or incongruence in their *interaction*;
3. Developmental and other theoretical frameworks should be used in assessment, and assessment should not be limited to common-sense and atheoretical approaches.
4. Use *multiple kinds* of developmental and other theoretical frameworks to increase the degree of individuation in environmental designs;
5. To determine whether environmental redesign is needed, use criteria derived from theories and your own educational values to analyze and make judgments on the interaction data;
6. If redesign is needed, the nature of the redesign also derives from the assessment data as evaluated by theoretical criteria; and finally,
7. The evaluation of designs or redesigns also should use theoretical as well as atheoretical variables applicable to a given project.

These recommendations were used in implementing an integrated campus ecology/student development project called the Olentangy Project. This project used multiple developmental and other theories (a) to assess students, their environment, and the degree of congruence in their interactions, (b) to redesign the environment, and (c) to evaluate the effects or outcomes of the redesigned programs over 3 years of implementation. This chapter describes the Olentangy Project and the research results regarding its effects, and thus illustrates the principles used in integrating campus ecology and student development.

THE OLENTANGY PROJECT

A modified ecosystems process (Aulepp & Delworth, 1978) was used in developing the Olentangy Project. There was a project coordinator and representatives of all levels of administration, staff, and students involved with the Olentangy halls. Moos's (1979) theory of person-environment interactions provided the basic conceptual framework for the initial assessments of the students and environment. Perry's (1970) theory of intellectual development and the Jung/Myers (Myers, 1980) theory of personality type were integrated into Moos's conceptual framework and the ecosystems use of the data.

Assessment of the Environment and Students Using Moos's Social Ecological Framework

Moos's (1979) work on social ecology recommended that researchers assess environments in terms of the *physical setting, organizational factors*, the *human aggregate*, and *perceived social climate*. The *physical setting* refers to the nature and design of space and architectural characteristics. *Organizational factors* include size of organizational units, staff-student ratios, governance structures, political climate, and programming emphases. The *human aggregate* includes factors such as gender, age, cultural diversity, and expectations. The *perceived social climate* mediates the influence of the other three factors and includes perceptions of various dimensions of interpersonal relationships, personal growth and goal orientation, and system maintenance and change. In this project, all of these dimensions were used in the initial assessment, and perceived social climate also was used to evaluate the redesigned environment.

Physical Environment

The Olentangy residence halls consist of two 24-story towers, divided into three houses of 735, 1010, and 827 residents each. One half of one tower is taken for administrative space and contains the 735-resident house. The other tower contains the 1010- and 827-resident houses. Each house contains identical 16-person suites as the basic living unit for students (see Figure 1). Each suite contains a common living room, a bath, and study areas and bedrooms for four students.

Each floor (see Figure 2) contains six suites plus living space for a resident advisor and maintenance space. There are three non-suite floors in the building: one contains living quarters for the full-time professional staff as well as maintenance and housekeeping space, one houses cafeterias and kitchens, and one contains the

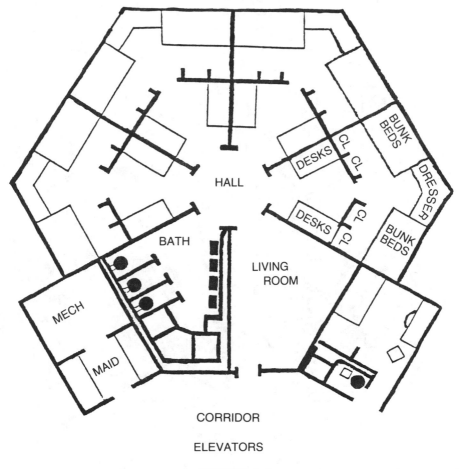

FIGURE 1
Olentangy Suite Plan

main office and some recreational and lounge space for residents. Recreational and lounge spaces have been kept at a minimum because a branch of the student union is located nearby, and the initial designers considered the branch union's public space to be "space for the residents of the Olentangy houses" (G.B. Carson, personal conversation, 1970).

In the suites where students live, all desks, bookcases, and chests are bolted to the walls or floors of the building. This allowed the furniture to be considered "part of the building per se," and thus the furniture was purchased with the same bond funds as the construction of the building at a very low interest rate. Movable furniture would not have been "part of the building" and such furniture would have had to be purchased from other funds at higher interest rates. The initial design decision was to save money with the lower interest rate and bolt the furniture to the building.

FIGURE 2
Olentangy Floor Plan

The internal walls of each suite are not highly sound-resistant. When a radio or records are played anywhere in the suite at moderate sound levels, the sound can be heard in all four study-bedroom areas.

Organizational Environment

Staffing

Each house has three senior staff, one full time director, and two half-time graduate student assistant directors. There is one undergraduate resident advisor on each floor. The resident advisor-student ratios are 1:91 in these houses, compared to 1:40, 1:12, and 1:67 in other residence areas on the campus. Senior staff-student ratios are 1:300 in these houses and 1:188, 1:250, and 1:275 in the other areas.

Programming and Governance Structures

Governance is organized through a house-wide council and floor governments. Suites per se are not part of the formal governance structure. Programming efforts have focused mostly on hall and floor-level events. Intramural teams are active and organized on a one team per floor basis. Suites are not the focus for governance, programming, or intramurals.

Resident advisors meet with each suite at the beginning of the year to review rules and regulations and to suggest that members of each suite meet and negotiate standards for living together in their suite. The suite mates are encouraged to meet on their own and negotiate these standards. The resident advisor does not participate in the negotiation sessions if they are held.

Policies on Use of Space

Students cannot paint or remodel their suites. Small refrigerators, pet fish, and personal pictures are the only personalized items permitted in the suites.

Political Climate

The director of housing is new, open to changes, and supportive of the ecological study and possible redesign of the Olentangy houses. He is prepared to provide financial support. The area director is new, open to changes, and willing to undertake the Olentangy Project. Hence, the political climate is supportive of the personal and environmental assessments and possible redesign of the environment. If the political climate had not been supportive, it might have been judged that an organizational intervention would have been needed prior to or simultaneous with any attempt at implementing an ecological project such as the Olentangy Project.

Human Aggregate

The students who live in the houses are 95% freshmen, 55% men and 45% women. All three houses are coeducational. The students come from mixed socioeconomic classes; 10% to 15% are Black and 85% to 90% are White. The mean cumulative American College Test (ACT) score is 20.

In Table 1, comparative information for contract renewals of freshmen, transfer requests to a new residence hall area, and damages in terms of dollars per student per year are provided. The Olentangy houses have the lowest renewal rates, highest rates of transfer requests, and highest rates of damage of any of the residence areas.

Perceived Social Climate

Using Moos and Gerst's (1974) University Residence Environmental Scales (URES), the perceived social climate of the houses was assessed and is summarized in Figure 3 for men, women, and both men and women combined. National norms also are included. These data were collected from 200 randomly selected residents of the Olentangy houses, proportionally by house and by gender. There were 170 usable

TABLE 1
Comparative Behavioral Data

Category	Ratio of Olentangy Houses to Other Areas
Transfer request to another area	2.5 to 1
Damages ($ per student per year)	2 to 1
Renewal of contract for same hall for next year (freshmen)	
Olentangy area	1 to 4%
Area A	65%
Area B	40%

responses. The results indicate that Involvement (the degree to which there is social interaction and feelings of friendship), Support (efforts to help each other with academic and social problems and to communicate in an open and honest way), Academic Achievement (extent to which classroom concerns are a priority in the house), Intellectuality (emphasis on cultural, artistic, and other intellectual activities in the house), Order and Organization (the amount of formal structure and organization in the suite), the Student Influence (extent to which residents control the running of the house and the rules, select staff, etc.) are *significantly lower* than in national norms. On the other hand, Competition (degree to which grades, dating, and other activities are competitive in nature) is perceived as being *significantly higher* than in national norms.

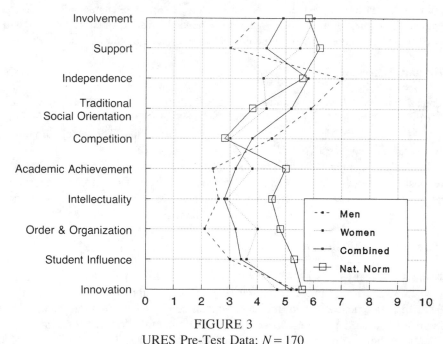

FIGURE 3
URES Pre-Test Data; $N = 170$

Analysis of the Moos Assessment Data Using
Personal-Environmental Theories

When person-environment interaction criteria associated with satisfaction and performance in physical environments are applied to these data (Schroeder, 1980), the Olentangy houses have many human and physical design problems. These criteria will be applied one at a time to the Moos assessment data.

Personalization of Space

Personalization of space means having the freedom to choose and arrange one's furnishings, lighting, decorations, color(s) of one's room(s), and so forth. Feelings of ownership, responsibility, and care for physical space seem to correlate positively with the degree to which space can be personalized (Schroeder, 1980).

Built-in or bolted-down furniture is called "hard architecture" (Sommer, 1974) because it does not permit personalization of space. Movable furniture, in contrast, permits a higher degree of personalization.

The absence of student room painting programs and strict rules about the use of a residence hall room or suite limit personalization of space. Policies permitting and programs encouraging students to paint their rooms and decorate and remodel their rooms, in contrast, lead to more personalization of space.

The Olentangy houses have mostly "hard architecture" and policies that limit personalization of space. There is no student room painting program, no remodeling, and a restricted picture hanging and decoration policy. These policies may be partially responsible for the high damage and transfer rates, low renewal rates, and students' lack of care about or feeling of ownership of the building.

Spaces for Stimulation and Privacy

Human beings apparently need space in their living environment for "stimulation," (e.g., space where recreational activities take place, music is heard, talking and dancing might be permitted) and "privacy" (e.g., space where no one else is present; it is quiet, reflective, and others keep out) (Schroeder, 1980).

The Olentangy houses maximize stimulation and minimize privacy. There is no public area on living floors and only limited public space in the building. Hence, the suite is the location for most human interactions. The design of the suites is such that privacy is difficult to find, especially given occupancy levels of 16 per suite and the fact that some walls are not sound-resistant.

Community Space

Floor and suite communities need a space where everyone can "fit" comfortably for meetings of all kinds. Space for floor meetings does not exist; hence, resident advisors must attend six separate suite meetings if they are to personalize com-

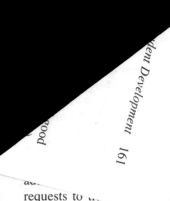

ːir floors. Suite meetings take place in the suite
ents are in the lounge, it is crowded.

sfaction

action with the houses seem to result from interactions
ɔccupancy levels, and the maturity levels of the young
ɑᴜ.   ᴊehavioral comparisons on renewal rates, damage, and
requests to ᴜ.   r areas seem to be manifestations of these interaction
problems (see Table 1).

Organizational and Programming Emphases

The organizational and programming efforts of the houses focus on the whole
building or the floor. The physical design and size of the building, however, mediate
against the effective use of these foci. Significant human interactions take place
mostly in suites rather than on a floor, and even less so in the building as a whole.
Hence, the organizational programming structures and emphases of the houses seem
to be misdirected.

Developmental Assessment of the Environment and the Students

In addition to using Moos's (1979) theory to assess the Olentangy environment,
the cognitive developmental theory of William Perry (1970) and the personality
type of Jung/Myers (Myers, 1980) also were used to assess *both* the *environment*
and the *students* of the Olentangy houses.

In terms of the Perry scheme, the positions of the students were assessed using
the Widick-Knefelkamp Sentence Stem and Essay Test (Widick & Rodgers, 1979).
The environments of the houses were assessed using the criteria that facilitate
development for persons at various Perry positions. These general criteria were
identified by Widick, Knefelkamp, and Parker (1975) as the *degree of structure* in
the environment, the *degree of diversity* presented by the environment, the *degree
of concreteness and abstractness* by which the diversity is presented, the degree to
which an *authority* is needed to model alternatives and define and facilitate the
processes to be used; and the *degree of personalness* in the interactions among
peers, and among authorities and peers.

If students are assessed as making meaning in dualistic ways (Positions 1, 2, or
3), then the residence hall environment would need to be characterized by the
following in order both to challenge the student appropriately and support him or
her as the challenge is experienced: (a) *high degrees of structure* with limited degrees
of freedom to change the structure per se; (b) an encounter with *moderate diversity*,
that is, experiencing two or three points of view on a topic and not just one or
more than three; (c) a *concrete and experiential* rather than abstract experience of
diversity; (d) an *authority to define the structure and help students process* their
concrete experience with moderate diversity; and (e) an *atmosphere as warm, trust-*

ing, and collaborative as possible in order for both positive and corrective feedback to be given and heard without defensiveness.

On the other hand, if students reason in relativistic ways (Positions 4, 5, or 6), the criteria alter radically. For these students, the environment would need to be characterized by the following in order to facilitate development: (a) *extensive diversity*, that is, two, three, or more points of view; (b) a *concrete or abstract* experience of diversity; (c) an *abstract processing* of the encounter and *narrowing toward commitment* on the topic; (d) *high degrees of structure* when a new topic is introduced followed by *low degrees of structure* with the *freedom to alter* the content or the structure per se; (e) encouragement of *self-generation* of the processes and the alternatives to control or resolve an issue; and (f) an *atmosphere* that is *as open, trusting,* and *collaborative* as possible in order for positive and corrective feedback to be given and heard without defensiveness.

The Jung/Myers (Myers, 1980) theory of personality type also provides a way of evaluating degrees of challenge and support in a person-environment interaction. In this theory, personality types are defined by preferences for either Extroversion (E) or Introversion (I) as an orientation toward the world, either Sensing (S) or Intuition (N) as a means of perception, either Thinking (T) or Feeling (F) as a mode of judgment, and either Perception (P) or Judgment (J) as an orientation for encountering and dealing with the external world of people and things. All of these functions and orientations are within every person; however, for each pair, one of the two is preferred, used most often, trusted more, and enjoyed more. If extroversion (E) is the preference of a student, for example, the student would prefer to spend time and energy in and would gain satisfaction from dealing with the external world of people, places, and things. If introversion (I) is the preference, however, the student would have an extroverted life but prefer the internal world of the mind, that is, internal thoughts, ideas, and understandings.

If sensing (S) is the preference for perception, then the student would prefer to use his or her senses in perceiving reality as it is. The student would be observant, detail-oriented, and realistic. The sensing-preference student might not trust his or her hunches about what might be. If intuition (N) is the preference, however, the student would prefer to perceive what might be, that is, the possibilities in a situation or set of ideas rather than the details of actualities.

If thinking (T) is the student's preference for judgment, then the student would tend to make decisions using impersonal, cause-and-effect logic rather than values and feelings. On the other hand, if feeling (F) is the preference, then the student would prefer to use a hierarchy of values and subjective feelings in making decisions rather than impersonal logical reasoning.

Finally, if perception (P) is the preference in dealing with the external environment, then the student would prefer flexibility and openness to new experiences in the environment, and would probably be slow to make final judgments. The student would tend to dislike highly organized, inflexible environments. Judgers (J), on the other hand, would tend to plan carefully, be organized, decide as soon as possible, and act. A judger would tend to be frustrated by lengthy debates and ambiguity.

In order to facilitate development, the Jung/Myers theory suggests strongly encouraging traditionally aged college students to seek experiences *consistent with* their type preferences, and only some experiences consistent with the opposite of their preferences. An ENFP personality type, for example, would be encouraged deliberately to seek the following kinds of experiences:

E = Actual experiences in the world or the use of ideas in the world rather than understanding ideas for their own sake;

N = Experiences that require imagination, creativity, and problem solving rather than experiences that deal with details and require realistic observation;

F = Experiences where judgments are made on the basis of sensitivity to feelings, care for another, or a set of values rather than experiences that require impersonal and logical judgment;

P = Flexible environments that do not require a lot of highly organized precise work or inflexible deadlines or schedules.

Returning now to the ecological perspective, to the extent that *other people* define the environments, Jung/Myers personality type theory can be used to define different degrees of congruence or incongruence in the person-environment interactions (Kalsbeek, Rodgers, Marshall, Denny, & Nicholls, 1982). Congruence is increased when the same types live together. Incongruence is maximized if exact opposites live together. In between are different combinations of similarities and differences. Increased degrees of similarity of type increase *support* because of the increased degrees of congruence. Increased degrees of differences in type result in increased *challenge* because of the increased congruence.

The Environment

When the Perry and the Jung/Myers criteria are used to analyze the Olentangy suites, the environment is characterized as basically *relativistic* in terms of Perry and maximally *challenging or heterogeneous* in terms of the Jung/Myers personality type theory.

In the Olentangy houses, students generally are assigned to suites randomly. This results in a maximum heterogeneity of different personality types living closely together in the 16-person suites. Heterogeneity of types introduces maximum diversity and conflict in learning styles, ways of judging interactions and activities, and preferred ways of organizing a "life-style" in the suite. Challenge is maximized; support is minimized.

In terms of Perry's theory, there are extensive degrees of diversity in the environment of a suite. When 16 rather than 2, 3, or 4 persons live together, both cultural and personality type diversity is maximized. Students intimately experience more than three (up to 15) cultural heritages and personality types.

Living in a suite is an experiential encounter; however, staff authorities are involved only somewhat with each suite. Resident advisors meet with suites to exchange information. They encourage suite mates to meet and negotiate conditions or standards for living together. They emphasize the need for standards of cleanliness in the bathroom, definitions and times for quiet hours, visitation policies, and the use of each other's possessions. Students are asked to negotiate standards for these topics on their own. The RA does not prestructure a suite meeting. Students must define their own structure for that negotiation without staff facilitation of the process. These conditions would be partially appropriate for students making meaning as Perry Relativists (Positions 4 and above). They would *not* be appropriate for students who reason in Positions 1, 2, or 3, nor would they facilitate achievement of the task of student development.

The Students

A random sample of 100 residents, proportional by gender and house, were asked to take the Widick-Knefelkamp Sentence Stem and Essay Test in order to assess their Perry levels. Sixty-five students completed and returned the instrument, and 59 of these responses were usable. The instruments were scored by two trained raters. The mean for this group was 2.546, with a ± .395 standard deviation. The qualitative modal score was 2(3). The mean was approximately halfway between Position 2 and Position 3 on the Perry scheme, and 85% of the group scored within Dualism (Positions 1, 2 and 3). These results were consistent with several years' data on random samples of 250 freshmen at the university (Rodgers, 1974–1988).

Students were also interviewed and asked to describe (a) life in their suites, (b) whether they had, in fact, negotiated standards for living together, (c) the processes used if standards had been developed, and (d) any follow-up meetings that were held on the standards.

Analyses of these data indicate that approximately 60% of the men's suites and 70% of the women's suites did attempt to negotiate standards for living together; however, 40% of the men's suites and 30% of the women's suites did not. Among suites that tried to negotiate standards, areas for which standards were developed were discussed; however, some of the students said they felt intimidated and most did not voice their opinions. Some men's and women's suites held follow-up meetings on their standards; most did not. Most suites soon failed to pay attention to their standards.

Generally, the data on life in the suites, whether standards were negotiated or not, were consistent with URES data discussed previously. Men's suites were competitive, and individualism was the norm. Support for academic and intellectual behaviors was low. Women's suites had more personal involvement and support among suite mates; however, academic achievement and intellectual concerns also were not central. Women's suites were more orderly than men's suites; however, the women in the sample expressed a desire for even more order and higher standards.

To sum up, living in the environment described with 15 other persons of this age and maturity level is very difficult. Challenge is maximized and support is minimized.

Analysis of the Developmental Person-Environment Interaction

The students, both men and women, made meaning in dualistic ways. The suite environment, both in terms of general life-style and the process used to negotiate standards, was mostly relativistic in nature. The interaction between these students and their environment is basically incongruent. Hence, one would predict dissatisfaction, attempts to escape the environment, polarization, alienation, and a lack of development. The behavioral data on requests to leave the hall, damage rates, and renewal rates are consistent with such predictions. On many dimensions, therefore, the environment seems to be *too challenging* for the students who live in suites.

To sum up, the assessment of the *environment* using person-environment interaction models and the assessment of the *environment* and the *students* using *developmental theories* both indicate problems and incongruencies between what *is* the case and what *ought* to be the case for increased satisfaction, improved performance, and development. Environmental redesign is needed if these outcomes are valued. The environment needs to become *more supportive* and *less challenging* in order for the person-environment interaction to be more developmental and satisfying.

ENVIRONMENTAL REDESIGN

In the assessments and analyses, developmental and person-environmental theories helped the staff to formulate goals and then redesign the environment in the Olentangy houses. The goals for redesign were as follows:

1. Increase support and decrease challenge as defined by the person-environment, Jung/Myers, and Perry theories;
2. Develop a sense of community in the suites and focus programming on the suites;
3. Facilitate psychosocial vector development as defined by Chickering's (1969) vectors;
4. Facilitate intellectual development as defined by the Perry (1970) scheme;
5. Provide more experiences and improve the quality of experiences among peers and between students and faculty and students and staff;
6. Lower the damage, judicial case load, and transfer request rates and raise the renewal rates.

Seven interventions were recommended in the environmental redesign. Briefly, they were as follows: (a) Remodel the physical space of all living floors; (b) Reduce occupancy from 16 to 8 students per suite if the suites cannot be remodeled in the short run; (c) If neither of the above can be done, or, in the interim, design a new process for negotiating standards for living together in suites; (d) Create Myers-Briggs suites; (e) Create Holland suites; (f) Create community using Chickering's vectors; and (g) Increase personalization of space through a student painting program. In this chapter, two of the seven interventions will be described along with outcome research on at least 2 and often 3 years of implementation.

Intervention 1: New Process for Negotiation of Standards for Living Together in a Suite

From the assessments we learned that members of suites were encouraged to negotiate standards for living together; however, the process used was basically relativistic in that it was voluntary, totally unstructured, not facilitated by an authority figure, and lacking in models of previously successful standards. Suites that chose to negotiate standards did so experientially; however, some residents were not drawn into the process.

Because the students seem to reason in dualistic ways, any new process for negotiating standards needs to be highly structured, experiential, and encouraged and facilitated by an authority figure. The process also needs to provide two or three model standards (moderate diversity) and a required follow-up session for evaluation and possible renegotiation facilitated by the authority figure. The *redesigned negotiation* process attempts to be congruent with these criteria and is summarized as follows:

1. The process is initiated early Autumn Quarter at a suite meeting with all residents and one staff facilitator present. The meeting is 2 to 3 hours in length. The following list describes the sequence of activities.

(a) Introduction, goals, and processes to be used are presented by a staff facilitator.

(b) A roommate-suite mate structured conversation modeled after Jones and Jones's (1969) structured dialogues is used with each of the four sets of four study-bedroom mates. The purposes of the structured conversation are to facilitate acquaintanceship, trust, and openness and to generate data on issues of living together.

(c) Two sample standards from previous years are given to the suite mates for consideration, and then the models and the students' opinions generated in the dialogues are discussed in a total group of 16 in the lounge. The staff facilitator guides the discussion and makes sure the opinions of less vocal students are solicited and discussed.

(d) Standards affecting all 16 residents are negotiated either by using a consensus process or a process involving one representative per study-bedroom with others observing. In the latter process, substitutions for the representative can be made, and written notes may be exchanged between a spokesperson and the study-bedroom mates. If the representative process is used, the standards negotiated by the four representatives are then tested for consensus with the total group by the staff facilitator.

(e) Students sharing the same study-bedroom then negotiate standards among themselves for their study-bedrooms. Their standards must be compatible with the suite standards.

(f) The topics covered include:

- Use and cleanliness standards for the lounge, bathroom, and bedrooms;
- Rules for visitation and overnight guests (consistent with university rules);
- Rules for study hours and conditions;
- Guidelines for social events in the suite;
- Procedures to handle personal conflicts and perceived violations of the standards;
- Use of each other's personal property;
- Personal hygiene; and
- Smoking and drinking (consistent with university rules).

(g) The negotiated suite and study-bedroom standards are committed to writing on a *Contract Form* and signed by all 16 students. A copy is posted in the suite, and the staff facilitator also keeps a copy.

2. After 2 to 4 weeks, the staff facilitator convenes another suite meeting in order to evaluate the standards. Changes can be negotiated. Individuals who may have violated the standards repeatedly are asked to account for their behavior. The staff member chairs and facilitates the meeting.

3. The process continues with at least two additional meetings on standards during the year. At these meetings, the elected suite representative to the house council chairs, and the staff member attends as an advisor.

Intervention 2: Myers-Briggs Suites

From the assessment it was learned that students are assigned to suites mostly in a random manner. This maximizes the cultural and personality type plurality in suites and contributes to making everyday interactions both diverse and challenging. Because the assessment seems to indicate that challenge needs to be reduced and support increased, this intervention uses various Myers-Briggs personality type strategies to assign students to suites in order to increase support. The intervention is summarized as follows:

1. Over the summer all residents assigned to the Olentangy houses are mailed a description of the Myers-Briggs suite mate assignment program and an invitation to participate. Participation is voluntary. Volunteers complete and return form G of the *Myers-Briggs Type Indicator*.

2. Personality types are used to assign the volunteers to suites using four different strategies. These are outlined in Figure 4.

In theory, these alternative strategies are points on a challenge-support continuum, with *pure* being the most supportive and *random* the most challenging. No other special programmatic efforts are made in these suites. The nature of the intervention, therefore, is consideration of the personality types assigned to the suites combined with the new process for negotiating standards for living together (i.e., Intervention #1).

Evaluation of the Redesigned Environments

Research design for the redesigned environments is summarized in Figure 5 on page 170. Program types included MBTI Pure, Dominant, and External strategies, ran-

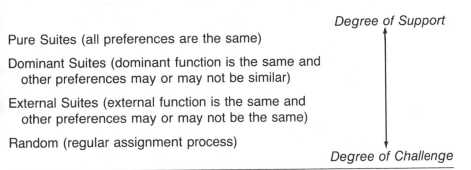

FIGURE 4
Myers-Briggs Suite Assignment Strategies

domly assigned suites using the *new* standards process, and randomly assigned suites using the *old* standards process. The outcome variables and measures were as follows:

1. Perry levels of intellectual development as measured by the Widick-Knefelkamp Sentence Stem and Essay Test (W-K) (Widick & Rodgers, 1979);
2. Perceived social climate as measured by the University Residence Environment Scales (URES) (Moos & Gerst, 1974);
3. The nature and frequency of peer, faculty-student, and staff-student interactions as measured by the Experience of College Questionnaire (ECQ) (Chickering, 1972);
4. Administrative reports needed to calculate the nature or rates of damages, judicial cases, transfer requests, and contract renewals.

Intellectual Development Outcomes

Changes in intellectual development of the combined Myers-Briggs suites compared to combined random suites over a 2-year evaluation indicate that residents of the Myers-Briggs suites seem to be progressing faster on the Perry scheme of intellectual development than residents in the random suites. Specifically (see Table 2), 28% of the residents in random suites showed positive developmental changes between October and May of their first year in college, whereas 65% of the Myers-Briggs residents showed increased intellectual development.

Although the Myers-Briggs suites had a higher mean than did random suites (2.67 to 2.55) on the pretest, the means were not significantly different (see Table 3), and both groups scored in the range typical of freshmen at the university. The posttest means were 2.59 for random suites, an increase of + .04, and 2.94 for Myers-Briggs suites, an increase of + .27. The within-group change for random suites was not significantly different, but was significantly different (p > .006) for the Myers-Briggs group.

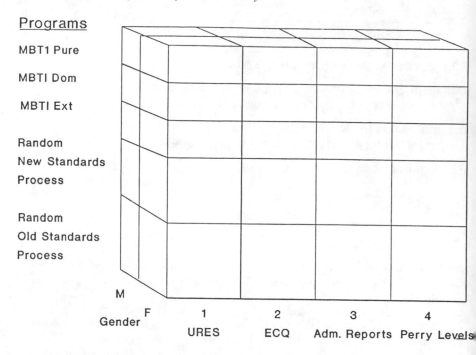

Outcomes

1 ▪ Community University Residence
    Environmental Scales (URES)

2 ▪ Interaction Behaviors (Experience
    of College Questionnaire (ECQ))

3 ▪ Administrative Reports of damages,
    judicial cases, transfer requests
    and renewal rates

4 ▪ Perry levels (Widick-Knefelkamp
    instrument   (W-K))

FIGURE 5
Evaluation Design

Hence, the Myers-Briggs new-standards combined environmental redesign seems to be associated with more rapid intellectual development than the redesign in the random suites. There may be systematic differences, however, between residents assigned to random suites and those who volunteer for Myers-Briggs suites. Volunteers, for example, may be more highly motivated. Current studies include a Myers-Briggs random control group in order to test for this possible difference.

TABLE 2
Random and Myers-Briggs Intellectual Development

Suite Type	No Change	+ 1/3 Stage	Positive Change + 2/3 Stage	+ 1 Stage
Random N–59	72%	21.5%	6%	—
Myers-Briggs	35%	49.0%	12%	4%

This control group includes students who volunteer for Myers-Briggs suites but are assigned randomly instead.

Perceived Social Climate Outcomes

Both the new-standards processes and Myers-Briggs suites were designed to increase support and decrease challenge. Selected dimensions of the perceived social climate can be used to evaluate whether or not these goals are being achieved. Higher scores on the following URES scales are indicators of increased support:

Scale 1: *Involvement.* Degree of commitment to the house and residents; amount of social interaction and feeling of friendship. ("In this house there is a strong feeling of belongingness.")

Scale 2: *Support.* Extent of manifest concern for others in the house; effort to aid one another with academic and personal problems; emphasis on open and honest communication. ("People here are concerned with helping and supporting one another.")

Scale 8: *Order and Organization.* Amount of formal structure or organization (e.g., rules) in the house. ("House procedures here are well established.")

Scale 9: *Student Influence.* Extent to which residents (not staff or administration) perceive that they control the running of the house, formulate rules, select staff, and so forth. ("Students enforce house rules here.")

Lower scores on the following scales are indicators of decreased challenge:

TABLE 3
Pre- and Posttest Intellectual Development Comparisons

	Random Suites	Pure	Myers-Briggs Dominant	Suites External	Combined*
Sample size	59	41	21	42	104
Pretest mean and SD	2.55 ±.40	2.59	2.94	2.75	2.67 ±.43
Posttest mean and SD	2.59 ±.34	2.80	3.11	3.07	2.94 ±.45
Difference	±.04	+.21	+.17	+.32	+.27

*Does not include Random Suites.

Scale 3: *Independence.* Diversity of residents' behavior allowed without social sanctions, versus socially proper and conformist behavior. ("Behaving properly in social situations is not important here.")

Scale 5: *Competition.* This subscale is a bridge between the Personal Growth and Intellectual Growth areas. The degree to which a wide variety of activities (such as dating, grades, etc.) are cast into a competitive framework. ("Around here, discussions frequently turn into verbal duels.")

The interventions were not deliberately designed to affect scores on these scales:

Scale 4: *Traditional Social Orientation.* Emphasis on dating, going to parties, and other "traditional" heterosexual interactions. ("Dating is a recurring topic of conversation around here.")

Scale 10: *Innovation.* Organizational and individual spontaneity in behaviors and ideas. ("New approaches to things are often tried here.")

Scale 6: *Academic Achievement.* Extent to which strictly classroom accomplishments and concerns are prominent in the house. ("Most people here consider studies to be very important in college.")

Scale 7: *Intellectuality.* Emphasis on cultural, artistic and other scholarly intellectual activities in the house, as distinguished from strictly classroom achievement. ("People around here talk a lot about political and social issues.")

The results comparing intervention and comparison groups over 3 years support the proposition that the redesigned environments were successful in significantly affecting the perceived social climate in the *desired directions* on most of the scales.

For the total group of men and women (see Table 4 and Figure 6), three of the four support scales did increase significantly. Involvement, Support, and Order and Organization all increased significantly in the Myers-Briggs suites and random/new-standards suites when compared to random/old-standards suites. For the Myers-Briggs suites only, the challenge of Independence significantly decreased compared to random/old-standards suites. The Myers-Briggs suites also significantly increased Academic Achievement and Intellectuality scores compared to both kinds of random suites. Hence, it seems that the combined-interventions and the new-standards process alone resulted in changes on the desired scales in the desired directions. The increase in Academic Achievement and Intellectuality for the Myers-Briggs suites may be related to the intervention, to some unknown characteristic of the Myers-Briggs group, or both. Studies including the Myers-Briggs control group should help clarify this issue.

For women (see Table 4 and Figure 7), both Myers-Briggs and random/new-standards suites showed significant increases on Involvement, Support, and Order and Organization. Challenge scales did not change. Innovation and Academic Achievement scores increased significantly. Hence, the interventions did increase support, but did not affect challenge scores for women. Because the Myers-Briggs and random/new-standards suite scores are so similar, it is possible that the new-standards process is especially helpful in increasing support for women. The increases in Innovation and Academic Achievement were associated with both Myers-Briggs and random/new-standards suites; hence, it is difficult to interpret the results. Perhaps more order brings a more academic study atmosphere to the suites.

TABLE 4
Perceived Social Climate Outcomes

	Significant Changes in the Desired Directions		
Population and Scale	Random Old Standards	MBTI New Standards	Random New Standards
Total (men and women)		*	*
Involvement		*	*
Support		*	
Independence		*	
Academic achievement		*	
Intellectuality		*	
Order & organization		*	*
Women only			
Involvement		*	*
Support		*	*
Traditional social orientation			*
Academic achievement		*	*
Order & organization		*	*
Innovation		*	*
Men only			
Involvement		*	*
Support		*	*
Independence		*	*
Academic achievement		*	*
Intellectuality		*	*
Order & organization		*	*
Student influence		*	

For men (see Table 4 and Figure 8), both the Myers-Briggs and random/new-standards suites significantly increased support scores on Involvement, Support, and Order and Organization, and the Myers-Briggs suites also increased on Student Influence. Challenge scores on Independence were significantly lower when compared to random/old-standards suites. There was no change or difference on Competition. Both Intellectuality and Academic Achievement scores increased for Myers-Briggs and random/new-standards suites compared to random/old-standards suites.

Evidently, it seems that the interventions had a special impact on the perceived social climate of men's suites. All of the support scores increased significantly for the Myers-Briggs suites, and all but one for random/new-standards suites. One of the two challenge scales was lower for both interventions compared to random/old-standards suites.

To sum up, the deliberately designed Myers-Briggs and random/new-standards environments seem to have achieved their desired goals. There seems to be decreased challenge and an improved sense of support in the social climate of these suites. In addition, academic achievement and intellectual interests seem to have progressed

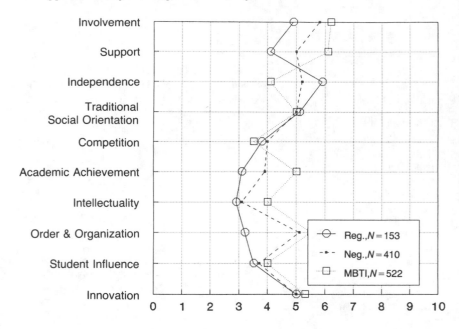

Reg. = Regular suites without any interventions
Neg. = Negotiated standards for living together in a regular suite
MBTI = Assigned to a suite based upon Myers-Briggs Type and negotiated standards for living together

FIGURE 6

URES Scores Men & Women Combined (3 Years)

more rapidly in the Myers-Briggs suites than in regular suites. Both interventions also seem to have had more influence on men's suites than women's; however, both men's and women's suites benefited from the interventions.

Outcomes on Student-Faculty/Staff Interactions

The Experience of College Questionnaire (ECQ) was used to ask students to report on their actual *behaviors in* rather than *perceptions of* (URES) the environment. Viewed together, the ECQ and URES data provide a picture of the nature of the perceived social community and the behaviors underlying the perceptions.

The first section of the ECQ examines student relationships with faculty, residence hall staff, and student affairs staff (other than residence hall staff). It asks *how many individual* faculty, residence hall staff, and student affairs staff the student has *talked* with for more than 5 minutes outside of class or scheduled conferences, and how *many conversations* they have had, *how many faculty or staff the student knows quite well and personally,* how many *activities, meals, or social occasions* have been held together, how many times students have been in staff or faculty *homes or apartments,* how many times faculty or staff have been in the *student*

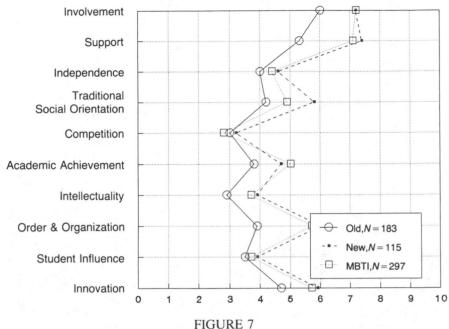

FIGURE 7
URES Scores Women (3 Years' Data)

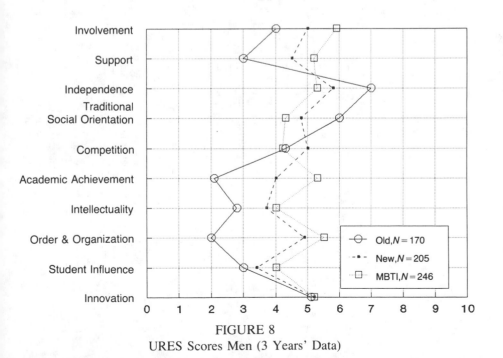

FIGURE 8
URES Scores Men (3 Years' Data)

TABLE 5

Experience of College Questionnaire: Male and Female Students Combined for 3 Years

	MBTI									REGULAR & NEGOTIATE								
	Year 1			Year 2			Year 3			Year 1			Year 2			Year 3		
	F	R	S	F	R	S	F	R	S	F	R	S	F	R	S	F	R	S
1. Number of faculty (F), resident staff (R) and student affairs staff (S) who residents have talked with for more than 5 min. outside of class or at a scheduled appointment.	X						X	X										
2. Number of conversations lasting more than 5 min.	X	X		X											X			
3. Number of F, R, and S the residents know quite well and the F, R, or S is personally interested in how the resident is progressing.	X				X		X											
4. Number of times residents have participated with F, S, or R in an out-of-class activity, meal, or social occasion.		X			X													
5. Number of times the resident has been in the home of F, R, or S.									X									
6. Number of F, R, or S who have come to students' suites for formal or informal gathering.	X				X		X											
7. How many F, R, or S really welcome the resident to visit them in their offices to discuss ideas or personal concerns.			X				X											

Note: X = Significantly higher number of behaviors; F = Faculty; R = Residence hall staff; S = Student affairs staff other than residence. Regular = Randomly assigned suites of students with no process of negotiated living standards; Negotiate = Randomly assigned suites of students with negotiated process for defining living standards.

176

suites, and if faculty or staff would *welcome the student to their offices for a personal or intellectual visit.*

As indicated in Table 5, the Myers-Briggs suites for combined men's and women's scores over 3 years had a higher frequency of desired behaviors than did random suites. There were no differences between random/new-standards and random/old-standards suites that used the former process. Generally, therefore, Myers-Briggs residents *interacted more often* and for *longer periods of time* with faculty members, residence staff, and student affairs staff than did both kinds of random suite residents.

Outcomes on Administrative Behaviors

Transfer Requests

In Table 6 the average frequency of requests to transfer per suite are summarized. For both men's and women's suites, there were no differences between random/new-standards and random/old-standards suites. For women, the Myers-Briggs intervention resulted in significantly fewer transfer requests than for combined random suites. Approximately 2.40 women per Myers-Briggs suite requested a transfer during an academic year, whereas in regular suites, 5.60 persons per suite requested transfers. This is a 54% reduction. For men, there were no significant reductions in transfer requests.

Figure 9 summarizes reasons for the transfer requests. The outcomes are consistent with the initial assessments. Random suite residents gave roommate and environmental problems as their most frequent reasons for seeking a transfer. The lower frequencies for these problems in the Myers-Briggs suites may indicate that the interventions are helping reduce roommate and environmental conflicts as they were designed to do.

Judicial Sanctions

Table 7 summarizes 3 years of data on judicial sanctions per suite per year. For women, there were no significant differences between the Myers-Briggs and random suites. For men, the Myers-Briggs suites did result in significantly reduced judicial sanctions. The reduction was approximately 50%. Hence, men with similar personalities seem

TABLE 6
Transfer Requests: Average Frequency of Requests
per Suite—3-Year Summary

Random/Old Standard & Random/New Standard		Myers/Briggs	
Female	*Male*	*Female*	*Male*
5.60 persons	3.80 persons	2.40 persons	3.60 persons
35%	25%	15%	23%

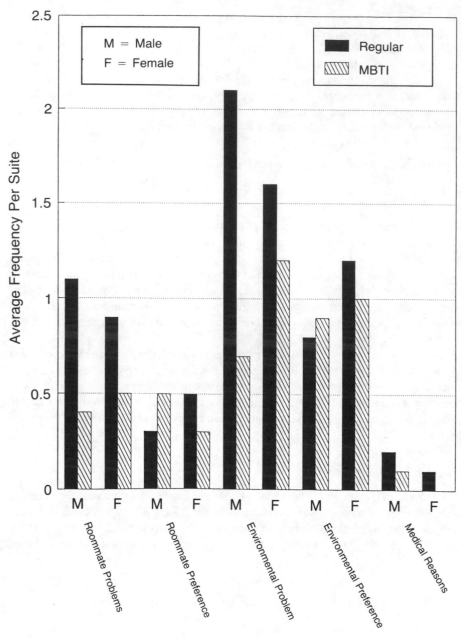

FIGURE 9
Reasons for Transfer

TABLE 7
Judicial Sanctions and Damages per Suite per Year Over 3 Years

	Topical		MBTI		Regular/Negotiate	
	Female	Male	Female	Male	Female	Male
Judicial Sanctions	.88	4.0	.50	2.50	1.1	4.2
Damages	$65	$75	$53	$91	$65	$95

to live together with fewer infractions of university and hall rules than men in random suites. Again, however, caution is needed in interpreting results. There was variance in the rigor with which minor incidents were reported over the 3 years.

Damages

Table 7 also summarizes damages per suite per year over 3 years. For women, the Myers-Briggs suites resulted in significantly less damage per suite per year, approximately $13 per suite per person per year. For men, there was a $4 per suite per person per year reduction. This was not a significant difference.

Renewal Rates

There were no differences in renewal rates among the various kinds of suites. Almost all students, whether residents of Myers-Briggs, random/new-standards or random old-standards suites, chose to move to a different residence area when given the opportunity to do so at the end of the year. Residents do not choose to remain in the Olentangy houses regardless of the kind of suite in which they lived during the academic year.

Summary

The deliberately designed Myers-Briggs/new-negotiation suites seem to have resulted in many changes consistent with redesign objectives. There seems to be improved support and a sense of supportive community in these suites. Challenge decreased, and relationships with faculty, residence staff, and student affairs staff were more frequent, lasted longer, and were more meaningful. Similarly, intellectual development progressed more rapidly in the Myers-Briggs suites than in random suites, and generally women in the Myers-Briggs suites had a lower incidence of damage and had fewer transfer requests, and men had fewer judicial sanctions.

The random/new-standards suites compared to random/old-standards suites showed improved perceived social climate on most of the desired scales. There were no behavioral differences in faculty or staff relationships, administrative indices, or intellectual development, however.

Hence, evidence supports the continuation of the interventions. Because students still choose to move out of the Olentangy halls at the end of the year, however, additional changes may be needed. For example, it may be desirable to reduce occupancy, increase soundproofing, physically redesign the floors and suites, and initiate personalization of space programs.

REFERENCES

Aulepp, L., & Delworth, U. (1978). A team approach to environmental assessment. In J. Banning (Ed.), *Campus ecology* (pp. 51–71). Washington, DC: National Association of Student Personnel Administrators.

Chickering, A.W. (1969). *Education and identity*. San Francisco: Jossey-Bass.

Chickering, A.W. (1972). Undergraduate academic experience. *Journal of Educational Psychology, 63*, 134–143.

Jones, J.E., & Jones, J. (1969). *Dyadic encounter*. San Diego, CA: University Associates Press.

Kalsbeek, D., Rodgers, R., Marshall, D., Denny, D., & Nicholls, G. (1982). Balancing challenge and support: A study of degrees of similarity in suitemate personality type and perceived difference in challenge and support in a residence hall environment. *Journal of College Student Personnel, 23*(5), 434–441.

Moos, R.H. (1979). *Evaluating educational environments*. San Francisco: Jossey-Bass.

Moos, R.H., & Gerst, M. (1974). *University residence environment scale manual*. Palo Alto, CA: Consulting Psychologists Press.

Myers, I.B. (1980). *Gifts differing*. Palo Alto, CA: Consulting Psychologists Press.

Perry, W., Jr. (1970). *Intellectual and ethical development in the college years: A scheme*. New York: Holt, Rinehart & Winston.

Rodgers, R. (1974–1988). *Perry level of entering freshmen*. Unpublished research studies. Columbus, OH: The Ohio State University.

Schroeder, C. (1980). *Redesigning college environments for students*. In F.B. Newton and K.L. Ender (Eds.), *Student development practices* (pp. 52–79). Springfield, IL: Charles C Thomas.

Sommer, R. (1974). *Tight spaces: Hard architecture and how to humanize it*. Englewood Cliffs, NJ: Prentice-Hall.

Widick, C., Knefelkamp, L., & Parker, C.A. (1975). The counselor as a developmental instructor. *Counselor Education and Supervision, 14*, 286–296.

Widick, C., & Rodgers, R.F. (1979). *Manual for the Widick-Knefelkamp Sentence Stem and Essay Test*. Mimeographed paper. Columbus, OH: The Ohio State University.

CHAPTER 8

Use of a Planned Change Model to Modify Student Affairs Programs

Don G. Creamer and Elizabeth G. Creamer

College student affairs programs often are not designed to promote specific developmental outcomes in students. They serve student needs using a traditional organizational blueprint for responding to expressed or inferred student requirements and often provide a valuable contribution to students' education. It is increasingly common, however, for leaders of student affairs programs to desire a more developmental focus for the programs under their administration, but they lack access to generalizable templates for action to ensure successful program reform. Making intentional changes in structured programs of service is neither simple nor guaranteed even when the leaders' motives and ideas are laudable.

Attempts to change significant elements of student affairs programs, such as the underlying philosophy, conceptual orientation, goals, or intervention strategies often end in frustration or outright failure. Although the causes of unsuccessful reform may run the gambit of explanations, they frequently are attributable to blunders resulting from a lack of knowledge about organizational behavior and change rather than to deficiencies within the innovation.

A felt need for change in student affairs programming is easily substantiated by the amount of literature in professional journals devoted to practitioner initiatives in new or reformed programs. At the same time, the literature also reflects a growing awareness of the need for the application of organizational development knowledge in student affairs to guide these changes. The knowledge of planned change and organizational development portrayed in the student affairs literature remains largely unfocused and atheoretical. Despite these weaknesses, the literature on planned change and organizational development shows much promise for improving practitioner capabilities to serve their institutions as change agents and reformers.

The application of knowledge of planned change may be especially important when attempting to infuse developmental theory and research intelligence into long-standing student affairs programs. Particularly in the case of initiatives with a developmental focus, expectations from constituents, including faculty and students, may be so shaped by tradition as to obstruct critical review of new proposals that seem either radically different in form from existing service programs or confusingly erudite. After all, debate about definitions contributes, in part, to the dissension within the student affairs professions about the adoption of developmental aims. Resistance to change from those who are outside the student affairs profession but who possess some authority to sanction its plans is not surprising and requires a skillful strategic offensive by innovators if it is to be overcome.

Skillful use of strategies to ensure needed program reform depends upon leadership knowledge about the forces that promote and those that inhibit change. This chapter focuses on some of this knowledge, but especially on a recently developed theoretical model of planned change in higher education and on some of its uses to facilitate programmatic change in student affairs.

PERSPECTIVES ON INSTITUTIONAL CHANGE

Organizational change is of two types—planned and unplanned. Planned change is purposive. It is an intentional effort to modify institutionalized policy, programs, curricula, processes or procedures, authority structures, technology, or culture toward the end of institutional renewal and improved organizational health. Organizational health is defined as the ability to solve problems and to achieve institutional goals. Planned change is only a part of the changes that occur in higher education, much of which happen in unsystematic and evolutionary ways, in contrast to a more revolutionary approach inherent in planned change efforts.

The number of theoretical models available to explain planned change in higher education is limited (Huse, 1975) and the literature ". . . is overwhelmingly descriptive rather than analytical" (Dill & Friedman, 1979, p. 412). Some literature directly relevant to student affairs is available (Blaesser, 1978; Borland, 1980; Hipps, 1982; Strange, 1981; Winstead, 1982; Woodman & Muse, 1982) but it, too, is descriptive and mostly atheoretical. Creamer and Creamer have reported work on the development of a theoretical model of change, called the Probability of the Adoption of Change (PAC) model, and it is this work that we wish to report here and to discuss its uses for practitioners.

The PAC model was developed from quantitative and qualitative analyses of cases in planned change in higher education and by use of grounded theory methods proposed by Glaser and Strauss (1967) and Glaser (1978). Findings from these analyses have been published elsewhere (Creamer & Creamer, 1986a, 1986b; Creamer & Creamer, 1988; Creamer & Creamer, 1989) and include descriptions of the PAC model. These descriptions also catalog nine key variables of the model that define conditions within an organization that influence the outcomes of planned change efforts. These variables and their definitions are presented in Table 1.

TABLE 1
PAC Model Variables and Definitions

Model Variables	Variable Definition
Circumstances	Refers to the source of impetus for change, whether internal or external; the nature of the environment, whether integrative and supportive of change; and the degree of felt need among constituents.
Value compatibility	Refers to the level of agreement between the values of the proposed project and those of the normative culture; includes harmony of procedures and facilities.
Idea comprehensibility	Refers to the degree of clarity, simplicity, and timing of the idea.
Practicality	Refers to the availability of resources, both fiscal and human, including appropriate skills, knowledge, and attitudes.
Top-level support	Refers to the strength and consistency of backing of project goals and strategies.
Leadership	Refers to the actions of "prime movers" or "changemasters" who focus energy and resources within the organization toward the implementation or adoption of the idea on a continuing basis, including the processing of and action on new information gained through feedback and monitoring systems.
Championship	Refers to the persevering advocacy by influential persons, other than the leader(s), who are empowered to assume responsibility for implementing the change.
Advantage probability	Refers to the perception of demonstrable gains, the likelihood of achievement of stated goals, and the probability of solving vexing problems many people feel.
Strategies	Refers to the interventions or actions taken to implement the idea, including the enhancement of integration among units of the institution toward common purposes, and intensity and forms of communication to inform constituents of the idea, plans proposed and undertaken, progress achieved, and evaluation of results.

THEORETICAL BASE OF THE PAC MODEL

Most administrators have experienced situations where a good idea never got off the drawing board, whereas a lackluster idea received support but was never implemented. Still others have witnessed the institution-wide adoption of a project based on an idea shelved for many years. The variables or conditions that influence these outcomes are the foci of the PAC model.

We identified three "leadership" variables that seem to play central functions in determining change project outcomes. To avoid redundancy in terms, we use the term "superintendence" when referring to the three variables collectively. Our original survey research findings from 170 reported change projects in student affairs underscored the importance of *leadership* and *championship* in project success. Further study of selected cases from that sample revealed a third superintendence variable that we called *top-level support*. In an even later study, using a meta-like procedure to study the relative contribution of PAC model variables to outcomes in four cases of student affairs innovation and three cases of academic reform, *leadership* and *championship* were found to be strong indicators of project success whereas *top-level support* was given moderate weight. The manner in which these three variables operate within a specific planned change project offers a powerful indication of whether it will be adopted by an institution.

The *leadership* variable in the PAC model refers to the multiple roles of the primary director of the project found in the most successful change initiatives. These roles include (a) formulating the vision, (b) developing top-level support, (c) selecting personnel, particularly the project champion, (d) allocating personnel and budgetary resources either from new or existing resources, (e) empowering a champion with responsibility to implement the project, (f) developing internal support, and (g) sustaining support throughout the life of the project (Creamer & Creamer, 1986b). Turnover of the leader was found to be a deadly element in change efforts, resulting in severe delays, if not derailment, of the project. Successful projects in student affairs were found to have a clearly recognizable leader with strong personal identification to the project. This kind of singular affiliation of an influential individual with a project also may serve as a source of opposition.

Championship in the model is defined as the role played by an influential advocate (or advocacy group) who is supportive of the idea during the planning stages and is responsible for implementing project goals during later stages. Advocacy groups seem to be more common in cases of change grounded in traditionally academic concerns than in student affairs. Project champions play a key integrative role in developing support for the change project within the institution. Additional roles for the champion are to implement the plan, negotiate participation from members of other units, particularly faculty, and monitor implementation. The most successful projects have a clearly identifiable project champion. As with project leaders, turnover of an effective project champion can seriously impede the adoption of project goals.

The third superintendence variable in the PAC model, *top-level support*, refers to the role of a chief executive officer or governing body. Top-level institutional leaders are instrumental in creating an environment conducive to change and supportive of experimentation. Official endorsement by the appropriate governing body and a clear, consistent articulation of support for a change project by top-level administrators are commonly associated with successful change projects. Yet, opposition to project goals may be fueled when power-coercive strategies are used by top-level leaders, such as in the issuance of a presidential directive. As with the other superintendence activities, turnover at this level may arrest the prospects of change.

The superintendence variables interact with the six remaining variables identified in the PAC model; that is, various roles of one of the three types of leaders serve to shape the influence of all other variables in the model. The project leader plays an influential role in successful change projects by perceiving conducive timing for change and by capitalizing on widespread perception of the need for change. Both timing and felt need are elements of the variable *circumstances.* Leaders play pivotal roles in identifying and shaping ways to address the perception of need compatible with existing institutional values. These elements compose the core of the variable *value compatibility.* Furthermore, project leaders are primarily, if not solely, responsible for *idea comprehensibility,* the shaping and articulating of the fundamental idea of the project and how to achieve its goals. *Advantage probability,* likely benefits to participants and other members of the academic community, also tends to be articulated by project leaders. The project leader often develops *top-level support* from the CEO and other influential institutional personnel and "gate-keepers" to the internal governance structure. The project leader works with them to marshal the resources necessary to accomplish the task, or to shape the *practicality* of the idea. The selection and empowerment of a project *champion* and the creation of an environment that allows the implementation of a project to be a top priority are common activities of project leaders. Finally, the choice of *strategies* that are collaborative and allow for broad information sharing across constituencies often is a decision of project leaders. These examples of *leadership* behavior serve to illustrate how any of the three types of superintendence may shape the force or impact of all other variables in the PAC model.

Superintendence roles were found to be influential, although in slightly different ways, in projects grounded in both student or academic affairs. Instructional faculty were involved in both types of change, and modifying their behavior often was at issue. In academic reform, the changes often were in instructional methods or attitudes toward new curricula. Innovations in student affairs were more likely to call for changes in faculty behavior in specific skills, such as advising or mentoring. We found that the channels of negotiation varied greatly between the two loci of change. The role of a clearly identifiable project leader was more instrumental in the cases of reform based in student affairs than those of academic affairs, where the leader was compelled to negotiate change through more formal, legislative-like processes. In these cases, success depended more on collaboration and facilitation than on the charismatic, visionary behavior of the leader instrumental in most successful changes in student affairs. Personal identification of the leader with the project often is intense in student affairs cases, but not in curricular affairs, where the leader is more likely to introduce the idea to the governance system without necessarily exhibiting strong ownership for it.

Pivotal superintendence roles are recognized in the literature on planned change (where they generically are referred to as leadership and sometimes championship), although different levels are not clearly identified as is the case in the PAC model. Glaser, Abelson, and Garrison (1983) listed championship by influential persons as a key variable influencing the acceptance of change. Championship by an influential person is recognized as part of the variable resources in Davis and Salasin's (1979) AVICTORY model. Similarly, Baldridge and Deal (1975) noted that change is more likely if championed by influential people. Moss Kanter (1983) identified distinct roles for both a project leader and champion. Several authors have recognized the key role of the superintendence variables in knowledge utilization or information linkages. Likewise, Lindquist (1978) characterized leaders of successful projects as cosmopolitans who are "top authorities well connected to information concerning external pressures, innovative models, and internal practices" (p. 233). The role of leaders to facilitate collaborative problem solving and information linkages to influential people and governance groups is recognized in many political models of organizational change, according to Lindquist.

The PAC model shares some similarities with other models of managed change in organizations, such as the action research model (French & Bell, 1984) and planned change model (Lippitt, Watson, & Westley, 1958). These models speak to the goal of improving organizational health and effectiveness through purposeful action or problem-solving strategies. Change in each model is directed toward the entire organization and is based on the application of behavioral science knowledge.

Some of the theoretical postulates of the PAC model differ, however, from those of other models of organizational change found in the literature. One major difference is the omission of an emphasis on the contribution of an outside consultant, change agent, or interventionist. Although change was effected without external consultants in all but one of the cases studied, nothing in the model precludes consideration of change agent roles as an element of leadership or championship. The role of external change agent is not considered central to the PAC model as it is in most models in literature about organizational development.

Additional differences exist between the PAC model and other models of change. Possibly because of the absence of consultants, the diagnostic phase of deliberate data collection characteristic of action research is not a distinct element of the PAC model. Although prescriptive, the model does not describe a linear process, with the possible exception of the multiple, distinct roles described for project leaders and champions. Although information sharing strategies are defined as part of the variable *strategies*, no reference is made in the PAC model to any specific intervention strategies, such as team building, which are common to the literature in organizational development. The emphasis of the PAC model is on the identification of influential variables or strategic leverage points for the implementation of change projects. Analysis of the role of the different variables can be used to determine if organizational change is likely. Unlike other models, the PAC model originated from the study of planned change in higher education. No assumptions are made about its generalizability to other settings, such as government or industry.

Resistance or opposition is not a discrete element in the PAC model. It is recognized, however, as a possible element of several variables in the model, including practicality, advantage probability, and value compatibility. Although resistance was present in varying degrees in all of the cases studied, it tended to be passive rather than overt and rarely took the form of active lobbying or forceful obstruction of the project. Resistance was more evident in change projects negotiated through formal faculty governance structures, such as in the change of curriculum. A theoretical assumption of the model is that resistance is more likely where values are more diverse than in student affairs and small liberal arts colleges, where the underlying value system tends to be more homophylic or consistent.

USES OF THE PAC MODEL

There are multiple possible applications of the PAC model. One of the most obvious applications of the PAC model is as a tool for strategic planning to weigh the forces in the environment that support and those that inhibit change.

Let us assume that a chief student affairs officer is considering a major reform of all orientation activities of the college to infuse developmental objectives and goals. She recognizes that such an initiative will require extending the activities to span at least the freshman year, and that the outcome measures will have to be refocused on actual student growth or change. She sees that the roles of the student affairs staff and of many faculty who help with the activities will have to be altered and that they may have to submit to specific retraining. She knows that the cost of the orientation program will be increased, that students' satisfaction with the activities may be affected, that the new initiatives may represent a major additional time commitment from students, and that the certainty of "success" is reduced by the added intricacy of program design and by the complexity of developmental outcomes. A checklist of questions framed using the PAC variables can be used as a planning guide. A checklist to evaluate an initiative with a developmental orientation follows.

CHECKLIST OF CONSIDERATIONS
FOR DEVELOPMENTAL ORIENTATION

Circumstances

1. Is there a widely felt need for this change?
2. What influential people or groups are likely to support or oppose the idea?
3. Is the environment generally supportive of changes like this one? Are other change projects currently being supported?

Value Compatibility

4. Are the underlying values of this idea for change consistent with those of the faculty and organizational culture? Will this change represent values contrary to prevailing beliefs, attitudes, and behaviors of faculty?

Idea Comprehensibility

5. Is the idea clear to all constituents?
6. Are the programmatic requirements of the idea simple enough to permit understanding by all constituents?

Practicality

7. Are there sufficient resources, both fiscal and human, to support the initiative?
8. Are there appropriate talents in the faculty and staff to implement the plans?
9. Is the timing of the idea appropriate vis-à-vis all other institutional commitments or initiatives?

Top-Level Support

10. How strong is the support from the president (and possibly the board) for the project? Can the support be depended on over time?
11. Is support for the goals of the project as well as the strategies required to implement it?
12. Will the president support necessary reallocations of resources?
13. What role is the president willing to play to support the project? For instance, is the president willing to endorse the project publicly?

Leadership

14. Can sufficient resources be deployed to implement the idea?
15. Can the idea be articulated clearly to all constituents?
16. Can the leader provide adequate oversight or supervision of the project?
17. Can qualified personnel be assigned to the project who can make the project top priority?
18. Are the talents of the personnel sufficient for the tasks of the project?

Championship

19. Is there one person available to assume responsibility for the execution of the project?
20. Is this person's commitment to the project strong enough to serve as a persevering advocate of the idea?
21. Does this person have the skills to defuse opposition to the project?

Advantage Probability

22. Can the benefits of the project be articulated clearly?
23. How can the benefits of the project be articulated, particularly to those whose jobs will be affected?

Strategies

24. What actions will be required to negotiate support for the idea?
25. What forms of communication will be required to "reach" all constituents?
26. What cooperative efforts between academic and student affairs will be required?

Thorough information about each of these items will yield sufficient data to decide whether the potential benefits compensate for the costs and whether the arguments in support of the initiative outweigh those opposing it. The checklist also can provide a way to identify sources of opposition and to consider ways to address them.

The distinctive features of developmental programming also suggest other uses for the PAC model. For example, it is essential in developmental programming to describe the problem to be addressed theoretically; that is, the affected students and certain environmental conditions must be explained from a particular theoretical perspective. (See other chapters in this volume for examples of this procedure, especially chapters 3 and 7 by Rodgers). The PAC model instructs innovators also to assess and describe numerous other factors that will have a bearing on the likelihood of full implementation or institutional adoption of the new practice. Even if the orientation program were conducted only once and produced all the expected consequences, this fact alone would not signal long-term success. It is likely, for example, that serious resistance to the effort may not coalesce until after the project is under way. Information gained from use of the PAC model may help leaders and champions of the project to identify avenues of support and resistance proactively and to target activities to redirect resistance and to optimize support.

Resistance to developmentally focused orientation programs is likely to come either from concerns over costs ("Couldn't the money be used better elsewhere?") or over leadership decisions ("Is a revamped orientation program what the academic and student affairs really need?"). Knowledge of the PAC model would help innovators to deal with concerns about costs through the use of negotiation and agreement strategies to prevent feelings of "losing out" by any group. By contrast, concerns about leadership decisions would call for strategies geared to participation and involvement.

A third use of the PAC model is to help design strategies directed at the entire institution to ensure the eventual adoption or institutionalization of the new approach to orientation if it proves worthy. The PAC model does not instruct student affairs professionals about how to conduct developmental orientation programs, but it does instruct the project champions and leaders about choice of strategies targeted on those outside the orientation program who may possess considerable power to decide whether the program shall be continued. Often, strategies designed to promote adoption of an innovation must include a variety of tactics aimed at many levels of the institution. Data gained from the use of the checklist as a diagnostic and monitoring device, as suggested earlier, also may serve as a basis for selecting specific approaches to enlist outside support and achieve approval for the permanent establishment of the effort.

Another use of the PAC model is as a guide to assess the applicability of an external model of service to a specific campus. Student affairs professionals often import "model" programs from other campuses virtually intact, and it is common that they do not work in the new environment as they did in the old. This likelihood can be anticipated, and the PAC model could be used to evaluate the degree of acceptance or fit of an external program prior to implementation. By use of the checklist suggested earlier to examine external programs systematically, modifications could be made to the program to increase the probability of adoption at one's home campus.

A final suggested use of the PAC model is to assist in the development and analysis of case studies of planned change efforts. The need to explain differential effects of environments on students' development compels professionals to study their practices scientifically. The PAC model has been used as a research tool to analyze case studies of change efforts in both academic and student affairs settings. It can be used to generate hypotheses, collect data around theoretical presumptions, and study programmatic effects on students in a context of intentionally designed strategies.

For example, the following illustrative hypotheses might be used to prepare for data collection to study the effects of the orientation program described above:

Adoption (or institutionalization) of the developmental orientation will depend upon:

1. the presence of a uniform perception of need for the program;
2. the harmony of the program with other similar educational initiatives already in place;
3. the clarity of the goals;
4. the ability of leaders to articulate the goals and the ways to implement them;
5. the availability of resources for the project;
6. the strength and persistence of top-level support;
7. the dependability of leadership for the duration of the project;
8. the effectiveness of project championship;
9. the capability of the project to resolve major problems for the institution; and
10. the potency of strategies employed to implement the project.

Broader theoretical constructs, such as those about the existence of multiple levels of leadership or superintendence in successful change projects, the centrality of information sharing as an intervention strategy, and the role of diversity or consistency in values also have been suggested as guides to further research.

SUMMARY

Despite the admirable purposes of designing and implementing developmental programs for students, the reality of institutional politics and organizational complexity makes their success less than assured. The goals of developmental education often are vague. The costs of developmental programming sometimes are excessive. The required time lines for developmental impact on students are not aligned with the academic calendar. Incentives for students to invest the added time even for their own benefit are scarce. Cooperation of faculty is uncertain where extrinsic rewards are limited and advantages of developmental programming are unclear. Just as good developmental theory is indispensable to design programs with growth consequences, good theory of organizational change is required to prepare the institution for ultimate adoption of new practices.

The theoretical base for the Probability of the Adoption of Change model was presented and the model's variables were described to suggest the use of the paradigm coterminously with developmental theory when charting reforms in student affairs. Several specific uses of the PAC model were suggested including institutional diagnosis of readiness for change, guidance for planning specific initiatives, instruction for monitoring and responding to events and conditions corresponding with change initiatives, assessing the applicability of external service models, and framing hypotheses for the study of change efforts.

REFERENCES

Baldridge, J.V., & Deal, T.E. (1975). Overview of change processes in educational organizations. In J.V. Baldridge and T.E. Deal (Eds.), *Managing change in educational organizations* (pp. 1–23). Berkeley, CA: McCutchins.

Blaesser, W.W. (1978). Organization change and student development. *Journal of College Student Personnel, 19*, 109–118.

Borland, D.T. (1980). Organization development: A professional imperative. In D.G. Creamer (Ed.), *Student development in higher education: Theories, practices and future directions* (pp. 205–227). Alexandria, VA: American College Personnel Association.

Creamer, D.G., & Creamer, E.G. (1986a). Applying a model of planned change to program innovation in student affairs. *Journal of College Student Personnel, 27*, 19–26.

Creamer, E.G., & Creamer, D.G. (1986b). The role of leaders and champions in planned change in student affairs. *Journal of College Student Personnel, 27*, 431–437.

Creamer, E.G., & Creamer, D.G. (1988). Predicting successful organizational change: Case studies. *Journal of College Student Development, 29*, 4–11.

Creamer, E.G., & Creamer, D.G. (1989). Testing a model of planned change across student affairs and curriculum reform projects. *Journal of College Student Development, 30*, 27–34.

Davis, H.R., & Salasin, S.E. (1979). Change: Decisions and their implementation. In S. Feldman (Ed.), *The administration of mental health services* (rev. ed.) (pp. 383–433). Springfield, IL: Charles C Thomas.

Dill, D.D., & Friedman, C.P. (1979). An analysis of frameworks for research on innovation and change in higher education. *Review of Educational Research, 49*, 411–435.

French, W.L., & Bell, C.H. (1984). *Organization development* (3rd ed.). Englewood Cliffs, NJ: Prentice-Hall.

Glaser, B.G. (1978). *Theoretical sensitivity*. Mill Valley, CA: Sociology Press.

Glaser, E.M., Abelson, H.H., & Garrison, K.N. (1983). *Putting knowledge to use*. San Francisco: Jossey-Bass.

Glaser, B.G., & Strauss, A.L. (1967). *The discovery of grounded theory*. New York: Aldine.

Hipps, G.M. (1982). Summary and conclusions. In G. Hipps (Ed.), *New directions for institutional research: Effective planned change strategies, No. 33* (pp. 115–122). San Francisco: Jossey-Bass.

Huse, E.F. (1975). *Organization development and change*. New York: West.

Lindquist, J. (1978). *Strategies for change*. Berkeley, CA: Pacific Soundings Press.

Lippitt, R., Watson, J., & Westley, B. (1958). *The dynamics of planned change*. New York: Harcourt, Brace & World.

Moss Kanter, R. (1983). *The changemasters: Innovations for productivity in the American corporation*. New York: Simon & Schuster.

Strange, C.C. (1981). Organizational barriers to student development. *NASPA Journal, 19*, 12–19.

Winstead, P.C. (1982). Planned change in institutions of higher education. In G. Hipps (Ed.), *New directions for institutional research: Effective planned change strategies, No. 33* (pp. 19–32). San Francisco: Jossey-Bass.

Woodman, R.W., & Muse, W.V. (1982). Organization development in the profit sector: Lessons learned. In J. Hammons (Ed.), *New directions for community colleges: Organization development—Change strategies, No. 37* (pp. 23–44). San Francisco: Jossey-Bass.

PART IV

MAJOR ISSUES IN PRACTICE

CHAPTER 9

Ethical Practice in College Student Affairs

Elizabeth Reynolds Welfel

During the last decade many professionals have "rediscovered" ethics. In particular, the literature on ethical issues in education and human services has grown rapidly during this period. Even the popular media have attended to unethical behaviors of human services professionals to an unprecedented degree. Professional associations, such as the American Association for Counseling and Development (AACD) and the American Psychological Association (APA) have revised and expanded their codes at least once during this decade (AACD, 1981; APA, 1981). In each case, the later version has placed a much stronger emphasis on ethics education for students and practicing professionals and has enhanced the organizations' efforts to enforce the ethical standards. APA in particular has provided clearer guidelines for graduate training in ethics and stronger sanctions against those who behave unethically in its revised statements. For example, training programs that seek to be accredited by the American Psychological Association must demonstrate that their students have attained competence in understanding the ethical standards. In addition, the names of APA members who have been expelled from membership for ethical violations are printed in annual dues statements mailed to all other APA members along with a reference to the portion of the ethical principles that they violated.

This increased interest in ethics has not escaped the attention of the American College Personnel Association (ACPA), the professional association to which most college student services professionals belong. ACPA published its first code of ethics for members in 1981 (ACPA, 1981) after a careful and deliberate process of obtaining broad-based input from members regarding its contents (Winston & McCaffrey, 1981) and will publish a major revision of the code in 1990. ACPA also devotes a column on ethical issues written by the chairperson of its Ethics Committee in each issue of *Developments*, its quarterly newsletter. Other professional associations to which college student services professionals belong have followed a similar course. The National Association of Student Personnel Administrators (NASPA, 1983) and the National Association of Women Deans, Administrators and Counselors (NAWDAC, 1976) also have devised specialized ethical standards for their members in the last decade, but have been less active in educating members about the provisions of their ethical codes.

Moreover, authors of counseling and student services textbooks now regularly include chapters on ethical and legal issues and place copies of the relevant ethics codes in the appendices for student reference, practices that were rare only a decade ago. Courses on ethics are becoming the norm in graduate training programs in counseling (Lipsitz, 1985), and papers and symposia on ethics appear more regularly at professional conferences. Finally, scholars have begun to develop sophisticated models of ethical decision making that can help practitioners cope more successfully with the ethical dilemmas they face (e.g., Kitchener, 1984; Rest, 1984) and educators have proposed more effective methods to teach ethics to graduate students (e.g., Kitchener, 1985, 1986; Pelsma & Borgers, 1986; Welfel & Lipsitz, 1983).

Taken together, all these developments offer promise for professionals, who are better informed about the ethical dimensions of their work, and thereby for a higher quality of service to students. Has that promise been fulfilled? Is the incidence of unethical behavior declining? Are the ethical standards being taught more effectively in graduate programs? In this chapter I address these questions, attending first to the causes and goals of the renewed interest in ethics, and then to the contributions and limitations of the current codes of ethics. In the third section, I review the research on unethical behavior as well as the theories of moral behavior and ethical decision making scholars have proposed. I also discuss the application of these comprehensive theories to college student services. The fourth section focuses on current practices in ethics education. In the last section of the chapter, I examine the emerging ethical issues for the profession that are likely to draw a greater proportion of the profession's attention in the future. Several recommendations for new directions for research and training in ethics are included.

The content of this chapter will focus on the literature from both student development and counseling. The reliance on the literature from both fields is grounded in the close alliance between the two fields and in the knowledge that the counseling aspects of the work of student affairs professionals often are ethically troublesome for practitioners in student affairs. Moreover, student affairs and counseling are helping professions that ethics scholars view as rooted in the same ethical principles (e.g., Kitchener, 1985). Finally, this attention to both professions is based on the availability of data-based literature in counseling and the paucity of ethics research in student affairs. It is my hope that the material in this chapter will provoke readers to initiate research on these crucial ethical issues facing student affairs professionals.

THE EMERGENCE OF ETHICAL BEHAVIOR AS A PRIORITY OF THE PROFESSION

Why has ethics moved into the spotlight? Several factors seem to have been especially influential. First, better documentation of the incidence of unethical behavior has clarified the nature and scope of the problem. In essence, some of these findings have shocked professionals into greater sensitivity. For example, the literature on sexual harassment of students by university faculty has demonstrated that this is a more common ethical problem than had been assumed (e.g., Glaser & Thorpe, 1986; Oravec, 1983; Tuana, 1985). Specifically, Glaser and Thorpe found that 31% of their sample of female psychologists reported experiences of unwanted sexual advances by faculty or clinical supervisors during graduate school. Moreover, 45% of those sampled believed that there would be punitive consequences for their training if they declined the advances. Oravec (1983) and Tuana (1985) suggested comparable levels of sexual harassment by college faculty in other disciplines. In addition, evidence that counselors sexually exploit their clients in the name of ''treatment'' has increased, along with the data suggesting that clients can be seriously harmed by such sexual intimacies (Bouhoutsos, Holroyd, Lerman, Forer, & Greenberg, 1983; Holroyd & Bouhoutsos, 1985). Moreover, these authors' findings suggest that the psychological harm engendered by sexual exploitation by therapists can be long-lasting and has, in some cases, resulted in chronic psychological problems and even suicide. Equally unsettling has been the finding that some therapists who sexually exploit their clients do so repeatedly with many different clients.

Second, the consumer rights movement has led those served by the profession to expect higher quality service and to be more likely to take action when the services are ineffective or inappropriate. Of course, the escalating cost of higher education has contributed to this consumer orientation. Fear of being sued by a dissatisfied student has caused some practitioners in counseling and advising roles to be more sensitive to ethical and legal issues even though the actual risk of litigation is low. In this case, the motivation to behave ethically may be based more on self-protective impulses rather than ethical ideals, but nevertheless, such realities have prompted greater awareness of the consequences of unethical behavior.

Third, the extreme economic pressures on higher education have placed a greater proportion of student services professionals in situations in which their obligations to their clients seem to conflict with their obligations to the institutions that employ them. What is cost-effective and what is most advisable for the students is not always identical. Student services professionals are particularly torn by such dilemmas because they must place the students' needs before their own but cannot ignore the impact of the college's economic difficulties on their own future employment and the lives of all students in attendance. Worries about declining enrollments and cuts in student services budgets have made the process of objectively counseling or advising students considering a leave of absence or transfer to another college a much more complicated matter. Moreover, administrators in higher education have not always demonstrated the level of sensitivity to the ethical standards of student services personnel necessary to a successful resolution of this problem. Consequently, practitioners themselves have become more aware of these issues and are more inclined to seek out appropriate ways to be loyal to both their clients and the institutions that employ them.

Legal rulings also have been an important force behind the renewed interest in ethics. Individuals who believe they have been victims of malpractice are more likely now to seek legal redress than before and are more likely to win their cases. The courts have supported clients' claims of malpractice against counselors who exploit clients sexually, who engage in other forms of dual relationships, and who fail to warn those who may be in danger of harm from their client even if such a warning means violating confidentiality (Hummel, Talbutt, & Alexander, 1985). The notoriety some of these cases have received seems to have awakened even the sleepiest counselors to the significant legal consequences of some forms of unethical behavior.

Finally, the research from developmental and social psychology increasingly offers more comprehensive and better tested theories of moral and altruistic behavior. Psychology better understands the process of moral reasoning and the social and psychological factors affecting moral behavior (See Rest, 1983, for example). Scholars in applied fields, particularly counseling, dentistry, and nursing, are translating their findings to their own domains. In similar fashion, ethicists are examining "real world" ethical dilemmas with greater frequency and have become resources for practitioners in medical settings. In other words, the quality of the scholarship has improved at the same time that the societal need has been recognized, thereby encouraging even more rigorous research into ethical issues.

In summary, social, political, economic, and philosophical factors have influenced the emergence of ethics as "the issue for the 1980s" in human service professions. It has been motivated both by self-protective impulses and moral idealism. In any case, the convergence of these factors has produced several positive outcomes for the profession.

THE ROLE OF ETHICAL STANDARDS IN INFLUENCING ETHICAL BEHAVIOR

One important outcome of this reawakening of interest in ethics has been the development of clearer and more detailed codes of ethics for student services professionals. The development, dissemination, and enforcement of a code of ethics is the hallmark of a profession, a feature that distinguishes professionals from other kinds of workers. A profession's endorsement of a code of ethics implies an understanding of the profession's responsibility to the public it serves, a commitment to educate its members, and members' willingness to monitor themselves and sanction those who fail to abide by the code. The ability of a profession to develop a set of ethical standards also implies a clearer, more universal identity, in this case, a more certain and widely accepted definition of the purposes and functions of college student services professionals. Thus, the publication of the American College Personnel Association's *Statement of Ethical and Professional Standards* in 1981 can be considered a critical point in the history of the professional organization, an event that symbolizes a new maturity of ACPA and a clearer vision of its goals and duties.

As Winston and Dagley (1985) pointed out, the publication of a code of ethics has several other values as well. Professional ethical responsibilities can provide objective means of evaluating performance. They can help individuals in other occupations better understand the role of the student services professional, and thereby offer a means of generating more respect for the profession. In addition, they can provide guidelines for decision making in practical situations and give stronger moral support to practitioners in evaluating their own and colleagues' behavior. Deciding how to handle an ethically sensitive situation is often an intellectually and emotionally demanding task, and the code offers a foundation on which to organize such decision making. It offers some support against the feeling of having to make a difficult decision in isolation and diminishes the worry about negative outcomes from an ethical decision. In addition, Winston and Dagley noted that an ethics code also can provide better safeguards for professionals against unjustified attacks on their conduct and, depending on how rigorously the code is enforced, can provide better protection for the public against unscrupulous practitioners. Finally, a clear, comprehensive, and well-publicized code of ethics is an educational tool, a valuable means of sensitizing those entering the profession to the ethical dimensions of their work. The contribution of the code in this area may be especially important because insensitivity to ethical issues during graduate training has been cited as a serious problem for the profession (Rest, 1984) and as a source of some kinds of unethical behaviors (Keith-Spiegel, 1977).

At the same time, it is important to acknowledge the limitations inherent in any code of ethics. First, ethics codes are designed to act as *guidelines* for professional behavior, not blueprints. They function as points of reference designed to answer many questions about ethical issues in practice, not as all-inclusive "cookbooks" for practice. Some provisions in the codes are specific in their requirements of practitioners, for example, the comments regarding sexual relationships with clients, staff, and students. Such relationships are expressly prohibited in Part 12 of *Section B: General Responsibilities* of the ACPA code. It states:

> Members maintain ethical relationships with colleagues and students and refrain from relationships which impinge on the dignity, moral code, self-worth, professional functioning, and/or personal growth of these individuals. Specifically, members are aware that sexual relationships hold great potential for exploitation. Consequently, members refrain from having sexual relationships with anyone to whom they act as counselors or therapists. Sexual relationships with staff members or students for whom one has supervisory or evaluative responsibilities have high potential for causing personal damage and for limiting the exercise of professional responsibilities and are therefore unprofessional and unethical.

However, other parts of the code are more abstract and present more general principles for behavior rather than requirements or sanctions. For example, *Section C3: Professional and Collegial Relationships* is framed more in terms of goals for professional interactions rather than statements of highly specific activities that are prohibited or mandated. In this and other sections, the code must be interpreted in light of the particular circumstances. Even when the code seems clear-cut there are still complexities the code does not address, such as the appropriateness of social/

sexual relationships with *former* clients, students, and staff. The standards, as currently written, offer a practitioner little help in decision making in this area. Therefore, no code can be a blueprint or recipe for behavior across all situations nor can it supplant the individual practitioner's responsibility for independent ethical decision making.

A related limitation stems from the nature of the process of writing a code of ethics. Because the development of a code is a tedious and time-consuming endeavor that entails compromise in order to obtain consensus, some provisions of a code can be "watered down" and idealism can be sacrificed to achieve ratification. Members of ethics committees also must wrestle with competing motivations for creating an ethics code. On the one hand, a professional association develops a code of ethics as a means of avoiding outside regulation and protecting its members from unjust accusations from others. On the other hand, it must keep in mind the needs and priorities of the public it serves. When self-regulation conflicts with consumer needs, ethics committees face their most difficult task.

Even though ethical standards cannot be equated with the legal requirements of professionals, ethics committees must keep current statutes in mind as they create and revise ethical standards. No professional association wishes to place members in the untenable position of having to violate the law in order to act consistently with its ethics code. Moreover, by the time a code is ratified and publicized it is well on its way to becoming obsolete. As Mabe and Rollin (1986) stated, no code of ethics is able to address "issues at the cutting edge," and ethics codes are least equipped to help practitioners where they often need the most assistance—as they move into innovative areas of practice and research. Frequent revision of the code helps to minimize these problems but does not eliminate them.

A third limitation that is especially obvious for college student services professionals is the lack of correspondence between the codes of conduct of the various professional associations. As Winston and Dagley (1985) detailed so rigorously in their work, the codes of NASPA, NAWDAC, and ACPA diverge from each other in several important ways. For example, ACPA's code (1981, Section B-1) identifies a member's primary responsibility as respect for the client and promotion of the client's welfare, whereas NASPA's code (1983, Section 5) states, "Members recognize that their primary obligation is to the employing institution." In addition, practitioners in college counseling settings are often members of both APA and ACPA. They are expected, by virtue of their membership in each association, to abide by the provisions of both codes. In situations where the statements in the codes conflict or are confusing, the moral and intellectual support the ethics codes ought to provide to the practitioner is seriously undermined.

In short, although the availability of professional ethical standards has clear benefits for practitioners, training institutions, and the public image of the profession, it is certainly not sufficient in itself to achieve the goals of the profession for ethical practice and consistently high quality of service to students. It is essential that practicing professionals be capable of exercising mature ethical judgment in interpreting the code in order for such goals to be realized.

RESEARCH ON ETHICAL BEHAVIOR

As mentioned earlier, the number of books and articles on professional ethics in the professional journals has increased dramatically over the last decade. In 1985, for example, Jossey-Bass published a book titled *Applied Ethics in Student Services*, edited by Canon and Brown (1985), as part of its series, *New Directions for Student Services*. The entire January 1986 issue of the *Journal of Counseling and Development* was devoted to the topic. APA recently published a revised edition of its casebook on ethical issues (APA, 1987), and one commonly used text on ethics for counselors is in its third edition in less than 10 years (Corey, Corey, & Callanan, 1988). In this section, I will present a brief review of the focus and findings of this literature.

Much of the literature published to date can be characterized as reviews of the literature or position papers attempting to sensitize professionals to the ethical dimensions of their work. These publications aim at helping readers develop a deeper understanding of the complexities involved in ethical decision making and the ramifications of improper decisions. Issues such as the relationship between personal values and ethics (e.g., VanHoose & Kottler, 1985), the relationship of moral philosophy to professional ethics (Losito, 1980), and the special ethical considerations when working with particular populations of clients and students (e.g., Fitting, 1986; Graham, Rawlings, Halpren, & Hermes, 1984; Huey, 1986) are especially prominent themes in this literature. VanHoose and Kottler, for example, discussed the notion of a counselor as value-free and argued that such a perspective is unsupportable and inconsistent with the highest standards of the profession.

Other authors have discussed the ethical dimensions in the use of specialized counseling strategies (Corey, Corey, & Callanan, 1982; Wilcoxin, 1986). To illustrate, Corey et al., (1982) provided a casebook of ethical issues for group leaders, delineating the unique ethical issues for practitioners who work with groups and presenting case examples that illustrate those special considerations. Other authors have attempted to sensitize readers to the special ethical issues in particular functions in higher education, such as recruiting (Fiske, 1981), financial aid management (Lenn, 1981), and administration (Chambers, 1981). The recommendations of all these authors stem from the application of existing ethical codes to their particular specialties and from their own professional experience. Very few rely on systematic and rigorous data-based investigations to inform their work. Thus, the contribution of these scholars lies primarily in sensitizing other professionals to special ethical issues and in providing important questions that future research needs to examine. None of these publications can be viewed as definitive, however, because they are not based on empirical research.

As indicated earlier in this chapter, researchers in psychology have documented the types of unethical behavior to which practitioners seem most vulnerable (e.g., Glaser & Thorpe, 1986; Pope, Tabachnick, & Keith-Spiegel, 1987). The major focus of the research has been on dual relationships and sexual exploitation. For example, surveys have found the incidence of dual relationships between psychologists and their clients varying from 2% to 7% of their samples (Holroyd & Brodsky, 1977; Pope et al., 1987). These studies suggest that the frequency of sexual intimacies with clients seems to be declining, perhaps in response to the significant peer and public pressure against such behavior that has developed over the last decade. Problems with inappropriate release of confidential information, biased judgments in forensic situations, and misdiagnosis on insurance claims seem to be continuing occurrences (Pope et al., 1987). The incidence of violations of confidentiality among psychologists seems to parallel that of dual relationships (Baird & Rupert, 1987; Haas, Malouf, & Mayerson, 1986), although one study found a substantially higher percentage of inadvertent release of confidential information in social situations (Pope et al., 1987). Because these surveys rely on self-report instruments, it is possible that these percentages may underrepresent the incidence of such behavior, but the consistency of findings across several studies lends a measure of credibility to these numbers.

Other authors have estimated the incidence of all kinds of serious violations of the ethical standards at 5% to 10% of practitioners (Welfel & Lipsitz, 1984). The data on sexual harassment on the college campus suggest that almost one third of female students may experience some level of harassment (Glaser & Thorpe, 1986). Other studies indicate that impaired or distressed psychologists may account for a portion of unethical behavior, and that some who behave unethically believe their behavior is wrong but cannot stop themselves (Butler & Zelen, 1977; Zelen, 1985). Researchers are beginning to pay more attention to impaired professionals as some authors suggest that at least 6% of psychologists nationally fall into this category (Laliotis & Grayson, 1985). Psychology researchers also have examined the capacity of psychologists to interpret the ethical code accurately (Baldick, 1980; Bernard & Jara, 1986; Bernard, Murphy, & Little, 1987; Lipsitz, 1985). In general, these studies have found weakly positive benefits of ethics education in promoting accurate interpretation of the code, but still inconsistent performance of practitioners.

In the counseling literature, much of the research has been of an analogue nature, using paper-and-pencil measures of ethical judgment. Unfortunately, few of these instruments provide any data supporting their reliability or validity, so that making meaningful interpretations of the results of these studies is next to impossible. However, a few trends are consistent. In general, factors like age, gender, membership in a professional association, or similar demographic variables show no consistent relationship with ethical awareness or ethical decision making. Some findings suggest that prior experience with a particular kind of dilemma increases the likelihood of making an appropriate ethical judgment. For example, those who have experienced the special ethical issues regarding confidentiality when working with minors seem better able to respond appropriately to similar items on the ethics instruments (Vafakas, 1974).

The research also shows consistently that those with more education do better on these instruments than those with less education. In other words, doctoral students score higher than master's students, who score higher than undergraduates. Conflicting results have been found when scores on measures of ethical judgment have been correlated with moral reasoning scores. An individual's stage of moral development was shown to be significantly correlated with ethical judgment in one study (Welfel & Lipsitz, 1983), but not in another (Royer, 1985). Conflicting results may result in large part from psychometric weaknesses in the ethical judgment measures used, as was found in one report by Doromal and Creamer (1988), who cited unacceptably low reliability of the Ethical Judgment Scale (VanHoose & Paradise, 1979).

Unfortunately, there are no published data-based studies in the literature on college student services that describe the kinds of ethical dilemmas practitioners in this setting face or the frequency with which their behavior may violate ACPA's code of ethics. The few studies that have been conducted focus exclusively on college counselors. For example, Vafakas (1974) examined the capacity of ethical judgment of community college counselors, and Hayman and Covert (1986) studied the attitudes of college counselors to the ethical dimensions of their work and the frequency with which they encountered ethical dilemmas in counseling practice. Hayman and Covert reported that counselors experienced ethical dilemmas regarding confidentiality and danger the most frequently and felt more confident about their ability to handle these issues appropriately.

This lack of data-based research on college student services professionals necessitates extrapolating from the research in related fields to estimate the scope of the problem of unethical behavior for this group. At this point, there is little reason to expect that the ratio of unethical or impaired practitioners would be substantially different than for psychologists or counselors, but until data become available, no definitive statements can be made. In the meantime, the figure of 5% to 10% of professionals who violate the ethics code is a reasonable estimate. Obviously, the need for data-based research on this profession is critical. Professionals in college settings also face unique ethical challenges for which extrapolations from the incidence in other professions are inadequate. Fortunately, the research designs developed by psychologists can be adapted for this purpose.

Still other scholars have presented models of ethical decision making, applying the literature from developmental psychology, philosophy, and biomedical ethics to counseling and college student services (Kitchener, 1984, 1985; Rest, 1984; Tennyson & Strom, 1986). The next section will discuss two of these models in greater detail.

Models of Ethical Decision Making and Ethical Behavior

In 1955, Milton Schwebel raised a question about professional ethics that has gone largely unanswered—"Why *unethical* behavior?" In 1984, Welfel and Lipsitz phrased the question somewhat differently, "Why *ethical* behavior?" Recent models of moral behavior and ethical decision making may provide more fruitful avenues for investigating this central issue. Two models from the literature are especially worth discussing in greater detail: Rest's four-component model of moral behavior (1983, 1984) and Kitchener's model of ethical justification (1984, 1985).

Rest's four-component model of moral behavior serves as a useful framework for understanding the complexity of ethical decision making and ethical behavior. His model is a description of the component processes of all moral behavior, but it fits ethical behavior because ethical behavior is one subset of moral behavior. Rest's approach to analyzing moral behavior is particularly helpful in addressing the issue of why people behave unethically and in providing a framework for guiding ethics education. Rest argued that in order for a person to behave ethically in a particular situation, that individual must have carried out the following four psychological processes: identify the situation as a moral one; plan a moral course of action; decide to carry out that plan; and, finally, implement the moral action. The following details each of the processes.

Component I: Interpreting the situation as a moral one. This component attends to the individual's ability to perceive the situation as one that affects the welfare of others. It also refers to the ability to trace the consequences of action in terms of the welfare of all involved. It addresses the question: Does the individual perceive that moral dimensions of the situation exist? When people fail to be aware, several factors may account for the lack of awareness: They misunderstand what is happening in the situation; they differ in their spontaneous sensitivity to the needs and welfare of others; or they may have strong emotional reactions to which they respond before they have time to reflect.

Component II: Formulating a moral course of action. This component involves the decision-making process, how one decides which course of action is morally right, fair, or closest to one's moral ideals. This, of course, is where the theories of moral reasoning are applied. In essence, one's stage of moral reasoning acts as a filter influencing how one understands what is moral and how competent one is to integrate the often complicated considerations involved in ethical issues.

Component III: Deciding what to do. This component focuses on deciding what one will actually do and whether the moral judgment made gets carried out in the face of competing values such as the need to advance one's own career or the desire to avoid criticism from colleagues. In essence, it deals with the motivation to act morally. In reality, of course, the motive to act morally often gets preempted by other considerations.

Component IV: Implementing a plan of action. This component deals with carrying out the moral behavior despite the difficulties it may entail. Old-fashioned words like character, perseverance, and resoluteness are particularly fitting at this point. The psychological concepts of ego strength or self-regulation are alternative ways of explaining factors that influence the actual implementation of the moral behavior.

It is important to note that Rest referred to these components as *processes*, not traits. He stated, "The four components are not presented as four virtues that make up the ideal person, but rather, they are the major units of analysis in tracing out how a particular course of action was produced in the context of a particular situation" (1984, p. 20). The failure to act ethically can be traced to a failure in one of these four component processes. For example, recent studies by Volker

(1983) and Lindsey (1985) indicate that some counselors have difficulty with component 1, recognizing an ethical issue when confronted with one. More than one third of the participants in these studies failed to recognize the ethical issues embedded in the counseling scripts when listening to tapes of counseling sessions. They seemed to be attending instead to the counseling and diagnostic issues, even though some ethical issues represented in the tapes dealt with issues of "duty to warn" and possible sexual abuse of a minor—ethical problems that have received a great deal of attention by the profession. In other words, many counselors never identified the counseling situation they listened to as one with ethical components despite cues that might seem obvious. Thus, they might be highly vulnerable to unethical behavior in a similar situation because of their lack of awareness.

Component 3 of the model also provides a framework for understanding the research results of Bernard and his colleagues (Bernard & Jara, 1986; Bernard et al., 1987). These researchers reported that psychologists were able to recognize the appropriate ethical response to a written dilemma as defined by APA's *Ethical Principles*, but indicated that almost half the time they would not actually carry out the ethical behavior they had just identified. In other words, almost 40% of the combined sample stated they *would* do less than they knew they *should* do. It is likely that other motivations took precedence over the motivation to act ethically as described by Rest in component 3. Unfortunately, Bernard and his colleagues did not ask respondents their rationale for choosing not to perform the action they had just identified as the most ethical, so that we can only hypothesize about their reasoning. Perhaps they responded as they did because of fear of reprisals from colleagues, lack of information about how to file an ethics complaint, or worry about the tediousness of reporting ethics issues. Research currently under way (Nilsson & Welfel, in preparation) is investigating the competing values that may influence that decision-making process and may offer a more comprehensive understanding of the reasons ethical values get preempted.

The work of Kitchener (1984, 1985, 1986) focuses on levels of ethical decision making. In addition to illuminating the intricacies of ethical decision making, Kitchener's model is also helpful in understanding some of the published findings and in directing efforts to design appropriate ethics training. In essence, it delineates the process of Rest's component 2 (formulating a course of action) in greater detail. Building upon the work of ethicists Hare (1981) and Beauchamp and Childress (1979), Kitchener elaborated a model of ethical reasoning with two distinct levels. (See Kitchener, 1984, for a detailed presentation of this material.) The first level is called the *intuitive* level. This level represents individuals' immediate, prereflective response to ethical situations and is based on the sum of individuals' prior ethical knowledge and experience. These moral intuitions form the basis for our ordinary moral judgments and, of course, are critical to everyday ethical decision making. These intuitive decisions allow us to take immediate action in situations in which there is little time for reflection. They act as our moral "good" sense or our moral conscience. The findings of Hayman and Covert (1986) support the use of intuitive ethical reasoning in practice. They surveyed college counselors and found that they tended to make ethical decisions on the basis of what they termed "common sense" rather than through reference to formal codes or ethics committees' recommendations.

However, as Kitchener pointed out so clearly, the intuitive level of decision making is not always adequate. First, some ethical issues are highly complex and an intuitive response may underestimate their complexity and lead to an unwise decision. Second, in a rapidly changing profession like college student affairs, in which new ethical dilemmas arise regularly, ordinary moral sense may be of little value because the particulars of the case may not have a parallel in past professional experience. Third, there are times when an individual's moral judgment is in opposition to the values accepted by the profession, a circumstance well documented by the numbers and kinds of cases appearing before ethics committees. In other words, to quote Kitchener, "Not all persons have moral institutions that lead them to defensible moral choices" (1984, p. 44). Consequently, when one's ordinary moral judgment is inadequate, the next level of moral reasoning comes into play, the *critical evaluative* level. Within this level there are three hierarchically arranged sublevels of ethical justification: (a) ethical rules, (b) ethical principles, and (c) ethical theory.

Codes of ethics are the moral rules that apply in professional practice. When an ethically sensitive situation arises, a professional ought to use the code of ethics and the published cases to which it has been applied to help determine his or her ethical responsibility. In essence, professionals ask themselves what the codes say about the matter they are confronting and how ethics committees have interpreted the codes in similar cases they have adjudicated. The ethics casebooks published by AACD and APA are of particular value in this respect (APA, 1987; Herlihy & Golden, 1990). Often, all the direction a professional needs will be provided at this level and no higher levels of justification need be invoked. For instance, if a professor in a graduate program is approached by a student in one of her classes and asked if that professor would accept him as a client in her private practice, reference to the code will reveal the appropriate response. The code directs the professor to avoid dual relationships with students, and thus, provides her with a clear statement of the profession's position on this relationship.

In other cases, the available moral rules will not be sufficient, for all the reasons highlighted earlier in the section of this chapter on the limitations of ethics codes. In situations where the code is insufficient, one must turn to the next level of moral justification—the level of ethical principles. These principles are higher level norms that are more general and fundamental than rules. In fact, ethical principles usually serve as the foundation on which ethical rules are based. They represent the rationale for the specific provisions of the codes. Although there are many ethical principles, Kitchener identified five that are of special relevance to counseling and college student personnel work:

1. *Autonomy.* This principle includes one's right to act as an autonomous person, free to make independent decisions, as well as one's duty to treat others with the same respect. It implies respect for the rights of others to make their

own decisions even when some believe them mistaken, as long as the individuals are competent and their decisions do not infringe on the rights of others.

2. *Nonmaleficence.* This principle involves the avoidance of actions that inflict intentional harm on others or risk harming others. Its roots are in the history of medical practice and it is best summarized by the phrase "Above all, do not harm." Many ethics scholars argue that this principle takes precedence over all others.

3. *Beneficence.* This principle states that human services professionals have a positive obligation to contribute to the health and welfare of others. This concept of an ethical obligation to do good to others and to use knowledge for the benefit of the public is a cornerstone of the human services profession.

4. *Justice.* This principle involves human services professionals' ethical obligation to treat persons fairly. Its formal meaning has been traced to Aristotle, who argued that justice means treating equals equally and unequals unequally in proportion to their relevant differences.

5. *Fidelity.* This principle is best explained by the word "faithfulness." It also involves issues of promise keeping and loyalty. It is the foundation for human services professionals' ethical obligation to be faithful to the contracts or agreements they make with their clients and employing institutions.

Kitchener advocated using these ethical principles when one is confronted with an ethical problem that the code cannot fully resolve. An example of such a problem is the appropriateness of establishing a counseling relationship with a former student. The code as currently written is mute on this point. Usually, careful consideration of these ethical principles will provide a suitable resolution. However, these principles do not represent ethical absolutes and often conflict with each other. For example, Kitchener noted situations in which the duty to do good (beneficence) conflicts with the duty to avoid harm (nonmaleficence) or with the responsibility to be faithful to contracts (fidelity). Other examples of such conflicts include the dilemma of researchers whose responsibility to do good and advance knowledge may conflict with their duty to avoid harm to the participants in their experiments, or the dilemma of counselors whose duty is to keep their promise of confidentiality but who also have responsibilities to protect society and the client from harm.

In a 1985 chapter, Krager outlined how these principles apply to the work of college administrators and student personnel educators. For example, she delineated how the principles come into play in five different roles of administrators—planner, resource manager, organizer, staff development facilitator, and evaluator—and in five different roles of educators—advisor, instructor, program planner, researcher, and mentor. Her work provides a model for selecting ethical issues for practice in specific positions in higher education and for fostering discussion about how these principles apply to particular circumstances. For instance, Krager highlighted how the ethical principle of autonomy should guide behavior in advising situations, recommending that an educator's responsibility to provide guidance to students must be tempered by an awareness of students' right to make independent decisions about what may be in their best interests.

Situations in which ethical principles conflict occur with less frequency than instances when the codes are insufficient for proper ethical reasoning. When this happens, the third level of ethical justification must be invoked, the level of ethical theory. At this point, professionals need to refer to the ethical theories, such as utilitarianism or formalism, that ethicisits have presented. Such theories provide a rationale for giving precedence to one principle over another. A complete discussion of the content of these ethical theories is beyond the scope of this chapter. See Kitchener (1984) or Beauchamp and Childress (1979) for such a discussion.

CURRENT PRACTICES IN ETHICS EDUCATION

The number of courses on professional ethics has increased dramatically over the last three decades. In psychology, for example, since the first survey of training in ethics in graduate programs (DePalma & Drake, 1956), there has been a sevenfold increase in the availability of formal courses in ethics. Recent research indicates that in psychology it is now almost universal for students to have formal training in ethics. Lipsitz (1985) reported that only 6% of his sample of counseling psychology students indicated no formal training in ethics. In fact, Lipsitz suggested that the trend is toward offering a separate, required course on ethics. Unfortunately, little information is available regarding either the content of such training or its impact on students. Moreover, the results that have been published are conflicting. For example, Baldick (1980) found that separate, formal courses enable students to interpret the ethics code better, but Lipsitz reported no significant differences in the scores of students who had formal courses in ethics and those whose training in ethics was integrated into existing courses or those who had no ethics training at all. Neither of the researchers controlled for the variability in the content of the ethics training, therefore it is possible that their failure to examine the nature and quality of the courses masked existing differences in ethical reasoning. However, such a conclusion awaits further research.

In the absence of documentation on the practices in ethics courses, we can only hypothesize about the teaching methods used. It is reasonable to expect that most courses review the relevant codes of ethics. Some even may use one of the few instructional models for teaching ethics published in the literature, such as those of Abeles (1980), Pelsma and Borgers (1986), or Tennyson and Strom (1986). It also is reasonable to expect that case situations are examined in light of the ethics code and that recent legal rulings are discussed. In addition, it is possible that the work of Rest and Kitchener has been used to organize the curriculum in some recent courses. Obviously, the need to test these hypotheses empirically is critical. The importance of such data-based research is highlighted by the findings that most current faculty have had little training in ethics (Stadler & Paul, 1986) and that in many training programs ethics courses are considered to be of secondary importance and appropriate for any faculty member to teach (Welfel & Lipsitz, 1983).

Moreover, no published research has yet examined the frequency of separate ethics courses in college student personnel programs or the content of such instruction. In addition, no research in psychology or college student services has explored the outcomes of such training on actual behavior in the workplace, thus we have little information regarding its success in increasing ethical awareness after graduation. On the other hand, several scholars have proposed guidelines for ethics education that can be used as the basis for research. In general, these scholars make several recommendations for training in ethics (Kitchener, 1985; Rest, 1984; Welfel & Lipsitz, 1984).

First, they call for courses that go beyond values clarification exercises and review of existing ethics codes. Values clarification exercises often fail to do more than articulate the intuitive level of ethical reasoning, and ethics codes are likely to change at least every 10 years. Second, these authors recommend attention to the process of ethical decision making, not just the outcome. Students need to know not just what is ethical, but why it is so. Third, these scholars propose that courses integrate findings from research on morality and social and developmental psychology more effectively. Too often professional ethics courses are taught in a vacuum and students are not given a sense of the context of ethical issues. The fourth recommendation from this literature is for ethics education to emphasize that ethical issues arise frequently rather than in rare and isolated events. Many students seem to expect that they will never confront ethical problems and thus are ill-prepared to cope with such issues when they arise. In short, the dramatic change in the number of ethics courses reveals a new commitment to ethics education, but the lack of systematic research into the design and outcomes of these courses is a significant problem. Fortunately, the profession now has specific models of ethics education that can be tested empirically, as well as research tools for longitudinal follow-up of students in such courses, so that this gap in the literature need not exist much longer.

EMERGING ETHICAL CONCERNS
IN COLLEGE STUDENT SERVICES

Forecasting future developments in ethical issues is a risky undertaking. Obviously, the decade of the 1990s is likely to include many changes that we cannot envision at this time. Several ethical issues, however, seem to be of increasing importance. In this section, I will present four of the most critical issues. The first one I touched on earlier in the chapter—the conflict between the professional's responsibility to be loyal to individual clients and students and her responsibility to be loyal to the college for which she works. Consider the following case (adapted from Welfel, 1986):

> A college counselor learns from the Vice President for Student Services that unless enrollment trends change dramatically, student services budgets will be cut by 15%. She is also informed that along with heightened recruitment efforts, the college is giving special attention to retaining those students already enrolled. The Vice President has specifically requested that student services personnel make retention their first priority. It is quite clear that the long-term survival of the college is at stake. Soon after being informed of these developments, the counselor has an appointment with a sophomore with good grades who is considering withdrawing because of a lack of motivation for studying. As the counselor conducts the intake interview she thinks of the Vice Pres-

ident's directive and the college's gloomy financial outlook. She wonders whether it is ethical to include her boss's directive and the college's economic problems in her decision making about this client.

As the numbers of college-age students in the population decrease and economic pressures on higher education increase, such scenarios will occur more frequently. Counselors will feel pressure to influence their clients' decision making to stay in school unless there are compelling reasons not to. It is possible that merit increases and productivity measures will be overtly or indirectly tied to counselors' success in keeping tuition-paying students in school. Even if administrators act with sensitivity to the ethical dilemmas embedded in this issue, counselors themselves will feel an internal pressure to retain students (or to recruit unqualified ones) to keep their jobs. Furthermore, the ethics codes make it clear that counselors do have ethical duties to be loyal to the institution that employs them and to the college community at large, so that the most ethical course of action is not always unmistakably clear. The task of placing one's obligations to the client ahead of other obligations will become much harder than ever before in the history of the profession. How can the college student services profession prepare itself for this emerging issue? Several courses of action are available.

First, scholars can help practitioners view their ethical responsibilities more broadly. Their choice is not between passively accepting or defiantly ignoring institutional proprieties, but rather one of becoming involved in shaping them and in designing recruitment and retention programs to help move the college beyond its economic crisis. For instance, the counselor in the above dilemma can make use of her knowledge of program development and organizational behavior in working with university administrators to develop services that supplement individual counseling. These services might help students finish school, or might provide prospective students with a clearer picture of what the college can offer them. Such services might include study skills programs, peer advising services, in-service training for faculty, and staff development programs for residence hall staff. Professional organizations also bear a responsibility to assist practitioners develop more sophisticated responses to this dilemma through continuing education programs and sponsored research.

The second emerging ethical issue is an especially uncomfortable one for college student services professionals—the issue of sexual harassment. The evidence that sexual harassment is a serious problem on campus is increasing. Moreover, data also show that even when graduate students enter personal relationships with faculty that they perceive to be without coercion, they often perceive a degree of coercion after the relationship is over, or otherwise come to view the relationship as harmful to their professional development (Glaser & Thorpe, 1986). Although no data exist regarding the exact frequency of coercive relationships between college student services personnel and students, there is little reason to believe this group is any less vulnerable than others in higher education to such unethical behavior. It is possible that college student services professionals may be at greater risk because their contacts with students often are more frequent, more friendly, and sometimes more personal than those between teaching faculty and students. It also is possible that the student might be especially vulnerable to misperceive his or her ability to consent freely to an intimate relationship because the power differential between student services professionals and students is usually less obvious than that between teaching faculty and students. In this case, students may be more likely to express regrets about the relationship after the relationship has been terminated rather than during the relationship.

Regardless of the exact level of risk, the problem of coercive sexual relationships is a critical one for the profession because it contrasts so strikingly with its espoused beliefs. The history of the profession is replete with references to serving students and promoting their welfare above the professionals' own, and with individuals who exemplify that tradition. Sexual harassment represents malicious, self-serving behavior that compromises the respect that the profession has earned. If the challenge of reducing the incidence of sexual harassment is to be met, it requires comprehensive education of practitioners and students to the seriousness of such behavior, vigilant and careful enforcement of the ethics code, and serious efforts to rehabilitate those who have violated it in this way. Furthermore, it requires more encouragement and support for professionals to intervene when they learn of sexual harassment by colleagues. Practitioners need to be better informed of reporting procedures, more aware of the ethical consequences of not reporting, and better trained to cope successfully with the uncomfortable future interactions with the colleague at question.

A third emerging issue also deals with the relationships between professionals and students. The need for faculty and student services professionals to develop mentoring relationships with students is well documented in the literature. The benefits to both mentor and student are equally clear. The difference between a mentoring relationship and a "dual relationship," however, is not always clear. How can professionals act as mentors without having personal relationships with students? If all personal associations are inappropriate, how can the relationship truly function as a mentoring one? On the one hand, the profession calls for practitioners with multiple roles and diverse life-styles to demonstrate their diversity and to encourage a wide range of students to consider similar careers. But, on the other hand, recent statements in both ACPA's and APA's codes of ethics make the discrimination between appropriate and inappropriate sharing less clear. The severity of recent rulings of the APA ethics committee regarding dual relationships makes professionals concerned about any personal interactions with clients and students. Needless to say, the impact of dual relationships on clients mandates that professionals be extraordinarily cautious regarding this issue. I am not advocating any loosening of sanctions for violators. Serious harm does indeed come to clients whose counselors engage in dual relationships with them. What seems needed instead is clearer guidance from the professional associations lest practitioners jeopardize the effectiveness of their mentoring relationships with students by avoiding all personal and social contacts with them.

The fourth issue that will attract increasing attention in the 1990s is the conflict between the legal and institutional pressures to violate confidentiality to protect the greater good and the duty to honor the special trust between counselor and client. In a now-famous ruling (Tarasoff v. Regents of the University of California, 1976), a California judge ruled that "privilege ends where the public peril begins." Since that time the concept of the "duty to warn" has become part of the ethical code of psychologists and counselors. In essence, counselors are obliged to reveal information gathered confidentially if others are in danger or if the client is in danger of harming self. Subsequent court rulings have broadened the concept of the duty to warn, and counselors are often caught in the difficult position of attempting to predict violence or of cautioning clients about revealing such information to them. In warning clients, counselors jeopardize the future of the therapeutic relationship and damage clients' ability to trust counselors. Second, it is often impossible reliably to predict which threats will be carried out and which threats will never be acted upon. Ironically, counselors also may be at legal risk for a malpractice suit on the grounds of violating confidentiality if they reveal information obtained during counseling and the client never carries out the threat. In short, counselors are confused about how to proceed with such troubled clients and are greatly worried about malpractice claims or ethics charges against them.

Such dilemmas are not limited to practitioners in college counseling centers. Other student services professionals who regularly function in counseling and advising relationships are increasingly aware of the need to hold confidences even though the confidential nature of their relationships is not so clearly established as for counselors. They are subject to pressure from faculty and administrators to reveal confidential information and have little guidance about what is appropriate ethically. They also have less legal protection when they claim confidentiality than to professionals with clear counseling functions and a less well developed professional support system for coping effectively with students who threaten harm. Obviously, the profession needs to clarify the ethical responsibilities of student services personnel in such cases and offer all practitioners better guidelines for decision making.

The final emerging issue I wish to address is that of the weakness of ACPA and AACD in enforcing their ethics codes and in sponsoring continuing education about professional ethical issues. This gap is all the more evident because the ethics codes themselves are clearly written and as comprehensive as possible in a rapidly changing and diverse field. The ethics committees deserve recognition for the comprehensiveness and accessibility of the standards, but still, these committees have failed to take a proactive stance in other ways. For example, only a handful of complaints come before the ethics committees annually. We can be certain that more than a few professionals violate the codes each year, so how do the committees explain the paucity of cases brought for adjudication? What have they done to address this issue? Why aren't the activities of the ethics committees published each year in the journals as they are published by APA's ethics committee in the *American Psychologist*? Is anyone ever expelled from membership in AACD or ACPA for unethical behavior? The lack of information regarding the activities of the committees, and even more basically, the lack of activity by these committees, will become an issue of greater importance, especially as research on the scope and outcomes of unethical behavior expands and the legal pressures on practitioners increase.

Perhaps part of the lack of activity can be traced to the dual role of the professional association. On the one hand, it acts as a vehicle to protect the profession from undue outside influence. Its role is to prevent nonprofessionals with little knowledge of the profession from exerting undue influence on its members. On the other hand, its role also is to protect the public it serves from unethical actions of its members and to promote the public good. These roles sometimes conflict. "Undue outside influence" can be difficult to distinguish from reasonable public concern, and legitimate self-protective impulses easily can be diverted into self-serving complacency. The publication of such carefully crafted codes coupled with the failure to educate members to their contents fully or enforce the codes vigorously testifies to the lack of resolution of the conflict. If the profession is to reach its ethical ideals, or even to protect itself from more forceful outside influences, resolution of this dilemma is crucial.

Other ethical dilemmas also will draw the attention of the college student services profession in the 1990s. Several of these will focus on the unique ethical considerations of particular subspecialties of college student services professionals, such as residence hall directors, and particular types of institutions, such as the community college. Legal rulings in malpractice suits and economic pressures on higher education will continue to influence the definition of ethical practice in ways that cannot yet be envisioned. The best preparation for these changes and for ensuring that professionals act in compliance with current ethical standards is carefully crafted research, comprehensively designed educational programs for students and practitioners, and stronger leadership by the professional association in monitoring the standards of practice of its members. These actions will help college student services practitioners be more sensitive to ethical issues in the normal course of their work and will provide them with the capacity to make more appropriate ethical decisions in the face of increasingly complex and confusing ethical dilemmas.

REFERENCES

Abeles, N. (1980). Teaching ethical principles by means of value confrontations. *Psychotherapy: Theory, Research and Practice, 17*, 384–391.

American Association for Counseling and Development. (1981). *Ethical Standards*. Alexandria, VA: Author. (Originally published by the American Personnel and Guidance Association.)

American College Personnel Association. (1981). Statement of ethical and professional standards. *Journal of College Student Personnel, 42*, 184–189.

American Psychological Association. (1981). Ethical principles of psychologists. *American Psychologist, 36*, 633–638.

American Psychological Association. (1987). *Casebook on ethical principles of psychologists*. Washington, DC: Author.

Baird, K.A., & Rupert, P.A. (1987). Clinical management of confidentiality: A survey of psychologists in seven states. *Professional Psychology: Research and Practice, 18*, 347–352.

Baldick, T. (1980). Ethical discrimination ability of intern psychologists: A function of training in ethics. *Professional Psychology: Research and Practice, 11*, 276–282.

Beauchamp, T.L., & Childress, J.F. (1979). *Principles of biomedical ethics.* Oxford, England: Oxford University Press.

Bernard, J.L., & Jara, C.S. (1986). The failure of clinical psychology students to apply understood ethical principles. *Professional Psychology: Research and Practice, 17*, 313–315.

Bernard, J.L., Murphy, M., & Little, M. (1987). The failure of clinical psychologists to apply understood ethical principles. *Professional Psychology: Research and Practice, 18*, 489–491.

Bouhoutsos, J.C., Holroyd, J., Lerman, H., Forer, B.R., & Greenberg, M. (1983). Sexual intimacy between psychotherapists and patients. *Professional Psychology: Research and Practice, 14*, 185–196.

Butler, S., & Zelen, S. (1977). Sexual intimacies between therapists and patients. *Psychotherapy: Theory, Research and Practice, 14*, 139–145.

Canon, H.J., & Brown, R.D. (1985). *Applied ethics in student services.* New Directions for Student Services, No. 30. San Francisco: Jossey-Bass.

Chambers, C.M. (1981). Foundations of ethical responsibility in higher education administration. In R.H. Stein (Ed.), *Professional ethics in university administration* (pp. 1–12). San Francisco: Jossey-Bass.

Corey, G., Corey, M., & Callanan, P. (1982). *A casebook of ethical guidelines for group leaders.* Monterey, CA: Brooks/Cole.

Corey, G., Corey, M., & Callanan, P. (1988). *Issues and ethics in the helping professions* (3rd ed.). Pacific Grove, CA: Brooks/Cole.

DePalma, N., & Drake, R. (1956). Professional ethics for graduate students in psychology. *American Psychologist, 11*, 554–557.

Doromal, Q.S., & Creamer, D.G. (1988). An evaluation of the Ethical Judgment Scale. *Journal of College Student Development, 29*, 151–158.

Fiske, E.B. (1981). Ethical issues in recruiting students. In R.H. Stein (Ed.), *Professional ethics in university administration* (pp. 41–48). San Francisco: Jossey-Bass.

Fitting, M.D. (1986). Ethical dilemmas in counseling elderly adults. *Journal of Counseling and Development, 64*, 325–327.

Glaser, R.D., & Thorpe, J.S. (1986). Unethical intimacy: A survey of sexual contact and advances between psychology educators and female graduate students. *American Psychologist, 41*, 42–51.

Graham, D.L.R., Rawlings, E.I., Halpren, H.S., & Hermes, J. (1984). Therapists' need for training in counseling lesbians and gay men. *Professional Psychology: Research and Practice, 15*, 482–496.

Haas, L.J., Malouf, J.L., & Mayerson, N.H. (1986). Ethical dilemmas in psychological practice. *Professional Psychology: Research and Practice, 17*, 316–321.

Hare, R. (1981). The philosophical basis of psychiatric ethics. In S. Bloch & P. Chodoff (Eds.), *Psychiatric ethics* (pp. 31–45). Oxford, England: Oxford University Press.

Hayman, P.M., & Covert, J.A. (1986). Ethical dilemmas in college counseling centers. *Journal of Counseling and Development, 64*, 318–320.

Herlihy, B., & Golden, L. (1990). *AACD Ethical Standards casebook* (4th ed.). Alexandria, VA: American Association for Counseling and Development.

Holroyd, J.C., & Bouhoutsos, J.C. (1985). Biased reporting of therapist-patient sexual intimacy. *Professional Psychology: Research and Practice, 16*, 701–709.

Holroyd, J.C., & Brodsky, A.M. (1977). Psychologists' attitudes and practices regarding erotic and nonerotic physical contact with patients. *American Psychologist, 32*, 843–849.

Huey, W.C. (1986). Ethical concerns in school counseling. *Journal of Counseling and Development, 64*, 321–322.

Hummel, D.L., Talbutt, L.C., & Alexander, M.D. (1985). *Law and ethics in counseling.* New York: Van Nostrand Reinhold.

Journal of Counseling and Development. (1986). *64*(5) [Entire issue].

Keith-Spiegel, P. (1977). Violation of ethical principles due to ignorance or poor professional judgment versus willful disregard. *Professional Psychology: Research and Practice, 8*, 288–296.

Kitchener, K.S. (1984). Intuition, critical evaluation and ethical principles: The foundation for ethical decisions in counseling psychology. *The Counseling Psychologist, 12*, 43–56.

Kitchener, K.S. (1985). Ethical principles and ethical decisions in student affairs. In H.J. Canon & R.D. Brown (Eds.), *Applied ethics in student services* (pp. 17–29). San Francisco: Jossey-Bass.

Kitchener, K.S. (1986). Teaching applied ethics in counselor education: An integration of psychological processes and philosophical analysis. *Journal of Counseling and Development, 64*, 306–310.

Krager, L. (1985). A new model for defining ethical behavior. In H.J. Canon & R.D. Brown (Eds.), *Applied ethics in student services* (pp. 31–48). San Francisco: Jossey-Bass.

Laliotis, D.A., & Grayson, J.H. (1985). Psychologist heal thyself. What is available for the impaired psychologist? *American Psychologist, 40*, 84–96.

Lenn, D.J. (1981). Ethical issues in financial aid management. *The College Board Review, 121*, 11–25.

Lindsey, R.T. (1985, August). *Moral sensitivity: The relationship between training and experience.* Paper presented at the annual meeting of the American Psychological Association, Los Angeles.

Lipsitz, N.E. (1985, August). *The relationship between ethics training and ethical discrimination ability.* Paper presented at the annual meeting of the American Psychological Association, Los Angeles.

Losito, W.F. (1980). The argument for including moral philosophy in the education of counselors. *Counseling and Values, 25*, 40–46.

Mabe, A.R., & Rollin, S.A. (1986). The role of a code of ethical standards in counseling. *Journal of Counseling and Development, 64*, 294–297.

National Association of Student Personnel Administrators. (1983, February). *NASPA Standards of Professional Practice.* Unpublished document approved by NASPA Executive Committee.

National Association of Women Deans, Administrators and Counselors. (1976, March). *NAWDAC Statement of Principles, Purposes, and Professional Standards of Conduct.* Unpublished document approved at NAWDAC business meeting.

Nilsson, K., & Welfel, E.R. (in preparation). *From the "should" to the "will": The influence of competing values in ethical behavior of psychologists.*

Oravec, C. (1983). Sexual harassment in academic settings: Implications for personal ethical behavior. *Association for Communication Administration Bulletin, 46*, 73–79.

Pelsma, D.M., & Borgers, S.B. (1986). Experience-based ethics: A developmental model of learning ethical reasoning. *Journal of Counseling and Development, 64*, 311–314.

Pope, K.S., Tabachnick, B.G., & Keith-Spiegel, P. (1987). Ethics of practice: The beliefs and behaviors of psychologists as therapists. *American Psychologist, 42*, 993–1006.

Rest, J.R. (1983). Morality. In J. Flavell & E. Markman (Eds.), *Cognitive development* (Vol. IV). In P. Mussen (General Ed.), *Manual of child psychology* (pp. 550–629). New York: Wiley.

Rest, J.R. (1984). Research on moral development: Implications for training counseling psychologists. *The Counseling Psychologist, 12*, 19–30.

Royer, R.I. (1985, August). *Ethical orientation of mental health practitioners: A comparative study.* Paper presented at the annual meeting of the American Psychological Association, Los Angeles.

Schwebel, M. (1955). Why? Unethical practice. *Journal of Counseling Psychology, 2*, 122–128.

Stadler, H., & Paul, R.D. (1986). Counselor educators' preparation in ethics. *Journal of Counseling and Development, 64*, 328–330.

Tarasoff v. Regents of the University of California, 551 P. 2d 334 (S.C. Calif. 1976).

Tennyson, W.W., & Strom, S.M. (1986). Beyond professional standards: Developing responsibleness. *Journal of Counseling and Development, 64*, 298–302.

Tuana, N. (1985). Sexual harassment in academe: Issues of power and coercion. *College Teaching, 33*, 53–63.

Vafakas, K.M. (1974). Ethical behavior of community college counselors. *Journal of College Student Personnel, 15*, 101–104.

VanHoose, W.H., & Kottler, J.A. (1985). *Ethical and legal issues in counseling and psychotherapy* (2nd ed.). San Francisco: Jossey-Bass.

VanHoose, W.H., & Paradise, L.V. (1979). *The Ethical Judgment Scale.* Charlottesville, VA: Author.

Volker, J.M. (1983, August). *Counseling experience, moral judgment, awareness of consequences and moral sensitivity in counseling practice.* Paper presented at the annual meeting of the American Psychological Association, Toronto.

Welfel, E.R., & Lipsitz, N.E. (1983). Wanted: A comprehensive approach to ethics research and education. *Counselor Education and Supervision, 22*, 320–332.

Welfel, E.R., & Lipsitz, N.E. (1984). The ethical behavior of professional psychologists: A critical analysis of the research. *The Counseling Psychologist, 12*, 31–42.

Welfel, E.R. (1986, August). *Emerging ethical dilemmas for counseling psychologists.* Paper presented at the annual meeting of the American Psychological Association, Washington, DC.

Wilcoxin, S.A. (1986). Engaging non-attending family members in marital and family counseling: Ethical issues. *Journal of Counseling and Development, 64*, 323–324.

Winston, R.B., Jr., & Dagley, J.C. (1985). Ethical standard statements: Uses and limitations. In H.J. Canon & R.D. Brown (Eds.), *Applied ethics in student services* (pp. 49–65). San Francisco: Jossey-Bass.

Winston, R.B., Jr., & McCaffrey, S.S. (1981). Development of ACPA ethical and professional standards. *Journal of College Student Personnel, 42*, 183–184.

Zelen, S.L. (1985). Sexualization of therapeutic relationships: The dual vulnerability of patient and therapist. *Psychotherapy: Theory, Research and Practice, 22*, 178–188.

CHAPTER 10

Student Outcome Assessment: An Institutional Perspective

T. Dary Erwin

How effective are colleges and universities? How effective are divisions of student affairs in higher education? How much do student development professionals contribute to the education of college students? Student affairs professionals have long mused over these questions. Today, they are posed by persons outside higher education, particularly legislators and the general public.

The movement toward accountability has now reached higher education. In the past, higher education was often exempted from external scrutiny of its quality; however, recent reports by the National Institute of Education (NIE) (Astin, Blake, Bowen, Gamson, Hodgkinson, Lee, & Mortimer, 1984), the Association of American Colleges (1985), and the National Governor's Association (1986) have motivated overseers to consider, and in some cases to require, assessment of students' learning. The student outcome assessment movement is flourishing, with new mandates, new policies, and exploratory activities in assessment.

According to a recent survey (Boyer, Ewell, Finney, & Mingle, 1987), about two thirds of the states have begun assessment efforts of some type. This survey reported a reduction in the states' specific requirements concerning how and what to assess. Assessment is instead becoming "a matter of institutional prerogative." Earlier ventures in assessment were much more structured in policy, with assessment results tied to funding (Bogue & Brown, 1982). On the other hand, El-Khawas's (1987) survey found that 7 of every 10 college administrators nationwide believe that assessment should be linked to the institutional budget process. The recent retreat from further state-level mandates brings a responsibility for institutions to initiate their own assessment programs. In other words, colleges must define their educational objectives and select or design their own assessment methods, or the state will do it for them.

The call for assessment is not limited to the states. Stung by criticism that professional associations and regional accreditation associations rely too heavily on circumstantial evidence of quality, or on input measures such as the size of facilities and the number or qualifications of staff, accrediting associations such as the Southern Association of Colleges and Schools (1984) have introduced guidelines for assessing students. Moreover, former Secretary of Education William Bennett spurred on these initiatives by making assessment a necessary activity for reaccreditation (Vobejda, 1987).

ASSESSMENT AND STUDENT AFFAIRS

In view of these trends, should the profession of student affairs actively involve itself in the issue of outcome assessment? Should it delay getting into assessment until it has to do it or should it move ahead into this new area? Because assessment is pervasive around the country, accountability through assessment is probably inevitable in student affairs. Thus far, the student assessment movement has been aimed primarily at academic affairs. Only one major report has highlighted the importance of fostering noncognitive development. *Involvement in Learning* (Astin et al., 1984) is the only report to address *student* outcomes and includes such academic outcomes as knowledge, intellectual capacities, and skills, but also other dimensions of student growth such as self-confidence, persistence, leadership, empathy, social responsibility, and understanding of cultural and intellectual differences (p. 16). The state of New Jersey places equal emphasis on student development and student learning in its assessment requirements (Morantes, 1987). The assessment guidelines of the Commonwealth of Virginia indicate that "cognition may be viewed as part of a broader college experience which includes changes in attitudes, values, or behavior patterns" (Potter, 1986, p. 7).

There are several arguments in favor of prompt action by student affairs professionals:

1. Some agencies are formulating guidelines for assessment. For example, the American Assembly of Collegiate Schools of Business (AACSB), the professional business accrediting association, has introduced a new outcome assessment battery to assess the effect of educational programs in such areas as "leadership skills, disposition to lead, decision-making, and self-objectivity" (AACSB, 1987).

2. State plans for assessment generally provide time to design individual models, methods, and assessment expectations from a student affairs perspective. Failure to respond to this opportunity could result in objectives and expectations being imposed from outside the profession (Boyer et al., 1987).

3. Student personnel professionals already have some knowledge of assessment because of training in testing and knowledge of empirical research described in professional journals. In this sense, assessment represents a deepening commitment to a direction already agreed upon and practiced.

4. Assessment represents an opportunity to demonstrate student affairs' contributions toward the primary mission of colleges and universities, that is, educating

students. If the profession fails to document its educational impact, the entire mission of student affairs could be redefined away from development and education and toward resource management functions.

DEVELOPMENTAL ASSESSMENT

What should be assessed in student affairs? Most student affairs departments have a variety of stated or implicit goals. Some of them pertain to maintaining services for the institution, such as registering students, processing applications, or overseeing facilities. These goals support the resource management function of the institution and are vital for its everyday operations. Caple (1987) referred to these as first-order goals. Accountability for resource management functions is often measured by counting the number of students served or items served. Quality is expressed or implied through greater frequencies; the more students processed, the better the job done. These goals are valuable, but the services do not necessarily enhance students' personal growth and are not directly related to the primary mission of educating students.

Other goals in student affairs pertain to implementing programs and activities for students. Aulepp and Delworth (1976) conceived of this practice as the creation or design of environmental influences on campus to nurture student development. For example, a career planning and placement department may conduct a career development workshop to help students enhance their decision-making skills. The environmental goal then becomes the effective structuring, funding, and implementation of the decision-making workshop.

Yet another category of goals is that of developmental outcomes, or ways in which students directly benefit from student affairs functions or programs. It is to this area that assessment is primarily directed. How does the student's life change while she or he is at the college or university? What personal and social changes occur within the student? What have students learned about themselves, about the world? In what areas has the college or university enhanced the student's life?

Several conceptual approaches are usually mentioned when thinking about ways students develop during college. These are discussed in greater detail elsewhere in this volume and include Chickering's (1969) vectors of development, Heath's (1968, 1977) model of maturity, Kohlberg's (1981) stages of moral reasoning, and Perry's (1970) positions of intellectual development. Wisely, Kuh (1984) encouraged student personnel professionals to think beyond psychological approaches to other social science frameworks.

IMPLEMENTATION ISSUES IN ASSESSMENT

Assessment is a process broader than just administering a set of instruments to students. For that reason, several issues concerning the process of assessment will be considered here before discussing procedures for initiating assessment. Each institution must create its own assessment plan that is sensitive to its unique qualities. Committees for this purpose may be formed at four levels within the institution.

First, most colleges and universities have formed or are forming an overall steering committee composed of faculty, staff, administrators, and students to determine the broad scope of assessment. It is important that student affairs departments be represented on these committees and be included in any overall institutional assessment plans. It is at this stage that student affairs is often excluded from assessment, and perceptions of its functions may shift to a resource management approach, supportive of but not directly within the primary mission of educating students. Ewell (1984) addressed the issues of overall institutional planning.

Second, some institutions establish a university-wide or college-wide committee to define developmental goals. Such committees represent an institutional commitment to developing and assessing the whole student. This committee should be composed of a wide range of persons including faculty, administrators, and students, as well as student affairs staff. Typically, the academic departments consider their own subject matter objectives, and an academic affairs committee defines liberal studies objectives, so the institution-wide development committee can consider the attitudes, personal and social dimensions, and general developmental issues important for all undergraduates. As will be discussed later, it is important to link the work of this committee with other assessment efforts of both academic and student affairs divisions.

Third, within the division of student affairs, it may be wise to establish a separate committee for determining student affairs developmental goals. In what ways does the division of students affairs as a whole have educational impact upon the student? This committee might consist of student affairs department directors, or at least of one representative from each department.

Fourth, each department in a student affairs division should establish developmental objectives that represent the unique mission of that department. These objectives will overlap with those of other student affairs departments and of the division as a whole. Collectively, these objectives may become the goals of the division. Determining developmental objectives for the student affairs department is as important as establishing objectives in the major academic departments. It is at the departmental level that the education of the student primarily occurs, so a clear definition of purposes is essential.

At any of these levels, formulating objectives is a process that typically takes several weeks. As previously mentioned, these objectives should focus on developmental outcomes, not on resource management functions or environmental programs and services. Objectives must be specific, using behavioral or performance terms to describe the desired activity. Instead of listing an objective such as "to enhance students' growth," it is important to define student growth. For instance, one aspect of growth may be the development of student independence and autonomy. Autonomy is more specific that growth, but still too global for assessment. Autonomy might be defined operationally in a number of ways. For example, independence might be the ability to become more assertive (counseling center), to finance one's education (financial aid), to choose an institution (admissions), to withdraw from school (dean of students), or to make one's own decisions about sexual behavior (health center). Each student affairs department then needs to specify and implement its developmental objectives. Concurrently, environmental programs or services should be tailored for each department to help students achieve a particular set of developmental goals. The environmental goals are driven by the developmental goals.

From an assessment point of view, the term "growth" is too vague and is open to multiple interpretations. If global terms such as growth, maturity, or leadership are used, they should be defined operationally. If there are multiple definitions, all the definitions that apply should be recorded in writing. This task is similar to the counseling process of clarifying a client's program. A clear, understandable definition of what is to be accomplished should be stated.

If the staff are unable to agree on an operational definition or if the terms are difficult to specify, it is helpful to write down global terms and keep discussing what they mean. It is natural for developmental objectives to undergo periodic revisions and modifications over several months. Developmental objectives should be formulated first; then environmental objectives can be formulated to meet developmental objectives. It is important to ask whether programs are nurturing intended developmental goals. At this stage, some departments may change the focus of selected environmental programs and services to be more supportive of developmental goals. If some of the developmental goals are not supported by a program or service, critical management questions must be addressed. Can additional resources be shifted or gathered to establish an environmental influence to meet the developmental goal? Or should the developmental goal be dropped because it cannot be met? The process of determining developmental and environmental objectives clarifies the focus of student affairs programs.

Role of the Vice President for Student Affairs

The role of the chief student affairs officer is crucial in the assessment process. If this person does not lead in a supportive way, the possibility of assessment could become threatening to some staff. Assessment is as much a process as a technical program. It can be used to energize and direct a department or division if approached openly, with wide staff participation. Assessment need not consist of a myriad of complex statistics for the process to provide valuable feedback.

The assessment process may be expected to be stimulating and challenging, and, in a sense, a staff development activity. But the venture can be overwhelming and threatening on some campuses. It is important to remember that discussions about assessment may often move in new directions, with no traditional guidelines to follow.

The assessment process is commonly a learning process, a time for questioning old assumptions, and a time for discovering new ways to conceive of student affairs work. From one perspective, the assessment process is developmental for higher education professionals. At many institutions, the assessment process begins with fears of evaluation ("Will my performance evaluation be linked to assessment results?''), with thoughts of program reduction (''Is this just a veiled effort to cut back my job or program?''), with feelings of disappointment (''What have we done wrong to warrant review?''), and with feelings of concern (''I do not understand these new theories of student development.''). These fears are natural for some people in the beginning but usually dissipate over the course of assessment activities.

The chief student affairs officer might carry out the following steps in undertaking assessment:

1. Ask the student affairs staff offices to formulate specific objectives about their *direct* impact on students. Refer to strategies about establishing developmental objectives mentioned above. This step may take several weeks of discussion.

2. Discuss with the staff ways to help students reach these objectives. Many programs or services probably already support new program objectives. Link programs and services with each developmental objective. Again, consider what environmental influences will help students change developmentally. There will be several programs and services for some objectives, and few for other objectives. Discussion often centers on a proper balance between developmental objectives and adequate environmental influences. Addressing developmental objectives is limited, of course, by financial resources.

3. Determine assessment methods and instruments. Examine existing instruments discussed in this volume. This area is discussed later in this chapter as well as elsewhere in this volume.

4. Discuss how the assessment information will be used. Explain that it will not be used for summative evaluation related to individual staff but instead for formative evaluation and program improvement.

Linking With Academic Affairs

How do the assessment efforts of student affairs staff relate to assessment in the academic arena? Can or should the assessment programs be kept separate?

Often, the work of student affairs is regarded as unrelated to that of academic affairs. My experience in assessment has shown that it is often difficult to separate student and academic affairs assessment efforts. In fact, assessment often brings the divisions closer. For instance, general education outcomes are often expressed as liberal arts objectives such as writing, speaking, and quantitative or problem-solving methods. Defined at an institution-wide level, such global developmental objectives as moral, intellectual, identity, and social development are just as important as the liberal arts objectives for the undergraduate education of all students. Probably most people in and outside of higher education would agree about the importance of developmental goals in the undergraduate experience. The development of interpersonal relationships, for example, is often listed as an institution-wide goal, and faculty commonly agree that it is an important college outcome.

Although they agree that such developmental outcomes are as important as other components of general education, faculty are often hesitant to agree about their own role in enhancing developmental outcomes. As in the past, many faculty will defer to student affairs for leadership in advancing developmental goals. In actuality, academic departments also may contribute to the nurturing of developmental goals. The assessment process may raise the consciousness of faculty as all explore ways to enhance students' personal and social development.

In recent assessment efforts at James Madison University, faculty have been asked to define developmental objectives by their academic department. The purpose in this process is twofold: To promote holistic education and to assess the contributions academic departments make toward developmental objectives.

The role of intellectual development in student affairs is unclear to some professionals in the field (e.g. Barr, 1986). However, if academic departments design their own end-of-program tests, intellectual developmental assessment within the major program should be considered. For example, Figure 1 illustrates a proposed model for a table of specifications in a test design.

Faculty are encouraged to adapt Perry's scheme of intellectual development (Erwin, 1982) and to design subscales for their content or subject matter areas *and* for a higher order thinking scheme. For example, Dualism may relate to the types of objectives that are didactically taught, such as facts, basic principles, or theories. Relativism might be operationally defined as comparing and contrasting designated theories in the discipline. Commitment leads to reasoned beliefs about the discipline or development of a professional identity through reasoned study. Empathy might be fostered through discussions of how the discipline contributes to the betterment of society and humankind.

Academic Subject Matter Subtopics

Developmental Level	1	2	3	4	5	6
Dualism						
Relativism						
Commitment						
Empathy						

FIGURE 1
Model for Program Test Design

Measurement Considerations

Although assessment has been discussed here primarily as a process, several measurement issues should be mentioned as factors to consider when planning assessment objectives. Some of the measurement concepts discussed here relate to reliability, validity, reference groups, and research designs.

Reliability of instruments, whether existing or locally designed, is essential. *Reliability* is the consistency with which people or raters respond to a measurement instrument. In nontechnical terms, is your gauge (instrument) measuring your objective in a precise way? Although reliability can be determined by comparing results from similar forms of the same instrument or from the same instrument administered twice within a short time span, it is more often determined in developmental surveys by a coefficient of internal consistency (Cronbach, 1981) or by a generalizability coefficient (Brennan, 1983). Appropriate values for reliability range from .60 to .79 for group evaluation uses and from .75 up for individual student use. An instrument can have high reliability and low validity, but if reliability is low, validity cannot be high; therefore, it is important to check reliability levels first. For interview techniques, the generalizability coefficient is a powerful reliability estimate for determining rater error.

It is often said that what student affairs departments do cannot be measured. In fact, any measurement of human behavior contains errors, or a degree of unreliability. This is true for a classroom test as much as for a developmental instrument. It is important to realize that any score or rating contains error from the student, from the assessment method, and from the scoring mechanism. Nevertheless, if these errors can be identified, results can still be valuable.

After an acceptable standard of reliability has been satisfied, consider the validity of the assessment instrument. *Validity*, a most elusive concept, generally refers to the worth or accuracy of the measuring instrument. Several types of validity exist, such as content, predictive, criterion-related, and construct validities. The reader is referred to Brown (1976) for complete explanations. The main query should be: Has the instrument been used successfully in a similar manner and with a similar population? Does it measure the developmental goal that has been established? If the instrument has not been used to measure this goal, it is important to treat its initial use as a research experiment and not as an accepted tool for program evaluation. Because many student development assessment tools are still new, there are few validity studies for most instruments.

The issue of appropriate *reference groups* to use in assessment has engendered much debate. Norm-referenced or criterion-referenced measures may be used. Norm-referenced scores are reported in relation to large numbers of other scores for comparative purposes; criterion-referenced scores are compared to a recommended level designating competence. Often, it is valuable to know how well students at one institution are developing compared to students at other institutions. Norms or percentiles related to scores on an instrument provide that frame of reference for geographical regions, for cultures, for genders, for minority groups, and for age groups. With criterion-referenced instruments, minimum scores or levels are designated to represent particular competencies, skills, or desirable attitudes. In both cases, various levels of scores have different interpretable meanings.

In the area of *research design*, the use of a variety of methods is recommended. Tests, surveys, checklists, interviews, portfolios, and unobtrusive observations should be considered as alternative methods for gathering outcome assessment information. Incidentally, most states that have mandated assessment are also requiring that assessment information be quantifiable, not just narrative or anecdotal.

Longitudinal studies are common in developmental assessment projects. Students assessed during summer orientation programs (before entry) are reassessed at various points during their undergraduate years. The academic assessment efforts refer to this pretest and posttest study as "value-added," attributing supposed gains or losses to an intervening program of study. Readers are cautioned to consult Linn and Slinde (1977) for problems of unreliability in change scores. Even in view of those problems, longitudinal designs are still preferred in development, as opposed to cross-sectional studies. Planned assessment studies should consider the impact of particular environmental programs and services as opposed to only recording developmental change over time. Consult Hanson and Lenning (1979) and Pascarella (1987) for more sophisticated research designs.

Storing Assessment Information

After you begin collecting information from students, storing it becomes another major task. You may collect several scores or ratings for each student, and it makes sense to retain this information through the undergraduate years and after graduation for later follow-up. Efficient and confidential storage mechanisms are necessary to ensure availability of assessment information.

Small schools may be able to use microcomputers and data base management packages to maintain information. However, most colleges and universities would be wise to consider the use of their administrative data base or computerized student information system to store assessment information.

Most colleges and universities have a computing data base that contains admissions information, grades, financial aid information, and other biographical information. I recommend that assessment information be added to this data base and maintained confidentially just like the more traditional information used to support resource management functions (Erwin & Miller, 1985; Erwin & Tollefson, 1982).

Using Assessment Information

Implementing an assessment program carries the responsibility for appropriate use of student information. Although the primary purpose that has been discussed so far concerns assessment for program review, assessment information also can be used for diagnostic feedback with individual students if reliability levels are appropriate. Counseling centers have tested students for years, and now divisions of student affairs can use assessment information for individual counseling and student advising on a broader basis. Student development professionals possess the background for interpreting information on personal and social characteristics and thus serve as an asset to the institution.

Student affairs professionals also carry a professional responsibility to ensure proper use and storage of assessment information. Not only does this mean that the information should be properly interpreted, but it also means the information should be treated in a confidential manner. The collection of information and its storage in a computer data base does not necessarily lead to data abuse. In fact, data base management systems are generally more secure than a file folder and cabinet system. However, developmental information should be viewed as sensitive and should be available only to trained, authorized professionals.

Future

Members of the community often challenge the inclusion of developmental goals. "What right does an institution have to interfere in the moral and ethical lives of students?" "As a parent, I resent the college promoting independence, an encouragement to set vocational goals apart from what I think is best!"

Student affairs professionals have often claimed these areas of development as a major thrust of their work, so they must be able to defend their value. In my experience, faculty and other instructional personnel realize the limits of educating for subject matter content and believe that "higher order" goals of general education are more valuable and lasting. For instance, leadership skills may serve the student better in the long term than facts and figures. The future for student affairs professionals is bright because its work carries a responsibility to nurture vitally important goals of student development. Assessment will not only help student affairs professionals to determine the effectiveness of their programs and services in meeting these goals, but it will help to define these goals more clearly. Is assessment here to stay and is assessment applicable to the profession of student affairs? Questions still linger about the effectiveness of student affairs programs in higher education. The public recognizes the importance in the workplace and in everyday living of the developmental growth student affairs claims to enhance. Accountability is an issue that rarely fades away; it probably will gain more momentum in the near future. Aside from the points already mentioned, what must the student affairs profession do to plan for the future?

1. The leadership of the major student affairs organizations must recognize the importance of the student outcome assessment movement. At the 1987 ACPA/ NASPA meeting, the ACPA senior scholars convened a session about future issues, and assessment was mentioned prominently. Leaders should continue discussions such as these through national program features, through support for instrument design and use, and through spotlighting institutions with student affairs assessment programs.

2. Leadership is needed on each campus from the chief student affairs officer to set the proper tone for assessment to begin. A recent report (Hutchings, 1987), depicting several successful assessment programs, noted support from top administrative officials in five of the six.

3. Emphasize assessment competencies in graduate training programs. Every graduate program should consider establishing a course or a major portion of a course that would relate basic measurement terms and existing assessment instruments and methods to student development.

4. Designate at least one person within each division of student affairs who can act as a consultant in technical aspects of assessment. Some schools may have to look outside student affairs for such expertise because the combined knowledge of developmental theory and measurement and statistics is difficult to find in a single person.

5. Respect the reliability and validity limits of assessment information. If possible, use multiple sources of assessment information in program evaluation and student feedback.

6. Regardless of resources and knowledge about assessment or development, divisions of student affairs should begin planning. Start discussing the purposes of current efforts. In addition to institutional services or resource functions, what can you do to have a direct impact on students? Begin to link your programs and services with these objectives. Are programs and services serving the purposes you intend? This step will involve much lengthy discussion before issues of how to assess these goals are addressed. Although many educators claim to perform assessment activities, few institutions have approached assessment with a systematic, deliberate approach. This is an excellent time for student affairs professionals to initiate their own discussions of specific goal setting, assessment methods, and possible uses of information. It is an opportunity to demonstrate their educational effectiveness. Students will benefit, student affairs will benefit, our institutions will benefit, and the public may eventually demand such a demonstration of effectiveness.

REFERENCES

American Assembly of Collegiate Schools of Business. (1987). *Outcome measurement project*. St. Louis: Author.

Association of American Colleges. (1985). *Integrity in the college curriculum*. Washington, DC: Author.

Astin, A.W., Blake, J.H., Bowen, H.R., Gamson, Z.F., Hodgkinson, H.L., Lee, B., & Mortimer, K.P. (1984). *Involvement in learning: Realizing the potential of American higher education*. Washington, DC: National Institute of Education.

Aulepp, L., & Delworth, U. (1976). *Training manual for an ecosystem model*. Boulder, CO: Western Interstate Commission for Higher Education.

Barr, M.J. (1986). Should we be surprised? *Journal of College Student Personnel, 27*, 304–305.

Bogue, E.G., & Brown, W. (1982). Performance incentives for state colleges. *Harvard Business Review, 59*, 123–128.

Boyer, E.M., Ewell, P.T., Finney, J.E., & Mingle, J.R. (1987). Assessment and outcomes measurement—a view from the states. *American Association for Higher Education Bulletin, 39*(7), 8–12.

Brennan, R.L. (1983). *Elements of generalizability theory*. Iowa City, IA: American College Testing Program.

Brown, F.G. (1976). *Principles of educational and psychological testing*. New York: Holt, Rinehart & Winston.

Caple, R.B. (1987). The change process in developmental theory: A self-organization paradigm, part 1. *Journal of College Student Personnel, 28*, 4–11.

Chickering, A.W. (1969). *Education and identity*. San Francisco: Jossey-Bass.

Cronbach, L.J. (1981). Coefficient alpha and the internal structure of tests. *Psychometrika, 16*, 297–334.

El-Khawas, E. (1987). *Campus trends 1987*. Washington, DC: American Council on Education.

Erwin, T.D. (1982). The scale of intellectual development: Measuring Perry's scheme. *Journal of College Student Personnel, 24*, 6–12.

Erwin, T.D., & Miller, S.W. (1985). Technology and the three r's. *NASPA Journal, 22*, 47–51.

Erwin, T.D., & Tollefson, A.L. (1982). A data base management model for student development. *Journal of College Student Personnel, 23*, 70–76.

Ewell, P.T. (1984). *The self-regarding institution: Information for excellence*. Boulder, CO: National Center for Higher Education Management Systems.

Hanson, G.R., & Lenning, O.T. (1979). Evaluation of student development programs. In G.D. Kuh (Ed.), *Evaluation in student affairs* (pp. 163–182). Cincinnati, OH: American College Personnel Association.

Heath, D.H. (1968). *Growing up in college: Liberal education and maturity*. San Francisco: Jossey-Bass.

Heath, D.H. (1977). *Maturity and competence: A transcultural view*. New York: Gardner Press.

Hutchings, P. (1987, June). *Six stories: Implementing successful assessment*. Paper prepared for the Second National Conference on Assessment in Higher Education, Denver, CO.

Kohlberg, L. (1981). *The meaning and measurement of moral development*. Worcester, MA: Clark University Press.

Kuh, G.D. (1984). A framework for understanding student affairs work. *Journal of College Student Personnel, 25*, 25–31.

Linn, R.L., & Slinde, J.A. (1977). The determination of the significance of change between pre- and post-testing periods. *Review of Educational Research, 47*, 121–150.

Morantes, E. (1987, April). *A statewide comprehensive outcomes assessment program*. Paper presented at the Fifth Annual Regents' Conference of the State University and Community College System of Tennessee, Nashville, TN.

Perry, W.G., Jr. (1970). *Forms of intellectual and ethical development in the college years*. New York: Holt, Rinehart & Winston.

Pascarella, E.T. (1987, March). *Some methodological and analytic issues in assessing the influence of college*. Paper presented at the joint meetings of the American College Personnel Association and the National Association of Student Personnel Administrators, Chicago.

Potter, D.L. (1986). *The measurement of student achievement and the assurance of quality in Virginia higher education*. Richmond, VA: Council of Higher Education for Virginia.

National Governor's Association. (1986). *Time for results: The governor's 1991 report on education*. Washington, DC: Author.

Southern Association of Colleges and Schools. (1984). *Criteria for accreditation: Commission on Colleges*. Decatur, GA: Author.

Vobejda, B. (1987, September 6). Evidence of learning sought: Bennett moves to make colleges document student achievement. *The Washington Post*, p. 8.